KV-638-826

A. Afou

City of Birmingham

Polytechnic.

30/4/76.

B.A. Bus. Studies

BUSINESS ECONOMICS

BUSINESS ECONOMICS

by

JAMES BATES

Professor of Business Economics,
The Queen's University of Belfast

and

J. R. PARKINSON

Professor of Economics,
University of Nottingham

BASIL BLACKWELL
OXFORD
1971

© BASIL BLACKWELL 1963

NEW MATERIAL IN THIS EDITION © BASIL BLACKWELL 1969

ISBN 0 631 12300 8

*All Rights Reserved. No part of this publication
may be reproduced, stored in a retrieval system,
or transmitted, in any form or by any means,
electronic, mechanical, photocopying, recording or
otherwise without the prior permission of Basil
Blackwell & Mott Limited.*

REPRINTED 1971

PRINTED IN GREAT BRITAIN BY COMPTON PRINTING LTD.,
LONDON AND AYLESBURY, AND BOUND BY THE
KEMP HALL BINDERY, OXFORD

CONTENTS

v

TABLES AND DIAGRAMS

TABLES

DIAGRAMS

PREFACE TO THE FIRST EDITION

THE idea of writing this book occurred to us independently. If it had been an individual project it would, of course, have been different; that it has been possible to align our thoughts is mainly due to the fact that the need for the book was felt in attempting to teach economics to students in industrial administration at Glasgow University. The final decision to write it was taken at the bar of the Gleneagles Hotel during a conference organized by the British Institute of Management, so that the book owes its origins to attempts to educate managers in more ways than one.

Those who have attempted to teach short courses in economics to students in industrial administration will appreciate how necessary it is to be selective in choosing material. Economics as it is taught is concerned largely with the economy as a whole and its organization and management; the theory of the firm is scarcely more than a step in this process; and much of what is taught in economics seems to have small relevance to the problems of those in business—particularly those in small business. A knowledge of the factors making for a high level of demand, an efficient exchange of commodities in international trade and the organization of world finance are sometimes relevant to the success of large businesses and can be considered by expert economic sections in relation to the general policy of the firm; but the small firm can seldom rise to these refinements and to a young general manager economics often seems to be either obvious in elementary exposition, inapplicable to real-life situations in its more sophisticated forms, or just plainly irrelevant. It is not easy to defend economics against these criticisms by arguing that the best form of education for management is general education, and that relevance is a secondary matter. Education for management covers a wide field and some, at least, of the matter imparted must be of use in a narrow technical sense in addition to contributing to general education.

In this book we have attempted to extract from the general body of economic thought some parts that seem to us to be particularly relevant to taking decisions in business. We do not, of course, think that we have covered every aspect of economics with relevance to business decisions; and we have deliberately abstained from treating some subjects of importance, for example, wages and industrial relations. We did not think that a short treatment of these subjects would be very helpful; much of the subject lies outside the usual boundaries of economics, and could not easily have been integrated with the main tenor of development of the book. For other reasons we have omitted other things: for example we have not included a discussion of the theoretical and quantitative aspects of production functions, largely because a reasonable discussion of these would involve technical economic and statistical considerations beyond the scope of this book. Similarly we have omitted decision theory, game theory, activity analysis and other recent developments in mathematical economics which are relevant to business economics but which could not be usefully discussed in a book of this nature.

The theme of the book is that while the economic situation is always changing, and the businessman is therefore operating in an uncertain world, it is nevertheless possible to take business decisions in a systematic fashion, and by using appropriate techniques and ways of thought to reduce the uncertainties involved. We anticipate that in future numerical analysis is likely to play an increasingly important part in the taking of business decisions; this is why we have devoted a section of the book to elementary quantitative analysis. This section is intended only to introduce readers to the possibilities of numerical analysis mainly by illustration, and does not, of course, take the matter very far, though we are conscious that, nevertheless, it does not make easy reading.

In the process we have attempted to achieve a certain mixing of the ways of thought and techniques used by economists, econometricians and accountants. Probably the resulting blend will suit no one; but there does appear to be a border area in the three subjects of study where those engaged should be discussing common problems from a common point of view.

In these and other ways the book is something in the nature of an experiment. We should like to acknowledge assistance from a number of people, and to start with Professor

A. K. Cairncross (as he then was) who encouraged us in the project and gave us the benefit of his advice on an early draft of the table of contents. We should also like to thank Mr Jim Houston and Mr Jim McGregor of Honeywell Controls Ltd who supplied us with some valuable information and extremely useful comments on early drafts of some of the chapters. Mr J. B. Stevenson, lecturer in Accountancy at Glasgow University made useful comments on some of the accounting aspects raised in the book. He is not, of course, responsible for the no doubt unorthodox remarks which still appear. Mr Gordon Fisher offered valuable comments on the chapter on forecasting, and other chapters on quantitative analysis; here again the faults that remain are our own. We should also like to thank Mr Peter Hart for comments on these and other chapters and Mr N. Robertson for helpful criticism of the chapter on demand. Again the remaining faults are our own.

We are grateful to our wives for their forbearance and help during the writing of this book; we also gratefully acknowledge the typing assistance of Miss A. Allen, Miss K. MacDonald and Mrs D. Ryder.

PREFACE TO THE SECOND EDITION

IT is gratifying to have the opportunity to prepare a second edition of *Business Economics,* not least because it gives an opportunity for improvement and to correct mistakes.

Parts of the text remain as before but the arrangement of the book has been greatly changed and several sections, including those on pricing and the investment decision, completely re-written. A substantial amount of new material has been added and there has been some extension of the sections dealing with elementary operations research techniques. But the book continues to be concerned with the application of economic thought to business problems. It is not intended to be a treatise on operations research and the amount of mathematics used has deliberately been restricted, as is appropriate in a basic introduction designed to arouse interest and to be easily read.

A place has been found for new material by tightening the text and by eliminating discussions that have more relevance for the economy than for individual businesses. The length of the book is thus little changed, which seems to us to be right in an era when books of over 500 pages are all too common.

Any hopes of producing an ideal text have gradually been abandoned in preparing the second edition. Perfection is a changing objective and we remain conscious of an unfinished task.

As with the first edition there is a long list of names of people who have helped us in many ways. Mr H. Harrison has given us much advice on the sections dealing with operations research and has contributed examples. The study of a simulation problem in queueing was kindly provided by Mr A. L. Woods, and we should like to record our gratitude to him and Radio Telefis Eireann. Mr Brian Buckley as always has helped to clear our minds with critical and fundamental comment. He and Mr J. Buckley have helped in the preparation of diagrams. Mr Desmond Rea has read the chapter on investment and helped to improve it by critical comment. The same is true of Mr André Gabor who read the chapter on prices. Mr David Graham kindly gave up valuable time to us in discussing control systems operated by Carreras and we should like to express our gratitude to him and his company. Miss Yvonne Harris, Miss Joan Humphreys, Miss Yvonne Rogers, Mrs J. A. Bates and Mrs G. Bates have all helped in the preparation of the manuscript and greatly lightened our task.

We thank the following for permission to reproduce copyright material: Methuen and Co. Ltd. for Table 3.13 from *Queues* by D. R. Cox and Walter L. Smith; the Controller of Her Majesty's Stationery Office for Table 7.2 from H.M.S.O.'s publication *Investment Appraisal*; and the American Economic Association for Table 8.1 from the *American Economic Review,* 1958, p. 921.

To our wives and families we express our apologies for lost evenings and weekends, for contrary to what is commonly believed, rapidly expanding Universities leave teachers limited time for writing and research.

Belfast
April 1969

RECOMMENDED READING

In general we have followed the practice of recommending further reading at appropriate places in the text, and the reader who wishes to follow up particular topics will find that these references provide a useful starting point. In addition there are a number of books which, between them cover approximately similar ground to that covered in this book : a brief selection of these is included for guidance.

W. J. BAUMOL *Economic Theory and Operations Analysis*
(Prentice Hall, 1965, Second Edition)
JOEL DEAN *Managerial Economics*
(Prentice Hall, 1951)
R. S. EDWARDS and H. TOWNSEND *Business Enterprise*
(Macmillan 1958)
P. SARGANT FLORENCE *The Logic of British and American Industry* (Routledge and Kegan Paul, 1953)
D. C. HAGUE *Managerial Economics*
(Longmans 1969)
J. LESOURNE *Economic Analysis and Industrial Management*
(Prentice Hall, 1963)
R. MARRIS *The Economics of Managerial Capitalism*
(Macmillan, 1964)
A. MERRETT and G. BANNOCK *Business Economics and Statistics*
(Hutchinson 1962)
M. II. SPENCER and L. SEIGELMAN *Managerial Economics*
(Richard Irwin, 1965, Second Edition)

CHAPTER I

THE OBJECTIVES OF BUSINESS

MOST business men assert when questioned that the object of their firm is to make a profit. The reply, though sincerely meant, is seldom the whole truth and it prompts some reflection on the nature and purpose of profits.

Profit arises when there is a surplus of revenue over costs in a period of trading. In a limited sense this is a definition, but it does not say anything about how or why profits arise, nor about their function and relation to other economic concepts. Moreover the concept of profit is open to dispute over the meaning of the terms 'cost' and 'revenue'.

For generations theoretical economists have sought a consistent definition of profits. Wages, rent and interest may be looked on as a reward for the corresponding factors of production, labour, land and money (or capital), but it has always proved difficult to isolate a specific factor of production to which profit may be said to accrue as a reward.

Several theories have been advanced. The best known of these is that profits are a reward for bearing risk and uncertainty.[1] There is no need to bear those risks of fire and other accidental damage to, or loss of, plant and stocks that can be covered by insurance, and they are not related to profit. But most of the risks of manufacture and trading are not insurable. Every businessman undertakes some risk when he manufactures a product in anticipation of demand and the more specialized is a form of business activity the more risk and uncertainty there is likely to be. Anything new involves the risk that the public will not buy it, and certain trades are recognized to be more susceptible to sudden swings in demand, and therefore to be more risky. Fashion trades are an example, and most trades and industries which deal in goods which have relatively

---

[1] Frank H. Knight, *Risk, Uncertainty, and Profit* (London School of Economics and Political Science, Reprints of Scarce Works No. 16. 1933).

B

high price or income elasticities of demand,[2] or for which there are several substitutes, are also risky. If profit is thought of purely as a reward for risk, however, it will not coincide with what most people would think of in a general way as profit, and it might be applied too widely. Certain wage-earning occupations (such as coal-mining, jobs in the cotton industry, etc.) carry not only physical risk but also a risk of a loss of employment; it is rarely suggested that an appropriate part of the wages of such employment should be thought of as profit. Even if the risk theory does not provide a complete explanation, there is little doubt that it would be difficult to justify economic risk taking without some prospect of gain or profit, which in capitalistic countries would accrue to the entrepreneur and the providers of capital.

A second closely related type of theory states that 'normal' profits are a sort of managerial wage paid to a specialized form of labour, and that any surplus of revenue over costs after that is a profit due to imperfections of the market. Such profits accrue to monopolies, and in general the ability to take advantage before anyone else of changes in economic circumstances yields a reward in the form of profits above the managerial wage. This type of definition is probably too wide, since it evades the problems of defining adequately the service for which the so-called normal profit is a reward and thereby fails to define the functions and aims of the normal operations of a business; but the concept of extra or abnormal profit is itself quite useful.

Another theory regards profits as a reward for innovation and enterprise, for seeing the possibilities latent in various fields of action and in new technological development. To some extent this is a variant of the risk theory, but reward for risk is not a necessary part of the profit from innovations. The theory may also be looked on as a variant of that concerned with 'imperfection', because it stresses that profit may come from the exploitation of a temporary advantage. When innovations, of technique or marketing or indeed in any aspect of business organization, are made there is a short period during which the exploiters of the innovation make large profits, which are eventually reduced and shared out by the forces of

[2] See Chapter IV.

competition. Since innovation is almost always taking place, profit is always earned somewhere in the economy, and profit is thus linked to change and growth. This is undoubtedly a particularly important aspect of profit in a growing and developing economy, but it fails to explain why profits arise which are not a function of innovation. This type of theory is really only a special case of the 'imperfection' or 'friction' type of theory, but since it implies that profits are a return to a dynamism in business operations, it is a useful and acceptable partial definition.

None of the theories is intellectually satisfying but fortunately it is not strictly necessary to define a watertight category of rewards called profits. It is clear that some of what is normally called profits in everyday life is part of the reward to the various factors of production, such as rents on property owned by the business or interest paid on capital borrowed (a proportion of the dividend on ordinary share capital is probably profit). One factor of production, management, a specialized form of labour, also receives its reward partly in the form of profit. The sole owner, who manages as well as owns the business, achieves a surplus of receipts over costs, some of which is in a sense his 'managerial income' (roughly, what he would have to pay someone else to do the job), some of which is 'pure' profit, or return to enterprise. But what matters to him is that he earns something for running the firm whether it be for enterprise, risk bearing or innovation, and he calls this his profit.

With the increasing difficulty in modern business life of identifying the entrepreneur, particularly in large corporations, it becomes harder to state which factor of production receives its reward in the form of profit. If, as is often the case, a business is run by professional managers on fixed salaries who use the capital of other people, the answer may well be that it is not possible to ascribe anything called profit to the firm as an institution. Some of the surplus will accrue to managers in the form of extra high wages, some will be paid to shareholders as interest and a reward for the risks which *they* bear; some will be put by for future expansion and nothing else will be left.

Profit, in the sense of reward of some nature for some special factor of production, does not exist in the modern corporation: it all goes in payments to other factors of production or provision for the future.

Profit, however, is different from other kinds of income because it is not contractual, like wages and rent or 'fixed' interest; it is a residual item accruing as a result of producing in anticipation of demand: the businessman may be able to estimate profit fairly accurately, but he rarely receives it from anyone else as something due to him as a result of a contract: the rare cases in which he appears to do so, as in certain contracts affording him a certain level or margin of profit regardless of cost, are really to be regarded as payment for services. Since profit is residual it runs the risk of being negative, and it is liable to fluctuations with changes in business conditions. Thus the element of uncertainty does distinguish profits from other components of the value added by the productive process.

There is a lot to be said for the common-sense notion that profit is a reward for the successful conduct of a business. Several things contribute to this, and theories of profits draw attention to some of them; it is not really necessary to go any further. For present purposes profits may be defined as *the monetary proceeds from and incentive to successful business activity*. This is not a watertight definition and it evades rather than solves the theoretical difficulties, but it is a convenient categorization of this complex source of income.

The aims of business men, however, are complex and the money to be got out of business is only one reason for being in it; non-financial considerations are more important than is often imagined.

An important reason for setting up a business has always been the desire for personal independence. But the way of small business is hard; it is not easy to get established and it is difficult to expand. Larger firms benefit from economies of scale which enable them to buy more cheaply, to use methods of production that are economical only for long runs and to push sales with all the resources of a specialized section of the firm. Personal supervision often does not suffice to offset these advantages and many small proprietors get less from their businesses than they would be able to earn in alternative occupations. Many farmers in Northern Ireland who have not gone in for intensive livestock units make less than a farm worker's wage on farms of less than 40 acres. Many small shopkeepers must be little better placed. The occupation of such people is part of their way of life and this fact determines the conduct of their business. They must be regarded as maximizing the net advantages of their occupation, in this case the value of independence sustained by a modest income; it would be misleading to regard them as struggling to maximize monetary earnings alone or to judge their success or failure by this criterion.

Much the same kind of consideration applies in the case of a proprietor whose business is successful and capable of expansion, but who prefers to keep it at its present size. Expansion requires effort; it involves worry and risk; the rewards are cut by taxation; if present profitability is sufficient to provide for an acceptable and customary standard of living in line with the family position and the aspirations of neighbours, there may be no desire to expand further. This attitude of mind, while understandable, and perhaps even commendable as denoting a refusal to be preoccupied with material considerations, may be at odds with the evolution of society, for there is some truth in the assertion that business must expand or die.

The reasons for business expansion are not always economic. The tycoon bent on expansion may be more concerned with the prestige, political influence and power conferred by control of a large business. At this stage in the development of an enterprise profits may be sacrificed to expansion. But the reasons for expansion may also be predominantly altruistic. Mr Thomas Coughtrie, Chairman of Belmos, started to expand his business with the intention of creating employment in Lanarkshire during the depression; he was so successful that expansion became essential in order to retain young managers of promise and promote them to positions of responsibility.

Business is also creative; nursing and teaching are not the only occupation in which a sense of vocation may appear to be more important than pecuniary considerations. There are many dedicated businessmen who rank the satisfaction to be obtained in business with that obtained from practising in the professions. It is fortunate that this is so because it is no longer realistic to depict business as being run by some imaginary race of entrepreneurs owning their own firms and personally retaining the profits.

Even large businesses do not concentrate on maximizing profits to the exclusion of other objectives and they are unlikely to put considerations of growth on one side. Professor Baumol, writing from his business experience,[3] points to management's preoccupation with growth and the rate of growth of output that can be sustained having regard to the availability and cost of capital and the risks inherent in expansion. Many businessmen attempt to maximise growth rather than profits. Firms in communistically-organized economies have to conform to plans and objectives laid down by the State; these objectives have laid far more emphasis on the growth of output than on other criteria for success. Sometimes managers in such countries may be given a mutually inconsistent series of targets and have to effect some reconciliation between them. They too may be engaged, as managers in capitalistically-organized countries have been said to be engaged, in attempting to satisfy a series of criteria rather than in attempting to maximize profits or growth. Professor Herbert A. Simon points out that many businessmen concentrate on 'satisficing'[4] rather than maximizing and the way in which economies might be expected to operate would depend to some extent on whether management did one or the other.[5] In capitalistic and communistic economies managers do not lose sight of the fact that the more they do, the more may be expected of them, whatever the objectives they are expected to fulfil, and it is tempting to satisfice rather than to maximize. Professor Baumol has described how the management of one company, realising a few weeks before the preparation of their annual report that profits were likely to be spectacular, launched an energetic spending programme involving legitimate but optional expenditure on modernization, so as not to spoil the shareholders.

Growth and maximization of profits may not be incompatible. Profits may be both the means to and the consequence of

---

[3] *Business Behaviour, Value and Growth*, Harcourt Brace and World Incorporated, Revised Edition, 1967, Chapter 10.

[4] Satisficing is to accept any solution which is good enough in relation to various criteria such as survival, aspiration or avoidance of shame.

[5] See his article on 'Decision Making in Economics', *The American Economic Review*, June 1959.

growth; it is not suggested that growth is possible without profits or that profits are ever entirely sacrificed for growth. Even when maximization of profits is the objective it may sometimes be necessary to limit profits in the short run in the interests of expanding them in the future. The Acts creating public corporations generally give some indication of the character of the objectives they are expected to pursue. They are not told, however, to maximize profits, partly because they are in a position to exploit consumers by the exercise of monopoly power, and partly because it is frequently thought inappropriate for publicly owned bodies to make profit. Neither have their objectives been laid down in terms of growth, although this might have been a more reasonable criteria of success for some of them. The United Kingdom telephone service for example, has been neither specially profitable nor growth-conscious; the least satisfactory aspect of its post-war performance has been its failure to provide the services expected of it by actual and prospective customers. If it had been given the objective of expanding the telephone service, costs would have fallen as a result of economies of scale as its operations expanded, thus improving its financial performance.

One of the difficulties of nationalized industry is that it is not normally given one objective but several. These may range from the obligations of a common carrier or a good employer to statutory requirements to carry out some function without close regard to the cost of doing so. Consequently public corporations are required to satisfice. Varied criteria make it difficult to judge performance and it is all the more necessary to give public corporations clearly defined functions. In redefining the obligations of nationalized industry over the years greater emphasis has been placed on the need for them to be profitable in a financial sense. The original criterion set for financial success was that of breaking-even taking the good years with the bad. It was only after some experience of the effects of this kind of objective on performance that it was accepted that they ought to make reasonable profits by comparison with non-nationalized industries. This was desirable partly to inculcate a greater sense of the need for efficiency and to ensure that they realized the importance of finding money for capital investment from their own resources, and partly to put them on the same footing as private enterprise.

Increasing emphasis on profits does not mean, however, that they are re-established as the only test of efficiency. As in all industries operating in non-competitive conditions, efficiency must be judged by other tests, such as comparisons with similar industries elsewhere, evidence of a progressive outlook and the maintenance of an adequate quality of service. Similar tests may also be applied to private industry. Amongst businessmen themselves profitability is only one test of success and there is high regard for the firm that is known to be progressive, technically advanced, and receptive to ideas.

In practice large firms as well as public corporations must have regard to the public interest as well as to the interest of their shareholders, and this may mean some sacrifice of profit. Many business decisions involve moral as well as monetary judgments and such decisions are often difficult to make because a balance has to be struck between different interests. Maximization of profit is unlikely to override all other considerations. Private industry is likely to exploit monopoly situations to some degree but, irrespective of fears of retaliatory action from potential competitors or of regulation by the government, a company may deliberately attempt to refrain from exploiting its monopoly position to the full, preferring to follow some concept of a fair or reasonable price. Charging what the market will bear is frequently regarded as profiteering and a lower price based on cost may therefore be charged on ethical grounds.[6] For similar reasons a firm's policy in relation to, say, redundancy may be more generous than would be dictated solely by considerations of self-interest. Small firms may take a similar point of view.

COMPANY CONTROL

In a formal sense public corporations are controlled by government. Their objectives are laid down and they may be given some indication of how they are to attain them. Control may be further reinforced by making key appointments. There might appear little further to be said but control, whether it is applied to public or private corporations, is not a simple thing; there

[6] See P. J. D. Wiles, *Price, Cost and Output* (Blackwell, 1962).

are overlapping circles of control and a firm's policy can be influenced from a number of directions. Even in capitalistically-organized economies, business enterprise does not operate independently of the State. While directors and managers try to make their firm perform in the way they think desirable, government also frames policies with the intention of making firms achieve the objectives of its policy. Intervention is direct when firms are told that they must carry out some particular policy or when nationalization is adopted as a device to enforce government control. In spite of growing direct intervention most of the methods used by Government to influence business are indirect, and this applies to nationalized industries as well as to private firms. The reason for the choice of indirect rather than direct intervention is not solely ideological but reflects considerations as to how best the economy can be administered.

One reason why government rarely intervenes in the affairs of particular firms is that they are too numerous to be considered individually; in addition there are many decisions that are better taken at lower levels of control than by some centralized authority. The higher the level of control the less detailed can it be and the more it must be exercised by indirect means. In the United Kingdom government regulations normally apply to all firms or firms in particular industries; they have the effect of altering the economic framework in which business works. The most common method of control is by means of fiscal and monetary measures. Taxes may be raised or lowered to alter the level of demand for goods and services; they may be brought to bear on certain sections of industry, for example those producing consumer goods, or may be used through remission to give encouragement to export. Subsidies may be given to particular industries such as shipbuilding or agriculture, thus making life easier for them and encouraging them to increase output. Such discrimination may be combined with measures making it easier or more difficult to borrow money.

All economic measures operate imperfectly. Government cannot be sure that any measures will produce the desired effects. Our understanding of the working of the economy is incomplete; altering the conditions in which business works sometimes produces unexpected results, and the broad administrative methods of control used by government cannot be refined sufficiently to produce more than a close approximation to what is intended.

Control by government is over-riding in the sense that it has the effect of prescribing the general conditions in which business can function. Within this framework other bodies and individuals exercise control because they too have some say in what the enterprise is trying to do and in the means employed to accomplish its objectives. These interests include financiers and shareholders who provide money, and directors and managers who decide how it shall be used.

In the first half of the nineteenth century it was possible to think of firms as being small enough to have been built up, financed and controlled by one man, the entrepreneur. There are still many small firms in industry, in agriculture and in the service industries. But in manufacturing industry, and increasingly in agriculture and services, large firms are dominant, their small number being more than offset by their large size. The typical form of organization is either that of the public corporation or of the joint stock company with limited liability.

The administration of private companies is not essentially different from that of public corporations. The objectives of private companies are defined in memoranda and articles of association and they seek to attain these within the legal and other restrictions laid upon them. How control is exercised over the operations of such companies is an interesting matter. Legally, shareholders control the companies they own but their rights are limited in some ways; they cannot, for example, require higher dividends to be paid than those recommended by directors and in practice their influence may be weak because of the impossibility of a large number of shareholders making their views effective in day to day business.

The potential influence of individuals or groups of individuals in determining company policy is not just a question of seeing whether an absolute majority of votes can be mustered; the ways in which control may be exercised are subtle. Dominance does not necessarily imply a majority of votes in any walk of life, nor does a substantial holding of shares necessarily imply active intervention. The ultimate responsibility for the appointment of directors and indirectly for other appointments rests with shareholders; can they, and do they bring their weight to bear in this respect? Directors or managers may not be substantial shareholders and so may not represent the shareholders' point of view, but once appointed they have a major say in company policy.

A holding of more than half the shares in a company gives a clear majority for the exercise of control which can scarcely be gainsaid except at law. Sometimes quite a small minority holding can also be effective provided it is of some minimum size and the majority are indifferent to the issues being determined. Work by Professor Penrose[7] suggests that with a 1,000 voting shares, 6 per cent of votes could carry a decision with 96 per cent probability. Moreover, within groups that could command 6 per cent or more votes a small number of shareholders may themselves be dominant. This might arise also when members of a family were substantial shareholders and prepared to concert their views and actions. Family holdings in Marks & Spencer might be a case in point.

It is not easy to form generalizations about the many circumstances in which a small body of shareholders might exercise control. Registers of shareholders may show whether a limited number of shareholders come near to having either a majority vote or sufficient shares to enable them to exercise a controlling influence in practice. Professor Sargant Florence has suggested as one indicator of this whether the largest 20 shareholders command 20 per cent of the votes, but no-one would suggest that this is all that should be considered. If all possible forms of dominant interest are taken fully into account it might be possible to demonstrate that half of the companies in the U.K. or U.S.A. could be dominated by small groups.

But potentiality and actuality are two different things. The role of the shareholder can become largely passive. Even when there are dominant shareholdings it does not follow that these are used to influence company policy in normal circumstances. Insurance companies have large holdings in certain companies but appear to refrain in normal circumstances from attempting to intervene in the running of their affairs. It is doubtful how far such control is directed even to influence the

---

[7] Elementary Statistics of Majority Voting, *Statistical Journal*, 1946. Part 1. pp. 53–54. See Sargant Florence, *The Logic of British and American Industry*, p. 195.

appointment of directors or key personnel who will be concerned with the day to day direction of the company.

When shareholdings are widely spread even this form of control can seldom be exercised; if it is, the reasons are generally that the company is making losses and that some shareholder is sufficiently involved to be prepared to organize a body of opposition to the existing board of directors, or sees a way to forward his personal ambition by doing so. In continental countries there is greater opportunity for intervention on behalf of shareholders, for it is more usual to appoint banks as proxies to vote at meetings than to appoint nominees within the company; because of this a more unified view of shareholders in relation to the company which they own may emerge.

The present system of company law provides a framework for the extension of control to subsidiary companies, without need for any individual or group to own 50 per cent of all the shares involved. The parent company can ensure control over subsidiaries by holding 51 per cent of the subsidiaries' shares; it is possible to extend the process further because the subsidiaries in turn may control still another company or companies by acquiring a majority shareholding. At the end of such a chain a shareholder controlling a subsidiary company may have subscribed indirectly through the parent company's holdings for only a very small percentage of the subsidiary company's shares, but may, nevertheless have as complete a control as if he owned all the issued shares.[8]

Directors exercise control through their office rather than through their shareholdings. Professor Sargant Florence found that in very large companies the shares held by the Board of Directors exceeded 2 per cent of total shares in only 43 per cent of the companies examined, and exceeded 20 per cent of total shares in only 13 per cent of companies, while there was only an average of $1\frac{1}{2}$ directors amongst the largest twenty shareholders of large companies.

Effective control may be extended by the use of interlocking directorates, and the question of ownership of shares may have little relevance for control operated in this fashion. In fact

---

[8] Under the 1967 Companies Act, Subsidiary Companies have to be listed for the information of shareholders and the Board of Trade.

most relatively shareless directors are probably full-time 'inside' executive officers of the company, and the holding of office is certainly a more frequent ground for appointment to director-ships than shareholding, particularly where boards are small.[9] Succession to the board thus tends to be arranged within the firm by existing directors, and while formal approval must be obtained this is often no more than a formality when share-holdings are widely diffused and the votes of shareholders are assigned to existing directors as proxies. It is not unusual for institutions to work in this way; many of them are self-perpetu-ating and indeed must often be so if continuity in operations and management is to be assured.

Control over industrial operations is something which concerns government closely. On the one hand it is feared that centralization of control in limited hands will lead to too great a concentration of industrial power, which may be inimical to the consumer and harmful to the development of the economy through the exercise of monopoly powers and in other ways. This view has given rise to much legislation aimed against agreements between firms to limit competition, and also to measures designed to frustrate the establishment of large groups. On the other hand it is recognised that scale of opera-tion is increasingly important, and this led to active enc-ouragement, through the Industrial Reorganization Corpor-ation,[10] to firms with similar interests to merge and operate on a larger scale.

Control of a company or companies must be exercised with skill. Control is more often the power to influence the actions of others than a means to prescribe them. Indeed the first requirement of the successful controller is the realization that his powers are limited, for he must work by combining the activities of individuals or bodies in a constructive way. Often this can best be done by setting broad objectives and prescrib-ing certain limits of action, leaving others to change, initiate and shape on their own responsibility within their own spheres of control. This sort of control with its attendant devolution of authority is frequently more difficult than attempting to attend to all the details personally. One of the tests of the

[9] Sargant Florence op. cit. p. 105.
[10] See Chapter VI, Appendix II.

good manager is his ability to delegate while still maintaining broad control; even more important is his ability to devise a framework of control which will produce results.

So-called control exercised by the City has resemblances to control exercised by government over the economy. General impressions about the economic scene and more detailed views about the prospects for particular products, industries and firms are the starting point. Control consists of fashioning the flow of finance in line with these views, so that money is available for promising ventures and not for those that offer little prospect of success. This may be combined with influencing the appointment of suitable people to positions of responsibility. Once this is done the future of the enterprise may be left to its directors, further intervention being necessary only if the members of the board do not fulfil their promise.

This also sets the pattern in many cases for control of subsidiary companies; the board or the holding company may see its function as being that of setting objectives and laying down certain broad policies to be followed, and it may combine this with exercising influence over the appointments made in subsidiaries. There is room for variation. In some cases subsidiaries may be free of most control so long as they continue to function successfully according to some criteria: Lord Thompson gives the impression of controlling his newspapers mainly in this way. The control of Elliott-Automation, a collection of small businesses, appears to be closer than that exercised by Lord Thompson. As Sir Leon Bagrit has described[11] the divisional manager has complete authority and responsibility for the activities in his division from design, manufacture and cost accounts to sales and service, but his powers are limited in a number of ways, particularly through budgetary control. This is a common approach to the control of a collection of enterprises which can be varied and adapted to suit particular circumstances. In contrast, the description of the organization of Boots given by Mr F. A. Cockfield[12] emphasizes that the company is run as a single unit. It is vertically integrated and merchandise is bought centrally, although branch managers have a large measure of autonomy in determining sales effort

[11] In *Studies in Business Organization*, edited by Ronald S. Edwards and Harry Townsend Macmillan 1961, p. 63.
[12] Ibid. p. 127.

and range of goods stocked. Thus there are degrees of autonomy and degrees of control. If indeed we take the view that the character of a firm is decided by the right to make decisions rather than by ownership, it becomes very difficult to be precise about what is meant by a firm. For different matters the firm may alter its composition. In law it may have one constitution; in trade union bargaining another; while for the purpose of investment decisions still another identity may be involved.

THE SUCCESSFUL FIRM

If businesses are to succeed they must be capable of initiating and responding to change. Sometimes the changes involved will be radical, such as the introduction of a new product or process or a major extension of plant, but often change and reorganization will be no more than an attempt to catch up with what competitors have already done. A readiness to accept what is new to the firm is often as important as the ability to trace a new path.

The face of the world has changed completely since the Industrial Revolution. The advanced countries of the world have moved from being predominantly agricultural to being predominantly industrial in little more than a century. Change in even the last 50 years has been prodigious; we have reached a stage of industrial development where many things are out-of-date almost as soon as they have been produced, and often before quantity production has been started. This is true of aircraft production, where any programme is always a compromise between long runs of existing types at low cost and small quantities of technically superior but more expensive aircraft.

In some industries change is more gradual and the same articles may be produced for some years without radical alteration, but the pace of change must not be under-estimated. Experience has shown that economies are capable of increasing output of all kinds over long periods at a rate of 3 per cent or more per annum. The rate of increase in industrial production is generally much greater, and at certain stages of development it may increase at the rate of even 10 per cent per annum.

On the other hand nothing is more likely to perpetuate itself than industrial decline. Many areas in the United Kingdom have suffered because the industries on which they depended have declined, either because their products became outdated or because competitors were able to outsell them. The cotton and shipbuilding industries are cases in point. Often the process of decline is slow; the cotton industry reached the peak of its activity in 1913 and it is only recently that it appears to have been reorganized on a more effective basis. From the social point of view the protracted decline of industries is all the more dangerous, because through interrelations between firms it exercises a cumulative effect on the community, and once the number of stagnant or declining firms becomes large it is difficult to establish offsetting points of growth. It is seldom sufficient to rationalise those industries in which decline has been taking place; it is necessary to diversify and establish new types of industry or products which have good prospects of success. Sensing such opportunities is an important managerial function. It is often calls for practical insight and even intuition as well as analytical skill.

Few things are more difficult than the anticipation of some new need perhaps as yet unfelt by those for whom a product is intended; new departures are fraught with difficulty and no one can be sure that they will be successful. If the initial difficulties can be overcome a period of expansion may open up increasingly profitable opportunities. However, all innovators have their imitators and emulators; once the flush of newness is over competitors may gain an increasing share of the market, or profitable opportunities may disappear for other reasons. The introduction of colour television was welcomed by manufacturers of sets because saturation of the domestic market for black-and-white sets was being reached. Other new products such as synthetic fibres which have enjoyed an expanding market over the years have suffered considerable ups and downs. The ability to keep one step ahead of competitors is just as important as newness. New entrants are frequently better placed than those first in the field because they have not been put to the cost of developing new processes; they can take a fresh look at what is needed and can develop better production facilities.

Although there are no golden rules for the identification of favourable market opportunities, economic reasoning, market research and appreciation of current trends can help to eliminate unlikely possibilities. It would clearly be a mistake to attempt to outsell India or Pakistan by producing jute sacks for use in Asia but it might be quite profitable to sell highly sophisticated jute products in competition with them in the United States. The market for linen textiles is a contracting one but it is profitable to fly linen handkerchiefs to certain Mediterranean markets. At the same time it may pay to change from processing linen to processing synthetic fibres. It is always difficult to know whether it is better to improve existing production processes while continuing to manufacture the same products, or to adopt some radically new method of production, or to attempt to produce some new product. Many firms in declining industries recognise that they are operating in unfavourable circumstances, and attempt to diversify their activities. Thus a firm producing domestic boilers may branch out into the provision of canteen equipment, perhaps by the acquisition of a subsidiary, and another engaged in textiles may decide to supplement its activities by producing plastic materials. Similarly, shipbuilding companies faced with a recession of markets may branch out into the production of caravans, hovercraft or prefabricated houses—often with disastrous results. The success of these innovations will depend on whether the companies concerned can command the managerial skills needed to direct new enterprises. This is particularly important if existing facilities are being used for some new purpose under the operation of the same personnel; but it also applies if diversification is being carried out by acquiring existing going concerns. A new company is not faced with the problem of reconciling its past inheritance with future opportunities, but it is not without its difficulties. Tradition may be no drag but its own experience is no guide.

Progressive companies have recognised that one of the functions of management is to seek new profitable opportunities. The function of economic intelligence divisions in larger firms is not just to deal with day to day events, more often they are asked for long-term studies in the hope that these will suggest such opportunities. Research and development may be given great emphasis with the intention of assuring the company's future by developing new products. Thus, the power to

c

innovate may be built into the company's structure in the knowledge that experienced managers are available to exploit new ideas and that new companies can be established for the purpose.

The need for firms constantly to adjust themselves to their changing environment has relevance to the composition of company boards. Many talents are needed in the board room and a well-balanced team of specialists needs to be sought, but at least one of the directors must personify those characteristics of energy, initiative and readiness to pioneer that are characteristic of the mythical entrepreneur. Industrial development is a process of change, re-organization and consolidation; if these three steps are essential to development the Board of Directors should include individuals who are particularly adept at guiding the enterprise through the various stages. The qualities of directors capable of initiating change are different from those who are most capable of putting the changes into effect, and the responsibility of supervising a period of consolidation probably calls for a third type of director, possibly an older man with the patience and experience needed for putting the finishing touches to some innovation.

Economic considerations are only one aspect of business operations and it is necessary to look at the men concerned as well as what they are expected to do. Some part of the differing economic performance of countries and the varying success of firms may be explained not by differences in economic conditions but by differences in outlook.

A study by Political and Economic Planning[18] laid stress on the effect of managerial attitudes on the performance of firms. It lays down over sixty criteria for distinguishing progressive and non-progressive firms according to their attitudes, and reaches the view that these are highly relevant to economic performance.

Many of the criteria considered lie outside the scope of this book; they are concerned, for example, with views expressed by managers about industrial relations, selection of salesmen and training. But many of the criteria throw light on how firms take economic decisions.

[18] *Thrusters and Sleepers*, Allen and Unwin 1965, reprinted as *Attitudes in British Industry*, Pelican 1966

The margin between success and failure in industry is narrow : it is unusual to make a profit of more than 10 per cent on the value of turnover. There is no safe margin in which the inefficient firm can operate, and even the efficient firm cannot afford to be complacent if new products or new production methods or sales methods start to narrow profit margins. The basic philosophy of this book is that a decision should be reached only after a systematic analysis of the situation. It is not enough to list the factors that affect any given situation; it is also necessary to take the further step of assessing their quantitative importance. When the outcome of the decision to be taken is uncertain, as it generally is, an attempt must be made to delimit the uncertainty and to decide what policy to follow in the light of the possible outcome of the various strategies that can be followed. This approach applies to every aspect of business operations whether they are concerned with the location and scale of operations, the choice of product, expenditure on research and development or sources of finance.

In some cases location is self-determining; it is impossible to mine coal where coal does not exist and difficult to grow bananas cheaply in this country. Very few production activities are confined to a very limited choice of site such as the availability of some natural resource might imply. Other factors affecting costs may be more important, such as the cost or availability of labour or transport. Centres of population are both a source of labour and a potential market. Productive activities tend to gravitate to centres of population where modern social organization is facilitated by the economies that result from large-scale organization and where companies can expect to find ancillary facilities. Thus for some manufacturing processes the precise location of a factory, so long as it is near to some centre of population, is of little moment, but whenever it appears that location can affect costs by even 1 per cent it becomes an important factor, for 1 per cent of costs may be equivalent to 10 per cent of profits.

Investment decisions should be taken only after similar appraisal of their effects on costs and returns. What might be expected to be self-evident is clearly not so; the P.E.P study illustrated this abundantly. Some firms for example seem to regard the replacement of machines as being governed by serviceability rather than by considerations of profitability.[14]

All enterprises have their objectives and they seek to achieve these with limited resources and within constraints related to the environment in which they operate. If an optimal allocation is to be secured managers must adopt a rational and systematic evaluation of the alternatives in terms of what costs may be incurred, or what revenues or other benefits may accrue, as a result of the various courses of action open to them. It is this question of choice that makes economics so relevant to business decisions.

Systematic decision-making is vital for efficiency. This process starts with the specification of objectives; it should be followed with an analysis of the various courses of action open to the firm, bringing out all relevant factors and assessing their quantitative importance; the aim of analysis is to generate alternatives for consideration by management. It is not enough in practice to take decisions; policy must be executed and this calls for action and for administrative machinery designed to ensure that what is intended is actually carried into effect. As well as having economic implications this brings in administrative methods and the need for good human relations.

Carrying out these processes will help to reduce the uncertainty that is always present in business operations. Analysis itself reduces uncertainty by providing management with better data on which to base decisions; it may also contribute by reducing the range of uncertainty that exists. But uncertainty cannot be eliminated entirely, it can only be reduced; a further stage in decision-taking may lie in acknowledging this and adopting policies which will protect the firm from the uncertain outcome of reality. This does not mean that the firm is able to obtain the best of all possible worlds, but it enables it to appraise the consequences of the various courses of action that it can follow and to choose those courses that are likely to be consistent with the attainment of its objectives.

Statistical decision theory is an approach to this kind of problem; it may be illustrated in terms of deciding whether to hold a garden party indoors or outdoors. In practice such a decision might be reached intuitively without the trouble of ex-

[14] *Attitudes in British Industry*, p. 111.

amining what might happen in alternative circumstances. A better decision should result from a more analytical approach to the question. This might start with a rating in terms of points of the satisfaction that might be expected from the garden party in different circumstances. If the weather were fine and it were decided to hold the party indoors 20 points might be alloted; if the weather were fine and the decision were to hold it outdoors, 65 points; if rain fell and the party were held indoors, 40 points might be alloted; an outdoor party in the same circumstances would be given zero points, a complete washout. This system of scoring is set out in the pay-off matrix below (Table 1.1). The heading "Events (States of Nature)" is almost self-explanatory; it sets out the alternatives of weather over which there is no control. The strategies or courses of action listed in the left-hand column illustrate the power to decide whether the party will be held indoors or outdoors.

TABLE 1.1

PAY OFF MATRIX FOR GARDEN PARTY

Strategies or Courses of action	Events (States of Nature)	
	Fine	Rain
Indoor	20	40
Outdoor	65	0

If we were to think in terms of a simple business decision, pay-off in the matrix might represent profits in thousands of pounds, and the alternatives might represent prediction of outcomes if a new product were launched in conditions of boom or slump. Another matrix (Table 1.2) shows how the alternatives might look in terms of the pay-off.

TABLE 1.2

PAY OFF MATRIX FOR NEW PRODUCT SITUATION

Strategies	Events (States of Nature)	
	Boom	Slump
New Product	100	−20
No New Product	60	40

The decision that the businessman has to take is whether to launch a new product or not, given the uncertainty. Such decisions might be arrived at from different points of view. A very conservative manager might decide to play safe and make sure that if the worst comes to the worst he would secure the largest minimum pay-off possible. He would choose not to produce a new product, thus ensuring that his return would not be below 40. This is generally described as adopting a maximin criterion. At the opposite extreme a pure gambler might choose to launch a new product in the hope of making a killing, choosing in this case to produce a new product in the hope of gaining 100, even if a slump would result in a loss of 20. This is called the maximax criterion.

Another way of looking at the same alternatives is to consider what regret would be felt in various situations after the outcome was known. A regret matrix (Table 1.3) is shown below in relation to the launching of a new product. If the decision were taken to launch a new product and the state of the economy turned out to be that of boom, there would be no reason for regret because the maximum possible pay-off would have been secured. On the other hand, if the product were launched in conditions of slump, a regret of 60 would be felt. This is because the situation new product/slump results in a loss of 20, whereas had the decision been to launch no new product, and conditions of slump had still obtained, a profit of 40 would have emerged: The difference between the two situations is thus 60. Similarly, if no new product were launched and conditions of slump occurred, there would be no reason for regret because the best possible outcome in such circumstances would have been secured.

TABLE 1.3

REGRET MATRIX FOR NEW PRODUCT SITUATION

Strategies	States of Nature	
	Boom	Slump
New Product	0	60
No New Product	40	0

Another approach to this decision is to attempt to assign probabilities to the states of nature, estimating in what proportion of cases on the average one or other state would emerge.

It is then possible to estimate whether the business would gain on average if the decisions could be repeated in some kind of experiment; it would then be feasible to adopt that strategy which would give the biggest return on average. If we assign a probability of $\frac{1}{4}$ to the possibility of boom and $\frac{3}{4}$ to slump, the return expected from launching a new product would be $\frac{1}{4}$ of 100 *minus* $\frac{3}{4}$ of 20, amounting to 10; the return from launching no new product would be $\frac{1}{4}$ of 60 plus $\frac{3}{4}$ of 40, amounting to 45. There will be few circumstances in which industrial decisions take this simple form but the analysis is capable of considerable extension and development and may be applicable to more complex cases. Even when the theory does not lend itself readily to calculation and to clear-cut decisions determined by arithmetic, it has value in putting the nature of a decision into a form which can be understood and from which the consequences of various results can be assessed.

Nevertheless there is no analytical apparatus which can remove all the uncertainties from business decisions. It is a good plan to make some provision for alternative outcomes; to keep the arrangements flexible when this is possible; to spread risks in some measure; and to devise plans that do not hinge entirely on one set of possible circumstances.

This does not mean that all business decisions must be constantly reconsidered. Many of them may be of a nature that takes into account the effects of unforeseen changes. Controls that provide for the level of stocks to be related to production will automatically adjust stocks to fluctuations in rates of output, operating like a thermostat. The appropriate action to be taken when sales increase may also be built into the standing orders under which the firm operates. Some problems may occur so repeatedly that the solution to them is known, even though the outcome is uncertain, and the course of action to be taken in response to them can be prescribed as a matter of routine. Problems that once taxed the imagination, experience and judgment of senior managers can be reduced by mathematical techniques to matters of routine decision. Once such techniques are prescribed the problems with which they were designed to deal pass largely out of the field of managerial decision, and even though they are of quite basic importance to the success of the business, they can be regarded as minor decisions that can be left to subordinates.

The Board of Directors will be asked to take a great many decisions during a year and many issues will come up for examination. Some of the work of the board will be routine consideration of regular matters. But from time to time it will be necessary to consider the outlook for the whole of the firm's operations and to consider its prospects. Such an examination may be confined to considering the likely outcome of operations as they are currently planned or it may be more radical, setting new objectives for the firm, and exploring future opportunities for the business. This might start with a review of sales prospects and the measures necessary to effect an improvement. A tentative decision might be taken to aim at greatly increased sales. But such decisions cannot be maintained irrespective of the conduct of the rest of the company's affairs. A decision to increase sales must be related to increased production possibilities, financial requirements and cost functions. The process of decision can start with the consideration of any aspect of a firm's operations but it must complete the process by considering them all and their interrelations. It is not just a question of co-ordinating activities, but of co-ordinating the plan itself and testing its validity.

BUSINESS ECONOMICS AND MANAGEMENT

The growing awareness in recent years of the need for systematic management has led to the development of a number of approaches designed to instil in managers an appreciation of the ways in which business problems may be tackled. This is most commonly done through the employment of a series of devices leading to the production of check lists which help managers to identify the major problem areas of the modern business.

The job of the manager may be divided into a number of elements, which can be summarised as: planning, forecasting, coordination, organization and administration of the resources at his disposal; decision making, command (or the initiation and supervision of action by the communication of decisions and information), the fostering of good human relations and control. The efficient execution of these functions requires a great deal of expertise in a number of fields, and it is not surprising that the manager needs guidance in his task. Management by objectives and long range planning are two of the drills devised to assist the manager. Both of them proceed by listing a number of steps which assist in the statement and achievement of objectives; they point for example to the need to identify market opportunities, company strengths and weaknesses, to the need for a profit and so on. Management by objectives next proceeds through a drill by which objectives are set for individuals in the organization, in order that delegation may be efficiently carried out. A number of other drills, such as value analysis, critical path analysis, PERT (programme evaluation and review technique) have also been produced to assist the manager in some of the more detailed tasks of the organization.

Systems analysis is another such approach which, in its more advanced forms, presents both the need and the opportunity for sophisticated analysis. The basic philosophy of systems analysis is that all operations have to be seen as part of an overall system, which must be comprehended and coordinated if an optimal solution is to be achieved. Thus a business organization may be seen as part of a system in which *management* coordinates *men, material* and *machines* in order to produce *goods* which are sold to *consumers* in *markets* in which there are *competitors,* and in which the action of *governments* may have an important effect. The components of the system are in italics; systems analysis identifies, analyses and suggests courses of action suitable to the elements. It is similar in conception to the input-output analysis of the economist, which identifies and analyses interactions between different sectors of an economy.

Such approaches are extremely convenient to the manager in that they identify many of the main problem areas; their main shortcoming is that, in themselves, they neither suggest methods of analysis nor lead to operational solutions. Analysis, and the solutions which it suggests, require a conceptual approach which in turn implies a theoretical (or model-building) approach to problems. The check-list or cookery book approach to problems works well when the major constituents of a problem remain the same in all situations; in such circumstances a well-established drill can usually give a predictably workable answer. But there are few business situations in which such conditions regularly apply, and the ability to think through a problem from first principles is essential for a manager in a changing world. These first principles—economics, quantitative methods, human relations and organization theory—are the disciplines of modern management.

Operational research is a different matter; it has been defined in a number of ways, ranging from the epigrammatic "the art of winning wars without fighting" to the slightly apologetic "a study of administrative systems in the same scientific manner in which systems in physics, chemistry and biology are studied in the natural sciences'.[15] It is probably best described as a scientific study of the effectiveness of operations, an operation being defined as any human activity in which a certain set of resources is directed towards the achievement of a given set of objectives. The business applications of operational research may be regarded as an attempt to translate the subject matter of economics into practical recommendations.[16]

The methods of operational research are scientific; they are a combination of observation, experiment and deductive and inductive reasoning about relevant items. The main concern of operational research is optimization, or the best combinaton of the resources of the system in order to achieve the objectives of the organization. Optimal solutions are not always possible—the objectives, constraints and variables of a problem cannot always be uniquely identified and quantified—and in such cases operational research attempts heuristic solutions, designed to achieve the best possible solution given the limitations of the data and objectives of the problem.

One of the benefits of operational research is that it recognises the need for optimal solutions for the system as a whole. A solution which is best only in relation to one part of the system is sub-optimal; for example, a method of stock control which is optimal for a distribution point may place such demands on the factory supplying the stocks that the factory

---

[15] E. Duckworth, *A Guide to Operational Research*, Methuen 1965.
[16] Compare the definition of economics proposed by Robbins in *The Nature and Significance of Economic Science:* 'Economics is a science which studies human behaviour as a relationship between ends and scarce means which have alternative uses'.

is forced to work at less than maximum efficiency, with the result that such a solution would be sub-optimal for the system as a whole. This kind of approach to business decisions has many antecedents. Operational research developed most rapidly during the Second World War, but it really goes back to the devolution of control which has been a feature of the growth of modern industry; the problems of the giant concern cannot all be isolated into individual compartments and it is not a new thing to recognise the need for systems to cope with problems which span many functions and departments.

But major developments came during the Second World War when the British and American military services began to look at operations in the ways described above, and the need was recognised for a scientific assessment of the best ways of deploying resources. Assignments included optimum bombing patterns, patterns for depth charges, optimum spacing of ships in convoys, problems of minimizing delays in unloading ships in port, and the effectiveness of warning systems against air attack. Operational research teams were drawn from many disciplines; partly because of this tradition, and partly by intention, mathematicians and econometricians, economists and accountants, psychologists and biologists, scientists and engineers, have come to be associated in operational research teams.

Operational research is a recognition of the need for a new method for the study of systems which could draw from the experience of all sciences and could use this experience in the sphere of business. It is a method of approach rather than a collection of techniques. Examples of the practical use of operational research are used throughout this book in demonstration of the practical uses of business economies.

Chapter II

PRODUCTION AND COSTS

PRODUCTION is the organized activity of transforming resources into finished products in the form of goods and services; the objective of production is to satisfy the demand for such transformed resources. Coal and iron in their natural state in the ground are of little use to anyone until they are mined and worked on to produce steel for motor vehicles, bridges, ships and other goods.

To be specific, the productive process consists of taking materials,[1] and adding value to them by application of factors of production in form of labour, machinery and all of the other services of modern industrial organization. The addition of value means that goods are sufficiently different at the end of the productive process to justify charging a higher price for them; the rewards of production go to those factors (including capital and management) which add the value. Any activity which results in such added value constitutes production and, whilst we tend to think in ordinary life of production as being confined to manufacturing, strictly speaking the processes of marketing and transport are a part of production.

For practical purposes, however, it is usually convenient to think of production in terms of the two main categories of manufacturing and distribution.

Thus, the *net output* of an enterprise consists of the *value added* to materials by the processes of production; or, looking at it from the point of view of rewards to the factors which make up the productive process, it constitutes a fund from which charges are met, in the form of wages and salaries, rents, taxes, depreciation, advertising, etc.

The composition of costs and net output differs considerably from industry to industry, and even within the same industry

---

[1] Which are usually the products of some other processes—coal, for example, is the finished product of coal mining and a raw material of steel making, steel is a raw material for many other processes.

and among firms with essentially similar processes, differences between firms may be great. Physical and technological characteristics differentiate firms from each other, and there are also differences in the efficiency of utilization of factors and processes which affect cost structures. The main items of expenditure in most businesses are materials; the main costs of *production* proper (or net output) are wages and salaries. These are shown for the main manufacturing industry groups in the U.K. in Table 2.1 which illustrates the diversity of conditions. Wages are a relatively small proportion of net output in the 'food, drink and tobacco' group, a large part of net output being accounted for by advertising, selling expenses and depreciation; at the other extreme wages account for a high proportion of net output in construction and mining and quarrying. Net output as a percentage of sales is again low in food, drink and tobacco and high in mining. Industries in which net output is low in relation to the cost of bought-in materials and fuel often feel they have little control over costs because they depend so heavily on their suppliers. In fact when alternative sources of supply are available they are less dependent than might appear, because they can shop around and their ability to buy cheaply and effectively is one of the major tests of their efficiency.

TABLE 2.1

PRODUCTION AND COSTS IN BRITISH MANUFACTURING INDUSTRY, 1958

Industry	Sales £m	Cost of materials and fuels	Net Output	Wages and Salaries Per cent of net Output
		Per cent of Sales		
Food, drink and tobacco	4477	72.1	27.9	38.8
Chemicals and allied industries	2692	62.3	37.7	36.1
Metal manufactures	2479	66.7	33.3	56.9
Engineering and allied industries	9013	51.3	48.7	58.4
Textiles	3081	58.7	41.3	56.0
Other manufacturing	3771	48.2	51.8	55.0
Mining and quarrying	1031	25.1	74.9	66.6
Construction	3930	52.7	47.3	69.0
Gas, Electricity and water	1593	38.4	61.6	34.3
ALL industries	32,066	45.5	44.6	54.5

Source: Annual Abstract of Statistics, HMSO 1967.

The *Census of Production,* from which this summary table is taken, tells us a little about the costs of the productive processes, but not much about the processes themselves. These differ a great deal from trade to trade; some industries, such as light engineering, require a great deal of intricate and relatively expensive machinery; others such as shipbuilding, require heavy and expensive machinery; some industries need a lot of skilled workers to operate their machines; others, like the motor industry, with a lot of automatic processes, require a great deal of unskilled and semi-skilled labour, but a large expenditure item over the years is in respect of machinery. The clothing industry is different from all of these industries: it requires little machinery, most of it relatively inexpensive, and a large amount of semi-skilled labour; premises in the industry are usually small and an insignificant item in costs. In this industry the main costs are materials and labour.

If this diversity of conditions is taken to its extreme every firm is different, but there are some basic principles which help the economist and the businessman to sort out the meaning and efficiency of the productive process in general terms, without the need to consider each individual technique. In one sense the techniques themselves do not matter; what matters is the most efficient use of them, and this is both a technological and an economic problem.

PRODUCTION AND BUSINESS DECISIONS

In the productive process costs are incurred in payment for factors of production and resources, and the businessman has to solve two main problems. The first is to find the combinations and types of factors which will produce his output at least cost; the second is to find the most profitable or economical output at which to produce, and the proportions in which he will produce the components of his output. To put it at its simplest, he has to think in terms of costs and scale of production.

In the short run the production problem is to make the best use of available productive facilities; there is usually a variety of ways in which they can be employed profitably.

The cost of using given capital equipment to manufacture some product is measured largely in terms of the contribution which it could make to revenue if it were employed in producing some other product.[2] Thus, in a jute mill the cost of using machinery to spin yarn for carpet backing is to be measured in terms of the returns to be obtained from spinning yarn for the production of sacking. But these in turn have to be related to the availability of looms suitable for the weaving of the respective products. How the optimum use of machinery can be determined is discussed in Chapter III.

As time goes on there may be various opportunities of modifying capital equipment; these may range from the addition of comparatively small pieces of capital equipment to balance productive facilities, to a far-reaching and fundamental change in productive methods.

It is unusual to find that there is only one method of producing goods or services. In the production of electricity, for example, generators may be driven by water power, diesel engines, gas turbines or steam turbines, and in the case of the last the steam may be produced either by conventional fuel or through the use of nuclear power. The proportions of capital and running costs involved in the use of each of these methods differ appreciably. The construction of a dam usually involves large capital expenditure, but once it is completed the cost of keeping the turbines in operation is small. The capital cost of generating electricity by gas turbines on the other hand is much lower and the operating costs, in the form of fuel, much higher than for hydro-electricity.

The choice between these alternative methods of generation will depend on the precise circumstances encountered, but, for example, if interest rates are high and the cost of fuel low, the choice will be tilted against hydro-electricity and nuclear power and in favour of conventional stations.

Similarly, it is possible to construct roads using either modern machinery and limited numbers of men or by primitive methods involving the employment of large numbers of men. In underdeveloped countries, where wages are low and the cost of roadmaking machinery relatively high, the choice generally lies in favour of an intensive use of man-power.

Thus, the choice of productive methods is always affected by relative prices of factors or production or inputs.

[2] This is the rationale of the economist's definition of costs as alternatives forgone, or opportunity costs.

The technological relationships between inputs and outputs are frequently expressed as production functions, which normally take some such form as:

$$Q = f(I, J, K. . .)$$

which is a simple symbolic statement of the fact that Q is the maximum output of product which can be produced with i units of factor I, j units of factor J and so on. In formal terms a production function expressed the functional relationship between the inputs of a production process and the outputs produced.

The nature of the input-output relationship is the fundamental problem in the study of production and costs.

COSTS AND RETURNS

Underlying these observations are the Laws of Return, which depend on the facts (a) that factors of production are not perfect substitutes for each other; machinery cannot be substituted for labour indefinitely, grades of labour are not completely interchangeable and so on; and (b) that it becomes progressively more difficult to substitute one factor for another the further the process has already gone. The *Law of Diminishing Returns* (or Variable Proportions) is simply a statement about the returns which accrue to a factor of production, and says that, in a combination of factors of production, if the employment of one (the variable) factor is increased whilst the others are held constant, the additional units of the variable factor, will after a certain point in production, yield a smaller return than the preceding ones (this is conveniently summarized by saying that marginal returns will diminish). The total product of the group of factors will continue to increase, but at a decreasing rate in proportion to the increase in the variable factor; the reason is that the additional units of the variable factor, not being perfect substitutes for the fixed factor, cannot make up for the fact that fixed factors are not being increased. The law operates, *not* because less efficient factors are being employed, but because identical factors are being employed less efficiently: and this is so *not* because entrepreneurs make mistakes, but because in these circumstances no other result is possible.

The law may be illustrated by a simple hypothetical example (see Table 2.2). In the example all of the factors save one (labour) remain constant, labour input is increased in units (column 1). The total product increases, but after the sixth man is employed, the average product falls (i.e. average returns start to diminish); after the fourth man, marginal returns[3] (i.e. the additional return to each further unit of labour) start to diminish. For a while the marginal product of labour increases because it is possible to make better use of the fixed factors of production; this is no longer possible once four men are employed and thereafter the marginal product falls continuously. Following the change in marginal product the average product of labour at first increases but with the addition of the seventh man it too starts to fall.

TABLE 2.2

ILLUSTRATION OF THE LAW OF VARIABLE PROPORTIONS

Units of labour (man hours)	Total product (gallons of paint)	Average product of labour (gallons per man hour)	Marginal product of labour (gallons per man hour)
0	0	0	0
1	10	10	10
2	26	13	16
3	46	15.3	20
4	76	19.0	30
5	100	20.0	24
6	120	20.0	20
7	134	19.1	14
8	148	18.5	14
9	162	18.0	14
10	174	17.4	12

Several proofs and demonstrations of this law have been put forward,[4] but stated in this form the law is merely a statement of a physical fact: as each man is added he has less and less of the fixed factor to work with and cannot himself do the work of the other factors; therefore his product will be less than that of earlier men.

Formulation of the Law of Diminishing Returns in terms of

[3] Returns are not the same things as profits: returns are measures of output or product; profit is the surplus of revenue over cost.
[4] See G. J. Stigler, *Theory of Price* (Macmillan).

D

units of output is helpful in elementary exposition, but it is more convenient to discuss the application of the law to business situations in terms of costs which, being payments to the factors whose returns are measured, are merely the inverse of returns. Thus increasing costs mean the same thing as decreasing returns, decreasing costs mean the same thing as increasing returns; and the Law of Diminishing Returns may be restated as a statement of the tendency for average and marginal costs to increase beyond a certain level of output. Corresponding to fixed and variable factors respectively are the fixed (or overhead) and variable costs which are the rewards of the factors to which they are paid.

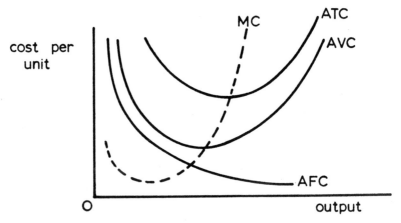

Fig. 2·1.   Average Fixed, Variable and Total Cost

It is usual to define fixed costs (sometimes called supplementary costs or overhead costs) as those costs which do not vary with output, and variable costs (or prime costs) as those which do; fixed costs therefore fall per unit of output as output expands, average variable costs tend, according to the law of diminishing returns, to fall initially and then to increase as output increases. At any level of output, therefore, average cost is made up of two parts—average fixed cost and average variable cost. A typical situation is depicted in Fig. 2.1, which shows average fixed costs declining with output,[5] average variable

⁵ The average fixed cost curve is always a rectangular hyperbola.

cost first falling and then rising, and average total cost doing likewise. The interesting thing is that there is a point of minimum average cost, at which the firm will be working at its best (or optimum) level of output, and where average costs are at their lowest because this is where the variable factors are used most efficiently (as a result of the operation of the Law of Diminishing Returns). Variable cost per unit of input (e.g. per man hour) is constant, but per unit of output or product, it first decreases and then increases. And even if the fixed factor were free (and fixed cost therefore zero) this would still happen. Where average total cost of a product is at its minimum production is being carried on at maximum efficiency, and this is the optimum scale of production.

This is the simplest possible case of a cost curve, and there are several complications which must be admitted in real life but the basic principles are as outlined here. The notion of average total cost reaching a minimum as a result of the operation of the Law of Diminishing Returns is fundamental to cost theory.

These fixed and variable costs are close to, but not precisely the same as what are usually known in business as indirect and direct costs respectively: the direct costs being wages of what are often called 'productive workers' (those whose contribution to output can be measured), indirect costs being all of the so-called 'overheads' of the business, including rent, rates, salaries of management and clerical staff and wages of 'indirect' or 'non-productive' workers (such as labourers, maintenance engineers and all whose performance or contribution to output cannot be measured or attributed directly to them). Perhaps the most useful operating basis of distinction is contained in the traditional definition of the economist: variable costs are those which can be avoided if production ceases entirely, whilst fixed or overhead costs cannot; but this definition is not quite appropriate to the practical distinction between direct and indirect costs in that several indirect costs (such as labourers' wages) are avoidable by stopping production (in business these are often called 'semi-variable' costs).

Another concept of the economist which needs to be introduced here is that of *marginal cost*,[6] which is the addition to

---

[6] The economist's concept of marginal cost is not the same as that of the accountant—the distinction is discussed later.

total cost of producing one more unit of output. Whenever average total costs are falling, marginal cost is lower than average cost (in other words it costs less to produce one more unit than it has done to produce all units to that point); when average cost is rising, marginal cost is higher than average cost because it is costing more to produce each extra unit than the average cost of all units to that point. It follows from this that when average cost is at a minimum (that is to say it is neither rising nor falling) it must equal marginal cost.

The cost curves outlined here are short-term cost curves, usually defined by the economist as the curves relevant in a time period when it is not possible to alter plant or methods of production. This time period differs from industry to industry and depends on the techniques and methods of production: in the rubber plantation industry, where it takes several years for a tree to come into full production the production period is long (this is true of most agricultural products and of many of the products of heavy manufacturing industry); in the clothing industry the period is relatively short. In the long run, of course, all costs are variable costs, since there is time for everything to be altered; it is convenient however to define fixed costs as those which refer to factors which cannot, within a defined period, be altered, and variable costs as those which can be so altered. In the short period the businessman similarly cannot normally alter many of his salaries, interest charges, etc., and these are also fixed costs. In practice it is not always easy to separate these, however, and the more complex is the production process and the more items of equipment there are at different stages of their lives and with different lengths of life, the more difficult the problem becomes. On the whole it is usually unrealistic to think of the cost of machinery as being entirely a fixed cost: depreciation through wear and tear is avoidable through stopping production, but obsolescence is a fixed cost. Accountants and economists usually treat machinery as a fixed factor depreciated through time rather than use, but the justification for this practice is convenience rather than logic.

RETURNS TO SCALE

In the long period, when plant can be altered, the situation is rather different. A series of average cost curves, each appropriate to a similar amount of the fixed factor(s) may be drawn, and the new long-run average cost curve may be defined as the lowest possible average cost of producing a given output when the businessman has time to make the necessary adjustments to his plant. The shape of the long-run average cost curve depends on the application of what are known as *Returns to Scale of Plant*. This is slightly more complex and realistic than the Law of Diminishing Returns, but it may be stated in fairly simple terms for three main cases: *constant returns to scale of plant,* under which, when all of the factors are increased in proportion, the product, too, is increased in proportion (this results in constant long-run average cost); *increasing returns to scale of plant,* when long-run average cost falls; and *decreasing returns,* when long-run average cost rises. Increasing and decreasing returns to scale are usually portrayed as different stages of the growth of the same firm, which is then assumed to operate at its optimum at the point of minimum long-run average cost.

Constant returns to scale are likely to occur in cases where it is possible to duplicate all services for each short-run cost curve or to share out equally between all plants any fixed services which may belong to the firm as a whole, so that from the *production* point of view, ignoring the problems of selling larger outputs and leaving aside questions of maximizing total profits, the businessman is indifferent to the scale of his output, because each plant is as efficient as the rest.

The main reason usually given for the fact that constant returns to scale are not to be expected in real life is the fact that certain productive services are indivisible and come in fairly large discrete units.

A machine may be able to turn out, say, 1,000 parts per day, and, if it is to be used efficiently, the other factors (labour and materials) will be so employed that the machine is utilized to that capacity. If output is to be increased by the use of the same methods of production, it is only economical to do so if a further 1,000 parts are required—if only 500 parts are required there is underemployment of the fixed factor (the machine) and decreasing returns to scale are the consequence. Much machinery in use nowadays is of this type: it is expensive to produce, and a machine with an output of 1,000 units may be no cheaper than one capable of producing a hundred times as much (small machines are usually much more expensive in relation to their output).

In terms of the hypothesis of constant returns to scale, it is not always possible to increase all productive services in a given proportion. It is often argued that the most important of these indivisible services is management, which sets a limit to the size and rate of growth of the firm: this is a point to which we shall return later to our discussion of the scale of production.

The distinction between short- and long-period cost is important in another context. Since, in the short run, fixed costs are irrevocable, they can, in certain circumstances, be ignored. In a period of falling prices and declining activity the price which can be obtained in the market may fall below the minimum level of average cost, but it may still be worthwhile to continue in operation so long as revenue is sufficient to cover variable costs and some small contribution is made to fixed cost; at any price which does not cover variable cost it is preferable to shut down. Ultimately however the fixed capital equipment will break down or wear out; at this point the firm will have to consider whether the equipment should be repaired or renewed or whether it would be preferable to go out of business because it is thought that additional capital expenditure cannot be recouped.

In the short run it is also possible to neglect other items of cost which need to be met in the long term if the firm is to continue in operation. A rush order may be met by running machinery without proper maintenance, and this may not matter much in the short run, provided that it is not done too often; in the long run to do so may be very costly. Running of machinery beyond its proper speeds comes into the same category. The efficient firm may temporarily behave in this way without impairing its efficiency, but the less efficient firm may well fail to take account of short-run neglect of costs such as overtime pay, excessive use of machinery and so on (some firms even neglect to take account of wear and tear).[7]

---

[7] Wiles in *Price, Cost and Output* (Blackwell, 1962) in this context distinguishes between what he calls *Immediate* and *Ultimate* costs, the latter being those which must eventually be met.

Although this distinction between short- and long-period cost is important, it is not always so clear cut in practice as in theory. The typical firm incurs costs over a wide variety of periods, and fixed assets wear out at different intervals, so that the distinction between the long and short period may be arbitrary. A realistic approach is to assume that there are certain factors which a firm possesses at any one time, which cannot easily be reproduced and which are fixed resources in a very real way; these set an upper limit to the amount of such resources available for use in that short period. But within these limits the amounts used can be fairly freely varied over time, and hence the proportion in which they are combined with variable factors can also be altered.

These, in rough outline, are the terms in which economics text-books usually discuss costs, and they provide convenient theoretical abstractions which serve the useful purpose of isolating some of the important factors affecting the cost structure of the business. Things in real life are rarely as simple as this.

A great deal of work has been done on the empirical determination of production functions. The pioneering econometric study was carried out in the 1920's by Cobb and Douglas who fitted a function to time series date series data of the form

$$P = f(L,C)$$

where P = the index of manufacturing output
    L = the index of employment in manufacturing industry
    C = the index of fixed capital in manufacturing industry.

The numerical value of the function for American manufacturing industry from 1899 to 1922 was

$$P = 1.01 \; L^{.75} \; C^{.25} \quad (R^2 = .9409)$$

The coefficient of determination (R^2) means that 94 per cent of the variations in the dependent variable (P) were accounted for by variations in the independent variables (L and C).

In logarithmic form the function is

$$\log P = \log 1.01 + .75 \log L + .25 \log C$$

This is a linear, homogeneous production function in logarithms, indicating constant returns to scale.

Although this function was originally calculated for manufacturing industry as a whole, it has been successfully employed, with modifications, for the measurement of production functions within firms and for comparisons between firms.

The main value of the work of Cobb and Douglas lay in its pioneering nature, and there have been many criticisms and further developments of their work.

For example, W. Nicholls[8] analysed the pork processing operations of a meat-packing plant in the U.S.A., and arrived at an equation

$$Y = -2.05 + 1.06\,X - 0.04\,X^2 \quad (R^2 = 0.92)$$

where Y = total live weight of hogs processed (in millions)
  X = total weekly man hours (in thousands)

The study was based on 52 weeks of single-shift working.

From this equation it is possible to construct an input-output schedule by substituting values of X (weekly man hours); from the production schedule it is then possible, as shown in the discussion of the Law of Variable Proportions, to derive average products of labour (Y/X) and marginal products of labour (dY/dX).

Production functions are not therefore merely theoretical and useless devices. They can be used as aids in decision making because they can give guidance in two directions: first is how to obtain maximum output from a given set of inputs; second is how to obtain a given output from a minimum aggregation of inputs.

Since production functions merely express physical relationships however, they cannot give guidance on factor costs; they may however be modified in order to include factor prices.[9]

Cost curves as they are conveniently drawn do not really refer to the business unit at all, but to a technical process

---

[8] W. Nicholls, *Labour Productivity in Meat Packing*.
[9] A consideration of this point would take us into realms of analysis beyond the objectives of this book. Economists have developed a system of *isoquant* analysis which introduces discussion of the effect of relative factor prices into production functions. The object of such analysis is to reach answers about two main sets of problems: the production of maximum output for a given set of resources and factor costs, and the production of a given output for a minimum combination of resources and factor costs. Interested readers may care to consult W. Baumol, *Economic Theory and Operations Analysis*, Prentice Hall, and M. H. Spencer and L. Siegelman, *Managerial Economics*, Irwin.

(or 'product line') and a firm may be made up of a whole group of such product lines.

The elegant simplicity of the conventional cost curve has led many economists to doubt its validity in real life, and, partly in an attempt to quantify cost data for research purposes, partly in the solution of practical problems, several quantitative estimates have been made. Many of the best known of these are presented, along with some of his own original estimates, in a research monograph by J. Johnston.[10] The general burden of these is that, although the initial stage of decreasing costs (or increasing returns) is very similar to that depicted in theory, once a stage of slowly decreasing, or constant, average costs is reached, cost curves show no inclination to turn upwards, and the typical short-run cost curves are of the shape shown in Fig. 2.2.

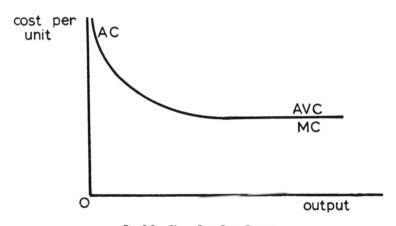

Fig. 2·2. Short Run Cost Curves

It is possible to argue against this that the reason why the curve never turns up again is that firms realize that they are in this position, and that to produce more would lead to decreasing returns (that is to say, they operate, as the theory says, at minimum average cost). But many of the studies imply more than this, and go on to say that there is a wide range over which average cost remains constant and at a minimum: in other words, there is no unique optimum position of minimum

[10] J. Johnston, *Statistical Cost Analysis* (McGraw Hill, 1960).

average cost, but a flat bottomed L-shaped long-run average cost curve.

The implications of this are important. It means that in a situation where average cost is constant over large ranges of output, marginal cost is the same as variable cost (because each increment of cost is the same as the preceding one), and is itself constant over these large ranges: this has important implications for price theory. It also means that many of the traditional arguments about diseconomies of scale[11] are of less force than has been held.

The reasons for this are to be found in a closer examination of the causes of economies of scale. A distinction may be drawn between technical and managerial economies of scale: technical economies refer to the plant, or product line and are concerned with the process of production; managerial economies refer to the business unit, and its economic administration.

Technical economies of scale arise for a number of reasons. One way of looking at them is as simple arithmetical economies arising from the spreading of overheads over greater output.

Underlying this process is the *indivisibility* of factors of production: many industrial processes need expensive equipment which cannot be produced economically, or which for technological reasons will not function, for small outputs. If it is to justify its cost such equipment should be used to full capacity, and all related operations must be so arranged that it is in fact so used. For example, if three main processes of production are required to manufacture a given product, it is possible to find out for each process the average output per process: thus, there may be a purely hand process which produces 60 units per hour per man (this may be, for example the delivery of bought-out billets of steel to the second process); a second semi-automatic process of, say, rough machining, may be able to produce 400 units per machine hour: a third purely automatic process, may produce finished goods from the roughly machined billets at the rate of 1,000 units per machine hour. The most efficient use of the whole combined process will

[11] Johnston sums up the new arguments: 'The empirical results on long-run costs seem to us to confirm widespread existence of economies of scale. The evidence on diseconomies is much less certain for, while there is in some studies a suggestion of an upturn at the top end of the size scale, it is usually small in magnitude and well within the range of variation displayed by the data' (op. cit. p. 193).

require that the machines operating the last two parts of the process should be fully utilized: this can only be done if an output equivalent to the Least Common Multiple of all the processes (6,000 units per hour) is achieved, requiring the use of 100 men in the first operation, fifteen machines (with their operators) in the second operation, and six of the last type of machine. Such an output is necessary because the machine for the last process cannot be divided to produce small enough units of output to allow the use of smaller quantities of the other factors.

As technology advances and as there is more and more plant of this type in use, so economies of scale tend to become an increasingly important feature of the economic scene, and the size of plants needs to grow. In the steel industry, for example, the most efficient size of blast furnace is very large and to some extent dictates the size of the steel works; in the motor industry[12] and others the growing use of expensive automatic machinery tends to set minimum size limits. Most modern industry is based on the large plant.

At the technical, or plant, level there are several other economies. Modern techniques have resulted in an increase in the number of specific or single-use machines and processes, designed to perform one operation more efficiently than by other means: these are frequently expensive and the small manufacturer cannot afford to use them, and although they are not necessarily large machines, there is a tendency for machines with large outputs to be more efficient. Small manufacturers often do not know of the best types of machinery and cannot afford to take big risks or to make experiments.

There are also what are sometimes referred to as 'economies of skill', or of specialization and the division of labour, which result from the fact that it is possible with large-scale production to assign each individual to the tasks for which he is best fitted, and in which he can indeed increase in efficiency by concentration on and repetition of the tasks.

At the plant level, too, there may be economies in the use of materials and utilization of by-products; the size of minimum stock requirements tends to fall as the scale of production in-

[12] For a discussion of economies of scale in the motor industry see G. Maxcy and A. Silberston, *The Motor Industry* (George Allen & Unwin, 1959).

creases; it is often cheaper to buy and sell in large quantities than small, because up to a point it is administratively no more difficult to deal with large than small quantities.

Attempts have been made to quantify economies of scale in practice and to develop empirical rules related to the theoretical considerations. The starting point is the relation between the volume of a container and the area of the material needed to manufacture it. In the case of a cube, of length of side *a* the volume is given by a^3 and the area of the material needed to contain it is $6a^2$. It is easy to demonstrate that large cubes need less material per unit capacity than small ones. For two cubes of dimensions r_1 and r_2 the ratio of the surface areas

$$\frac{S_1}{S_2} = \left(\frac{r_1}{r_2}\right)^2$$

The corresponding ratio of the volumes is

$$\frac{V_1}{V_2} = \left(\frac{r_1}{r_2}\right)^3$$

From which it follows that

$$\frac{S_1}{S_2} = \left(\frac{V_1}{V_2}\right)^{2/3}$$

Thus if we double the volume of the cube we shall need to increase the amount of material needed to form it in the proportion of $2^{2/3} = 1.59$. In other words doubling the volume can be achieved with a 59 per cent increase in material.

It is from reflections of this kind that the '6/10 rule' (approximated to 2/3) has been derived. At first sight such a rule may seem trivial and confined to one small aspect of production processes, but this is far from the case, and many industrial processes are affected by relations between area and volume. Blast furnaces are essentially boxes containing the ingredients needed to produce iron, and the reduction of surface area per unit volume that comes with increase in size has the added advantage that heat losses are reduced. Tankers too are essentially large boxes containing oil, and the area of the surface is important in relation to the surrounding environment—in this case the sea—because it affects the resistance of the ship to passage through the water in a rather complicated way related to powers of the vessel's principal dimensions. Chemical processes in the main are reactions carried out in vessels.

Another reason for attaching some importance to the '6/10 rule' is that the form of the relationship postulated (though not the value of 6/10) may be useful in describing empirically-determined relationships between size and cost. A number of attempts to develop such descriptions have been made.

S. P. Alpert[13] related the horsepower needed in milling operations to the amount of material to be removed and found that a useful approximation was $H.P. = kU^{0.75}$, where U measured the cubic inches of metal removed. S. C. Schuman amongst others has worked on similar problems relating to the chemical industry; in one investigation he examined the statistical relationship between capital costs (C) involved in producing a large variety of chemicals and the amount produced measured in pounds weight (S). The statistical relationship that emerged as a good fit to the data was

$$C = 0.126 \ S^{0.70}$$

Some distrust may be felt about the validity of a relationship applying to a collection of heterogeneous chemicals produced by different methods; nevertheless there may be common underlying factors governing capital costs.

The relationship outlined above can also be expressed in terms of capital costs per unit of product (K). In this form we have

$$K = 0.126 \ S^{-0.3}$$

This shows that the cost per lb. of product falls when output is increased. It will not, of course, fall significantly for an indefinite increase in output; after some point, although economies will still continue they will become less, as the form of the mathematical relationship indicates.

The kind of relationship can be extended to include variations in running costs with size of plant, by the establishment of individual relationships between various elements of costs and size of operation. It may be found that some costs vary proportionately with output while others fall to varying degrees with increase in scale of output, and the complete cost function will take account of such differences in behaviour.

On the basis of such empirical relationships and rules of thumb it is possible to relate investment decisions to the costs of production at various scales of operation. An example of this is given in Chapter VII.

Another aspect of the relationship between costs and scale of production is that expressed by learning curves. It is common experience that practice, while not always making perfect, results in improvements up to a point. The learning process has relevance to batch production, particularly of expensive units such as ships or aircraft. It is recognized by shipyards that producing, say, a score of fairly similar ships reduces shipyard costs quite substantially by the time the end of the run is reached.[14] For aircraft production more detailed investigations have been made in order to see whether the reduction in labour costs can be said to conform to a learning curve.[15]

One such curve relates the labour input of the nth unit of production to the labour input of the first unit produced. If L is the labour input to the first unit and r the learning factor, the labour inputs to the second, fourth, eighth and nth aircraft (where $n = 2^P$) respectively are Lr, Lr^2, $Lr^3 \ldots Lr^P$.

While such curves fall throughout their length the rate of reduction becomes progressively less, and with learning factors of 0.7 to 0.9 little further improvement in performance is to be expected after 100 units have been produced. Learning curves are of use in indicating on the basis of past experience how costs may vary with the expected length of run; they also provide some basis, when combined with other data, for determining price-output relationships, manpower requirements etc. For many types of production, labour costs account for a substantial part of total costs. In aircraft production labour costs may account for about 25 per cent of non-launching costs for the first unit produced and fall to about 10 per cent for a long run; learning costs are clearly important in such cases. Such savings are useful but on small runs they tend to be dwarfed by the costs of launching the aircraft.

[14] See J. R. Parkinson, *The Economics of Shipbuilding in the U.K.* p. 146, Cambridge 1960.
[15] Cost Curves and Pricing in Aircraft Production, S. G. Sturmey, *Economic Journal*, December 1964, p. 954.

MANAGERIAL ECONOMIES OF SCALE

Technical economies of scale provide an adequate explanation of the importance of large-scale operation at the plant, or product-line level; they are not sufficient alone to explain the growth of business units, which may have several plants. There are other economies of scale, which we have labelled *managerial,* which may refer to whole series of plants.

The market may well set the limit to the scale at which a firm may operate: if a market is small, or highly specialized, like the market for 'quality' motor cars, the technical economies of scale may not be realizable, because a firm could not sell an output which could achieve such economies. The application of this principle is more widespread than is sometimes realized: an interesting current example of this limit is in the British motor car industry, in which it is argued that significant economies of scale may still be achieved at levels of output which cannot be achieved in the British market. One of the arguments often put forward in favour of Britain's entry into the European Common Market was that such entry would give British manufacturers duty-free access to one of the biggest and fastest-growing mass markets in the world, which would enable the more efficient firms and industries to reap greater economies of scale and growth (the less efficient would not survive).

At the upper limit the necessary market size for the achievement of economies of scale may be so large that it cannot be realized in practice, and the firm may never be able to operate at the optimum. The statistical cost studies mentioned earlier indicate that this is a state of affairs which may be more common in manufacturing industry than is generally supposed. This provides a built-in incentive to growth which is greater in industries in which substantial technical economies of scale can be achieved. Sometimes economies of scale are so marked that there is room for only one producer in the market.

The lower prices which result from mass production may provide both the opportunity and the incentive to create new markets. In the early days of the motor car it was widely believed that motor cars were a commodity which, by virtue of their cost, could sell only to a limited market (this appears to have been based largely on a false analogy with the days of coaches, which could be sold only to a small and relatively wealthy section of the community). Henry Ford saw the fallacy, and mass-produced a cheap car which could be sold to a much wider group: in so doing he revolutionized the industry and created a new market. Mass production and low prices have repeated the trick so often and in so many different fields that it is no longer possible to accept without reservations and closer examination the old dictum that the market always limits the scale of operation: perhaps in the final analysis the market *is* the limiting factor, but it is doubtful in many cases whether the limit has any practical significance.

There may also be economies in the marketing process itself: it is often as cheap to sell a hundred units as it is to sell one unit, and the larger the scale of marketing the more economies there are. Advertising provides the classic example: it rarely pays to have a widespread and expensive marketing campaign for small-scale products, unless they are the 'prestige' products of a larger group.

Financial factors may also be important. As is demonstrated in Chapter VIII the large firm has advantages over the small firm in this field: it has access to capital markets and usually has substantial resources of its own, whilst the small firm frequently finds that, partly for institutional reasons, it cannot raise all the funds which it may need. Once a firm has succeeded in growing beyond a certain point (which is frequently though not invariably associated with its becoming a public company) these particular difficulties become less important, but it may still find it difficult to obtain further funds. The reason for this is usually that it is the most successful, or potentially most successful, firms which find it easiest to raise money, and frequently it is the big firm which is also the most successful. With the exception of the particular set of difficulties facing the small firm which are usually discussed under the heading of the Macmillan Gap,[16] the financial factors affecting scale of production are to a large extent reflections of the other factors; if all else is efficient, finance is not usually a limiting factor on the firm. There are, in fact, those who argue that the Macmillan Gap is a good thing in that it prevents funds from being channelled into occupations in which funds and the

[16] See Chapter VIII.

inputs which will be bought with the funds would be used at less than their maximum efficiency. This superficially attractive argument does, however, ignore the fact that, there are some occupations which can only be carried out on a small scale, and that many small firms are small merely because they are at an early stage of their growth and may require funds in order to grow.

Management is frequently cited as one of the main factors limiting the size of business units in that it is an indivisible and not easily reproduced factor of production subject to diminishing returns and, if the 'managerial optimum' is exceeded, managerial efficiency declines and increasing costs set in.

About the first stage of this process—the period of increasing returns to management—there is not much controversy. There are economies of scale in management as with most other factors and the larger the firm is the more it is able to employ specialists; in the small firm, for example, one man may be in charge of production, sales and finance, in the larger firm specialists can be appointed under one head man.[17] Improvements in management techniques and the development of more systematic management in recent years have proceeded *pari passu* with improvements in other techniques, and in particular the realization of the importance of delegation has meant that managerial economies of this sort are easier to achieve. Delegation is a form of specialization: it enables the head of a firm or department to pass on a great deal of routine and other work to subordinates whilst he concentrates on his own job of *managing* the whole firm or department; in turn his subordinates can delegate functions to their staff and so on.

Delegation is probably the key to managerial efficiency[18] and it explains why management in practice does not become progressively less efficient as firms grow. The school of thought which cites management as the limiting factor or size depends on an assumption that management efficiency is given and remains constant. In fact, however, it does not and management

---

[17] 'For any given degree of specialization, further economies may often be obtained by the spreading of managerial overhead cost, thus reducing average cost as output increases.' E. T. Penrose, *The Theory of the Growth of the Firm* (Blackwell, 1959).
[18] See Bates and Sykes, 'Aspects of Managerial Efficiency', *Journal of Industrial Economics* (July, 1962).

E

tends to become more efficient the bigger the firm becomes. There are managerial problems of size[19] but these are usually outweighed by the economies.

Sargant Florence[20] puts the case:

'Business enterprise is a corporate manifestation and its capacity to cope with large outputs is not fixed but expands with its structure.'

and

'most of those who have made a special study of organization differ from the economists. They come to the conclusion that no limit is set to the size of organization, if correct principles are adopted to enable a single leader to delegate control.'

The case against managerial diseconomies depends however on management being employed efficiently and adapting itself to changing economic circumstances; in real life one of the major problems of a business is to make sure that the whole management structure is efficient. Frequently it is not, and in such cases, bad management has set a limit. Management is probably the least homogeneous of factors of production. At the highest levels of entrepreneurship we find men like Lord Nuffield and Henry Ford,[21] but few achieve such heights and most managements operate at much lower levels; among the less distinguished the inability of such management to operate at higher outputs does restrict growth. Many firms remain small simply because their owners cannot or will not find and trust subordinates or partners with whom to share functions.

Without enterprising and efficient management a firm is unlikely to achieve its most efficient scale of operation. Management may not be the limiting factor in that it *can* be adapted to any size and rate of growth, but efficient management is a

---

[19] The problem of excessive centralization of control in the nationalized industries is an example. It is interesting, however, that one of the findings of the Fleck Committee was that the organization of the National Coal Board was in fact excessively *de*centralized.

[20] P. Sargant Florence, *The Logic of British and American Industry* (Routledge & Kegan Paul, 1953).

[21] Besides their entrepreneurial foresight such men also possess the ability to manage their firms efficiently and to choose the best men for various jobs. A distinction is often drawn between enterprise (which conceives plans) and management (which executes them) but in practice the one depends very much on the other.

necessary condition of growth.[22] Good management will ensure that the productive, marketing and financial sides of the firm are efficient, poor management will not.

There are also economies of *risk-bearing*. Large firms are usually less exposed to risk then small ones, because they can spread their risks. To the small manufacturer the breakdown of one machine or the accidental poor quality of a production batch may be a hazard which he cannot predict with certainty, but which may cause him a great deal of harm; the large concern on the other hand knows that a certain proportion of breakdown failures and low-quality batches are to be expected, and the probability of these can usually be predicted and allowed for. In any case, even if unpredictable, the loss of (say) 1 per cent of one's output is much less serious than the loss of 50 per cent or more. The risks of failure are small with large firms. The costs of total failure are, however, much greater and, whilst large firms can spread similar risks in this way, they are still vulnerable to the risks of depression and loss of markets.

Firms may seek to spread their risks in other ways by diversification, a practice which has become increasingly common in the last generation or so. A common objective of diversification is to ensure that a firm does not 'put all of its eggs in one basket': an age-old example is mixed farming, and in the sphere of manufacturing industry there are numerous examples of firms which produce a whole range of products which may have no apparent similarity of market condition or production method. Vickers Ltd, for example, make aircraft, ships, armaments, food processing plant, rubber, plastics, paint, instruments and a wide range of other products. Markets, too, may be diversified, even when firms produce only one product: the sale of fuels, for example, is for a variety of purposes—heating, lighting, power for vehicles, industrial and domestic use and so on—and this again is a way of spreading risk.

But risk-spreading is not the only motive for diversification.[23] Often new lines of activity may be suggested by research or technological change, which show a firm the way to make

---

[22] See Penrose, op. cit., *passim*.
[23] For a fuller discussion of the economics of diversification, see Penrose, op. cit., and Lloyd R. Amey. 'Is Business Diversification Desirable?', *District Bank Review* (June 1960).

better use of its materials and processes, by-products or market-ing facilities. A highly diversified output may, for example, be produced from one basic set of productive processes or materials: the chemical industry is like this and Imperial Chemical Industries have products ranging through paints, man-made fibres and explosives in addition to the chemicals themselves. Similarly, a whole range of goods which may be marketed through similar channels may be produced: Unilever supply a large range of manufactures which are supplied through the retail grocery trade—margarine, soap, vegetable oils, frozen foods, fish, etc.—some of these come from common raw materials, many do not. Sometimes the diversification occurs because of a firm's attempts at vertical integration (dis-cussed shortly); sometimes a firm may reach its market limit in one line of production and can expand only by diversifying its output.

Most big firms are diversified in some way. About two-thirds of all firms with over 500 employees operating in the United Kingdom have more than one plant.[24] Not all are diversified —Imperial Tobacco, for example, one of the biggest firms in Britain, was almost entirely specialized in tobacco products (though it now has interests in the paper industry, potato crisps and teaching machines)—but a high proportion are. An in-quiry by the National Institute of Economic and Social Research[25] showed that in the chemical industry only 79 per cent of persons employed by chemical companies were actually working in the chemical industry; in the metal goods industry, iron, steel and shipbuilding the proportion was 81 per cent; whilst in clothing and footwear and paper and printing the proportion was 97 per cent.

To some extent the risk-bearing economies associated with diversification tend to conflict with technical and managerial economies of scale, since diversification usually involves the presence of a proportionately larger number of specific fixed factors (equipment used in the manufacture and processing of plastics, for example, is not usually suitable for use in the ex-plosives industry) and in any case the different operations are

---

[24] *Census of Production.*
[25] See *Company Income and Finance* (National Institute of Economic and Social Research, 1956), p. 68.

usually carried out in separate, specialized plants. Increasing specialization is also called for in management. On the whole the attempt of a firm to achieve economies both of scale and of risk-bearing usually points to bigger and bigger business units. Small firms may diversify their output from common processes, this is true of the light engineering industry; mixed farming usually results in small farms with non-specialized labour and the use of an adaptable common factor (land); but these are special cases and more usually diversified firms are large.

EXTERNAL ECONOMIES

The economies of scale which we have been discussing so far are internal to the firm in the sense that they arise from the activities of the firm itself and are independent of the actions of other firms. There may also be external economies, shared by a number of firms, which arise when the scale of production of an industry (or group of industries) increases; in other words, they arise because of outside influences and occur when an increase in the scale of production of an industry brings benefits to individual firms. The main external economies arise from the common use and provision of certain services and factors of production: for example, in most industries there are trade associations which provide information and other services to members, and the identity of interests among firms in an industry makes it worth while to issue trade publications and information. The concentration of firms in a neighbourhood brings a series of mutual advantages in, for example, the growth of a pool of specialized workers, transport and ancillary trades. Clydeside, with its shipbuilding and engineering, the Birmingham area with its multiplicity of engineering trades and skills are both areas in which firms derive substantial external economies. A major disadvantage of such a process is that if there is depression in one of the major industries it soon spreads to all of the others, and this is a serious contingent diseconomy. There may be other diseconomies—the most popular example is that of several firms pumping oil from the same pool, a situation in which the more one firm gets the less is available for others—but such external diseconomies are frequently avoidable.

PRINCIPLES OF LARGE-SCALE PRODUCTION

Sargant Florence[26] summarises economies of scale in terms of three basic principles:

(i) *The Principle of Bulk Transactions* states that the cost of dealing in large quantities are usually not proportionately greater than the cost of dealing in small quantities.

(ii) *The Principle of Massed Reserves* is based on the statistical theory of large numbers, which may be simply stated as the fact that the greater the number of individual items involved the more likely is it that deviations will cancel themselves out and leave the average achieved results nearer to the expected results (this principle is the basis of risk-bearing economies).

(iii) *The Principle of Multiples* is an expression of the economies of specialization and large-scale production. In order for specialists to be used efficiently they must be used to their full capacity (in other words they are indivisible); and the more specialization is needed the larger becomes the size of firm required to make the most efficient use of them (the optimum size).

THE GROWTH OF FIRMS

A distinction may be drawn, after Mrs Penrose,[27] between economies of scale and economies of growth, and it is arguable that there is a limit to the *rate* at which a firm can grow without loss of efficiency, even though there may be significant economies at the size to which it wishes to expand. Mrs Penrose's own words[28] put it best:

'Economies of growth are the internal economies available to an individual firm which make expansion profitable in certain directions. . . . At any time the availability of such economies is the result of the process . . . by which unused productive services are continually created within the firm. They may or may not be also economies of size.'

The distinction is less obscure than it may seem. For any

---

[26] P. Sargant Florence, op. cit., pp 49–60.
[27] Penrose, op. cit., passim.
[28] Ibid., p. 99.

given scale of operations a firm possesses resources appropriate to that scale of output and to the type of products made by the firm. The fact that many such resources are indivisible means that a firm has an incentive to use them as profitably as possible, and the existence of indivisible resources provides a built-in incentive to growth. Such economies may exist for all sizes of firm and they need not be purely technical; the owner of a business may feel that he is not using his abilities to fullest advantage at a particular size and may wish to expand to utilize his own services to the full; the minimum amount of finance which it is worth while to procure may induce a firm to expand in order to use it; the necessity to advertise may dictate a larger scale of operation to absorb the extra overheads involved; in order to take advantage of opportunities for research and development, and the technological change which stems from them, firms seek to expand still further.[29]

The limit to a rate of growth at any one time may well depend on such factors; the rate of growth of a market may be limited, or the market may be resistant to sales pressures; a firm may wish to make sure of its reserves and its general financial position before it expands; it takes time to instal new plant. Mrs Penrose's argument is that the limit to the process is set by the ability of management to sustain the growth. It takes time for a firm to develop a new administrative structure appropriate to its new size, and this limits the rate at which a firm can grow if it wishes to maintain its efficiency. But the efficient firm with good management will evolve a new structure in time. The firm with bad management will not, and in this sense management is a limiting factor on growth, but it is not an inevitable limit and indeed it is quite likely that in the long run there is no natural limit to the size of business units.[30]

The straightforward desire for monopoly is another reason

[29] This produces what may be called the dilemma of growth: '... competition is the essence of the struggle among the large firms that induces and almost forces the extensive research and innovation in which they engage and provides the justification for the whole system; at the same time the large firms expect rewards for their efforts, but this expectation is held precisely because competition can be restrained' (Penrose, op. cit., p. 264).

[30] Even Adam Smith's limit of the market is, as we have seen, not inevitable; markets can expand, both spontaneously and under the influence of advertising, etc., and even if the market limit for one product is eventually reached, the firm can diversify.

why firms grow not merely or even mainly in order to charge excessive prices and reap excessive profits, but also in order to remove possible wasteful and unnecessary competition and because there may be room for only one firm if an industry is to operate without surplus capacity. These are what might be called the 'economies' motives for size which may produce monopoly and in certain cases there are sound economic reasons for growth to monopoly size. But whatever the reasons, and however good they may seem, there is always a danger that a monopoly which grows up for sound economic reasons may be perpetuated for wrong reasons and may result in the long run in exploitation.

THE DIRECTION OF GROWTH

Growth is not a homogeneous process, and firms may grow in any of several directions and by a variety of methods. They may, for example, grow spontaneously or by combination: spontaneous or autonomous growth occurs when a firm grows by adding to its own resources by capital expenditure on plant, equipment, etc. (the rationale of this sort of expansion has been one of the main concerns of this chapter so far); growth by combination occurs when several business units combine by formal mergers. Autonomous growth adds to the total productive capacity of an industry, unless by virtue of growth one firm achieves a superior competitive position and drives out other firms; growth by mergers merely involves a change in ownership and control. Most firms in practice expand in both ways.

Whichever method a firm uses, it normally results in some change in the scope of its activities by adding to (or occasionally subtracting from) the number and variety of its products and processes. The term *integration* is usually employed to designate the bringing of a group of activities under one single control.

Two main types and a number of subsidiary types of integration may be distinguished. Horizontal integration, which is the extension of the scale of production of similar products by combination or by plant extension, leaves the range of a firm's activities largely unchanged. Such integration was common in the coal and the cotton industries between the wars, and in the steel industry; it is also noticeable in the aircraft industry and electrical engineering. Horizontal integration may be motivated by the search for increased technical efficiency and large-scale production, or by the desire for monopoly, and it is the commonest form of integration in practice.

Vertical integration consists of an increase in the number of consecutive processes which are undertaken by one firm. Textile firms, for example, may undertake both spinning and weaving, iron and steel firms might (before nationalization in Britain) have their own coal mines, iron mines, furnaces and so on through the whole productive process; motor car firms may possess their own foundries and many manufacture components previously made by specialist manufacturers. Such integration may be backward towards the raw material and ancillary goods, in which case the motive is usually to secure supplies, or forward (in the direction of the market), in which case the motive is usually to secure outlets for a firm's products. The main economy to be expected from vertical integration is that processes may be linked together and so phased that continuous production of the right things is possible throughout the process, with insurance against the failure of supplies. Attractive though this form of integration may appear at first sight, however, it is less common than may be expected, partly because to some extent it works against the advantages of specialization and large-scale production and is limited by a lack of knowledge of the techniques of earlier or later stages of production (this may, of course, be overcome by hiring the right people when such integration is planned). In the past this form of integration has often been tried and abandoned— one of the most frequently cited cases is of Ford's purchase of rubber plantations—and the abandonment has usually been because independent specialist firms could do the job more efficiently, because they had the specialized skills and, probably more important, that by working for a large number of customers, they could achieve economies of scale beyond those possible for the large combine. On a relatively small scale vertical integration is common; for example many firms have their own transport. In general, the case for vertical integration is much less clear than for horizontal integration; in the last resort its effectiveness depends on whether a firm can operate on a large enough scale and with the necessary technical efficiency to achieve an optimum at each stage of production.[31]

Other forms of integration are possible. Lateral integration is fairly common, and consists of the combination of processes which may not be related directly to the same productive process. It occurs when a firm extends the list of its products: British Railways owns hotels to cater for passengers, aeroplane firms may manufacture motor cars, road and rail transport may combine to reduce risk and competition; firms may diversify for any of the reasons discussed under that heading. What Sargant Florence calls diagonal integration may be sought, and consists of the provision withon one organization of auxillary goods and services required for the several main processes or lines of organization,[32] (such as the provision of a firm's own power or repair services).

Integration is based, in one way or another, either on the materials which the firm uses, on its products, on its processes and services, or on its markets or on any combination of these. What matters is that integration should increase the efficiency of production or distribution.

METHODS OF GROWTH

As we have seen, whatever the direction of growth, a variety of methods is possible. We need not concern ourselves further at this point with autonomous growth; it is implicit in the investment discussion which underlies this form of growth, and is discussed later.

Cartels, trade associations, restrictive practices, market-sharing agreements, collective resale price maintenance (now largely illegal in Britain) are all ways in which firms may combine; strictly they are not methods of growth but ways of restricting competition or of achieving a growth in the size of the marketing unit. Mergers too may be motivated by the desire to reduce competition, but they are also a way by which the firm can achieve integration and growth.

---

[31] What is often called the 'make or buy' decision—whether a firm should buy its components out or make them itself—is a decision about vertical integration. The fact that so many firms decide in favour of buying rather than making, illustrates that the case for vertical integration is by no means straightforward or uncomplicated, and needs to be proved positively.

[32] P. Sargant Florence, op. cit., p. 45.

There is a variety of ways in which mergers may be brought about, but two main methods are important for this discussion. Amalgamation, often through the formation of holding companies, or a merger between 'equals' in one way; the other is by acquisition of a controlling interest in one firm by another, which may be in the form of a take-over or voluntary sale by one firm. The essence of the distinction is that the latter method involves the absorption of one party by another, the former does not. Both forms, however, result in formerly separate units of control becoming one, and they are usually aimed at securing economies of scale.

One advantage of combination with other firms, which is particularly important when a business is diversifying its operations, is that existing firms frequently have specialized staff, equipment and expertise which the business would have to develop for itself, possibly at great expense and over a long period of time if it attempted to grow by extension of its own plant. On the other hand, buying up another firm as a going concern may involve the purchase of 'goodwill' (which is usually supposed to represent the difference between the value of a firm's assets as a going concern and its value as individual pieces of equipment and buildings); this may well cost more than the alternative of autonomous development.

Take-over bids are a form of merger by acquisition which have attracted a great deal of attention in recent years, but they are by no means a new phenomenon. Any change in the control of a company by acquisition of its shares is technically a take-over; a distinction may, however, be drawn between cases where there is a willing buyer and a willing seller and cases where the seller is unwilling, or may not even know of the bid until it is too late to do anything about it. It is the second type of bid which usually makes the headlines. Although some take-over bids are undoubtedly the work of financiers manipulating the market for their own ends, most are the work of businessmen seeking to expand and strengthen their firms, to increase the scope for profitable operation, and sometimes to suppress competition.

Two main motives for take-overs may be distinguished. The first is the straightforward expansion motive; the second is the 'bargain' motive which induces a businessman to buy up a company for what he thinks is a bargain price. The taker-over may see, for example, that a company's assets are undervalued, or that excess profits have been retained in the past so that shares may be undervalued. There have been extreme cases where ultra-cautious firms, or firms which believe in financing all of their own development without going outside the firm, have acquired excessive liquid assets in the form of securities and cash (which, being the property of the company, are taken over when the firm changes ownership). When such firms have been bought out by the medium of share purchases, the purchase price of the firm has sometimes turned out to be less than the value of the liquid assets. Such extremes are rare, but cases of similar cash 'gifts' to take-over specialists are by no means uncommon.

Spectacular as these cases are, however, they are by no means the most important. Much more frequently a businessman sees that another firm has valuable assets which could yield big profits if efficiently managed: property take-overs are usually motivated by the desire of the bidders to acquire sites of high development value which are at present put to less profitable use; land used for public houses, for example, may be put to more profitable use as shoe shops, supermarkets and so on. Since the end of the war there have been big structural changes in British industry, which have had two main effects: on the one hand some industries have declined, either relatively or absolutely, and their assets have been used less profitably than they might otherwise; in addition even within industries the differences between the most efficient and the least efficient firms have become more obvious (this is always likely to be the case in a period of change, because some adapt themselves more readily than others). More efficient firms have taken over less efficient; growing firms have taken over the assets of declining or less profitable firms.

It is even argued that, by improving the allocation and distribution of resources in this way, take-over bidders perform a useful social service via the price mechanism. The claim may not be universally valid, but at least it is true that many take-overs are from legitimate business motives. Capital gains are often made as a result of the process, and these are frequently criticized, but against this it must be argued that a bidder will only offer more than the market value of securities if they have been undervalued in the past, for instance because of bad management or bad dividend policies, and there have been several cases in which bidders have withdrawn when market prices have gone too high. It is also argued that any capital gains which may accrue merely compensate for years of under-payment of dividends and low capital values. This argument would be more convincing if such gains went to the people who had held these securities through the bad period, whereas the gains frequently go to speculators or other people who have bought and shares just in time for the take-over gains to be made.[33]

Like every other form of business activity the take-over may be abused, (and it is arguable that there is a case for legisla-tion). The *City Code* has been drawn up by members of major bodies in the City of London, and members are expected to abide by it. In addition the President of the Board of Trade has the power to refer proposed mergers to the Monopolies Commission, and the Industrial Reorganization Corporation has the business of mergers as one of its main concerns. But take-overs are merely one form of merger, and one of the many ways in which a firm may grow in order to achieve economies of scale.

During the present century the tendency in Britain, as in all of the industrialized countries of the world, has been to-wards a growth in the size of business units.

To put the question of size into perspective, there are still many small firms in Britain and the concentration of employ-ment appears to be less marked than may be thought from a casual look at industry: but the biggest firms do account for most of the employment, assets and profits in the country, and their share is probably increasing. The trend is still towards an increase in the size of business units.

[33] See George Bull and Anthony Vice, *Bid for Power* (Elek. 3rd edn. 1961) and Paul Ferris, *The City* (Gollancz, 1960). These two books give entertaining, if superficial, accounts of some take-over bids in practice.
See also N. A. H. Stacey, *Mergers in Modern Business* (Hutchinson 1966); W. W. Alberts and J. E. Segall, *The Corporate Merger* (University of Chicago Press, 1966); G. R. Young *et al*, *Mergers and Acquisitions*, (Routledge and Kegan Paul 1965).

CHAPTER III

PRODUCTION AND COSTS IN PRACTICE

IN THE LONG run new technology contributes more to the efficiency of business than any other factor. But, given the state of technology, the application of economic analysis to the affairs of the enterprise can contribute a great deal. In essence the problem of production management is the improvement of efficiency and the reduction of costs. Techniques of economic analysis are helpful whenever there is a major element of choice between alternative courses of action and an optimal solution is sought.

METHODS OF PRODUCTION

One of the choices which needs to be made in practice is that of a method of production. Given available techniques, the choice is essentially an economic one related to costs and returns and depending on such factors as price and availability of materials, labour and capital and the size of the market.

In practice, production may be carried on in any of three main ways (or a combination of all three), the choice depending largely on the scale of production and length of run which can be achieved. The first of these, job production, is usually small scale; the second, batch production, is usually medium scale but may also be employed in large-scale production; the third, mass, or flow production, is almost always as its name implies, large scale. Large-scale production does not necessarily entail flow methods. It is rare to find a firm which uses one method to the exclusion of the other two, but product lines or part lines are frequently specialized on this basis.

Job production is common in small businesses, but many large concerns produce some of their lines by this method, the essence of which is that the firm manufactures single products (or at the most a few of any one product) usually to the requirements of the customer. This is sometimes referred to as a 'one-off' method of production: it suffers from the disadvantage that few economies of scale can be achieved (save for multi-purpose plant, building and staff) and unit costs are usually relatively high; where individual requirements have to be met, however, no other method is possible. Examples of this kind of production are to be found in the manufacture of special-purpose machinery, bespoke tailoring and similar trades.

Batch production is the typical method of manufacture in British industry. It consists as the name implies of the manufacture of a batch or 'lot' of products at one time, but is distinguished from flow production in that the process is not continuous. The manufacture of several different products for stock, as in the shoe trade and the clothing trade, or to fairly regular orders, as for components for the motor vehicle industry and the radio industry, are particularly suited to batch production. Some of the advantages of large-scale production are achieved; for example constant use of machinery, plant, skilled staff and so on, and the consequent ironing out of indivisibilities and the spreading of fixed costs; but complete specialization of inputs is not possible. This is the type of production which is most difficult to control; it is more difficult the larger the variety of products, and efficient production makes big demands on management. It requires good quality control, well-devised stock control and efficient programming.

Mass or flow production is frequently found side by side with batch production, but it depends for its success on large-scale operation. In general, the word 'flow' is preferable to 'mass' in this context: mass production is often treated both by economists and in common parlance as synonymous with large-scale production, but it is not necessary for flow methods to be used to achieve large-scale production, which may well be feasible for the production of large batches. Single-purpose plant and machines of large output capacity and high cost, like the automatic and semi-automatic machinery in modern motor car factories, is usually employed, and large outputs are needed to justify their installation. Products are usually highly standardized and they usually go through identical sequences of operations. Industries like oil refining, cement manufacture and flour milling have to be operated on a large scale and by flow methods in order to be efficient.

The advantages of large-scale production can usually be

summed up as the advantages of specialization of function, standardization of product and full-capacity use of large indivisible factors. The main danger of flow production in particular is that of over-specialization and susceptibility to economic fluctuations: closing a motor car factory is an expensive business and may be disastrous, but even a reduction of output to (say) 50 per cent of capacity may have equally serious effects.

Two typical problems associated with both batch and mass production are those of variety and length of run. A limitation of large-scale production is that specialization usually means standardization, because small changes in routine have to be ruled out. Further, the more complex is the mass-produced article, the more components it will usually have and the more the components themselves must be standardized, with the result that even minor differences in finished products are extremely difficult and costly to introduce.

From the point of view of the market, standardization has both its good and bad sides. Standardization makes choice easier, but there is a limit to the amount of uniformity that consumers will tolerate; in practice many large-scale producers have decided that the consumer will buy more of their produce if some variety is introduced. Product differentiation and advertising are the consequence of this, and they can be taken to extremes, both from the point of view of the consumer, who may become cynical about the whole process, but also, and more relevant to the present discussion, from the production point of view. The cost of variety in the last resort is the loss of benefits of standardization and specialization. In modern large-scale industry the tendency is for more and more reduction of variety where it costs most, in the large-scale production lines, and its introduction where it costs least, in the least specialized and the smallest-scale parts of the operation, such as the trimming processes of motor car manufacture. Usually the nearer to the finished product, the better suited is the process for the introduction of variety. Standardized products may make for duller living; they almost always make for cheaper living.

The 'length of run' problem is closely associated with the scale of production. At the extreme, the largest mass-production

units require the longest feasible production runs and fullest
utilization of fixed factors, maintained if possible until all of the
high-cost high-output plant can be written off. But even where
full-time long runs are not possible it is still desirable to use
fixed factors as fully as possible and the longest possible production runs are needed. Some motor car manufacturers aim for
a model which will run for several years with only minor modifications from year to year: the Volkswagen, the Morris Minor
and the Citröen have been conspicuous successes in this sense.
The problem also applies to batch production in which economies
of scale resulting from long runs must be balanced against the
cost of holding stocks, and the final answer may demand a
complicated operations research solution.

SHIFT WORKING

One way of achieving the maximum possible length of run in
relation to capital is by shift-working.

The main advantage of shift-working is that it economizes
on capital; its main disadvantage is that it increases the cost of
labour. The saving of capital arises because buildings and
machines may be used for 24 hours per day rather than for
8 or 16, and for 7 days a week rather than for 5 or 6. This
reduces the cost of capital to a limited degree because less
capital is required to produce a given output if it is used intensively rather than intermittently. Thus, if machinery is never
idle it will be used 168 hours a week rather than the 40 that
might be normal with single shift-working. Interest charges
on capital and buildings will be cut to a quarter in relation
to the output produced. Interest is the only charge that will
be cut in this striking manner; there may be small reductions
in insurance costs per unit of output (although in total there is
likely to be an increase); charges for depreciation or obsolescence
are likely to fall much less markedly. No hard and fast rule
can be laid down. Depreciation is to some extent the result of
using a machine and to some extent the result of general aging.
Even without use machinery deteriorates; it may rust or perish;
it may become out of date or obsolescent; Stephenson's Rocket
is a museum piece even though it could still haul a coach.

Some orders of magnitude may be assigned to the costs of
operating capital in the United Kingdom industry.

F

Depreciation and obsolescence	10
Interest charges or equivalent	10
Raw materials	50
Labour	30
	100

The figures given in the above table are illustrative; they are not meant to be exact and while they give an average view of industry as a whole there is no reason to suppose that they represent the situation in any specific industry or firm. A little arithmetic on the basis of the above figures demonstrates the effect of working two or three rather than one shift per day, while leaving the number of days worked per week unaltered. Since interest charges do not increase when output is increased, costs per unit of output on the second shift will fall immediately by 10; there may also be some reduction in the cost per unit of depreciation and obsolescence; a reduction of 2 may be taken to represent this. Thus costs on the second shift fall by 12 per unit of output. There will be no further reduction in interest charges by working three shifts; these have been eliminated already. But there may be a further small saving on account of depreciation and obsolescence per unit of output. More intensive working by, say, eliminating holidays or working the machinery faster would not be likely to effect much further reduction. Once interest charges are eliminated there is not much further scope for cost cutting by shift-working.

The savings in capital cost will almost certainly be off-set in part by the need to offer some incentive for second and third shift-working. Additional payments for shift-work vary; for an evening shift for the housewife no additional payment may be needed above ordinary rates of payment; second and third shifts are normally likely to involve additional payments equivalent to a quarter or third of earnings on the day shift even if the times of the shifts are adjusted to minimize inconvenience. The actual increase in labour costs is often higher than this; it is not always easy to maintain standards or provide adequate supervision on the night shift. Thus an addition of one-third to labour costs per unit of output is not an unreasonable estimate of the increase that would result. In the arithmetic example the savings in capital costs per unit of output would be slightly greater than the increase in labour costs, but there would not be much in it. Nevertheless, if this little were not absorbed by the need to make price reductions in order to sell more output, it would make an appreciable contribution to profits.

The above example approximates the cost structure of the cotton industry fairly well and partly explains why the United Kingdom cotton industry was slow to adopt double or treble shift-working when Japan and the United States found it advantageous to use their equipment more intensively. The Japanese had to be severely competitive to win world markets; it is less easy to explain why the United States, a rich country, has adopted shift-working. The feature distinguishing United Kingdom and United States practice was the relative modernity of their equipment. In the United Kingdom declining markets had provided little incentive to re-equip the industry. In the United States modern costly automatic looms were installed, and for these to pay, shift working was necessary. Those firms in the United Kingdom that re-equipped in the 1950s and subsequently were also keen to adopt shift-working.

One of the effects of shift-working is to reduce the ratio of capital to labour costs, because more labour is used when working two or three shifts with the same amount of capital. The effect is to open up new technological possibilities appropriate to a situation in which there is an economic incentive to substitute capital for labour; with shiftworking a worker can use two or three times the capital that would be provided without shiftworking. This would virtually give the British worker the same amount of capital as his opposite number in the United States.

Shift-working is favoured when:

1. Capital costs are high. This may be because a process uses a comparatively large quantity of capital in relation to output, because the cost of capital equipment is high relatively to, say, other countries, or because interest rates are high.

2. Depreciation is not closely linked to the output that is produced and is mainly the result of the ageing process. This, for example, is true of buildings but not of a high-speed cutting tool.

3. Obsolescence is a material danger and as much as possible has to be got out of the capital used before it is out of date.

4. Labour costs are low. This may be true when wages are low or because in a capital-intensive process very few men may be required.

5. Trade unions and their members do not require a substantial increase in wages for shift-working.

6. Difficulty is experienced in meeting demand because capacity is limited or because an unusually heavy flow of orders materializes.

7. More intensive use of capital opens up new technological possibilities.

In practice, the reasons for working shifts are often technological rather than economic. The industries in which shift-working is predominant are generally those working continuous processes such as metal manufacturing and chemical industries, or those that find it necessary to work at night, such as baking, newspaper printing, electricity generation and transport. But there are a number of other industries in which shift-working is important for economic reasons: the jute manufacturing industry is one, coal mining, where large sums must be invested in opening and developing pits, is another. Other industries, such as the motor car industry, may work shifts when demand is at a seasonal peak and occasionally a few machines or departments may work continuously because they use exceptionally expensive equipment.

In underdeveloped countries where capital is scarce, and therefore expensive, and where some forms of labour are cheap, there are strong reasons for shift-working. In the major industrial countries there is little reason to suppose that shift-working is ever likely to predominate. Higher real earnings make men more reluctant to work shifts and encourage them to exact a higher price for doing so. There is no reason to suppose that capital costs per unit of output will rise as time goes on and some reason for supposing that they will fall. Shift-working is thus likely to be confined to processes where it is unavoidable for technological reasons and to those exceptional industries or processes that require large amounts of capital.

COSTS AND BUSINESS DECISIONS

Cost data are needed for three purposes: as a record of the past, as a basis for planning and for control.

The businessman needs figures of costs if he is to be able to answer certain basic questions, such as the effect of using new techniques, whether products are paying their way, how much to increase prices as a result of an increase in costs, whether to accept an order and at what price.

Cost data cannot do everything, and the businessman needs to supplement them with information about markets, in order to determine whether with given production methods, or improved methods, he has a reasonable prospect of competing with others in the same field.

Several types of costing systems are used in practice, and the method employed usually depends on the nature of the productive processes of the firm; the principle usually employed is to analyse expenditure in such a way that costs can be allocated to individual activities. For present purposes we can confine ourselves to three main types.

The first main type attempts to cost each job, or batch, or contract separately, or to allocate costs to certain departments or processes. Several names are given to these systems (e.g. Job Costing, Batch Costing, Output Costing etc.), and although they differ in the accounting methods employed, they are all forms of 'record' or 'historical' costing. If properly constructed such records provide data for control and serve a useful but limited purpose.

The second type is 'standard' costing, which has grown up because of a dissatisfaction with historical and record costing. Perhaps the most important aspect of standard costing is its implication that it is not so important to know what a product has cost as what it can reasonably be planned to cost. The three most important elements are the allocation of overheads (or fixed costs) on a reasonable basis to each product, the use of costs as controls, and the importance of the *future* element of costs. Two authoritative definitions show the thinking which underlies the process.

Standard cost may be defined as : 'an estimated cost, prepared in advance of production or supply, correlating a technical specification of materials and labour to the prices and wage rates estimated for a selected period of time, with the addition of an apportionment of the overhead expenses estimated for the same period within a prescribed set of working

conditions.[1] Standard costing, as defined by the same authority, is 'the preparation of standard costs and their use to clarify
the financial results of a business, particularly by the measurement of variation of actual costs from standard costs and the
analysis of the causes of the variations for the purpose of maintaining maximum efficiency by executive action'.[2] Standard
costing may also be used as part of a system of budgetary
control.

The third main type is what has come to be known as
'marginal' costing. The choice of title is unfortunate because
it may imply that this is the process of ascertaining marginal
cost as it is understood by the economist : in fact this is not the
case. What the accountant means by marginal cost is variable
cost (cost which may be avoided by ceasing production entirely)
whereas the economist means the increment to total cost resulting from an increase in output of one unit. Although, as was
seen earlier in the case of firms with a flat-bottomed long-run
average cost curve, marginal cost is the same as variable cost,
the logic of the two definitions is different.

The philosophy underlying this principle of costing is that
fixed costs are unavoidable and that what matters is to cover
variable cost and make some contribution to fixed costs:
whether or not to accept an order to manufacture a product
depends on what 'contribution' will be made to fixed costs
after variable costs have been covered; the approach is an
attempt to take account of the fact that it is difficult to allocate
fixed overhead costs to production on a basis varying with the
level of output. The system has the virtue that it should allow
changes in costs which are the result of production to be
emphasized, but in practice there is a whole class of costs,
sometimes called 'semi-variable' costs which are difficult to
allocate, and even the variable cost is not always easy to calculate. In addition the concept of fixed costs is, as we have
seen, by no means unambiguous, and with firms in a state
of change such allocation is often arbitrary.

A useful product of the marginal costing approach is 'break-
even analysis'. A business may be said to break even when its

[1] An *Introduction to Budgetary Control, Standard Costing, Material Control and Productive Control*, The Institute of Cost and Works Accountants, April 1950.
[2] Ibid.

total revenue equals its total costs; this point can be calculated
via marginal cost analysis by working out the contribution per
unit of sales made to fixed cost, and from that determining
how many units of output are necessary for the firm to cover
its fixed costs and hence to break even; or alternatively this
may be done by means of a chart.

Figure 3.1 is a typical break-even chart. All businesses must
meet certain fixed costs irrespective of the level of output;
variable costs increase with output. The value of sales also
increases with output. As output and sales increase total costs
increase but, if the business is to be profitable, costs do not increase
as quickly as total receipts. In Figure 3.1 (overleaf) no profit
is earned until the plant is operating at about 40 per cent of
capacity; below this level sales are less than costs and increasing output serves only to reduce losses; above this level the
value of sales exceeds costs and with increasing output sales
increase more rapidly than costs, bringing increasing profit per
unit of output.

The main shortcoming of break-even analysis is that it
depicts profit as a single-valued or linear function of output.
In its simplest forms it ignores demand conditions in the sense
that it assumes that selling price is constant for all levels of
output; the discussion in Chapter IV shows that this assumption is frequently unrealistic. In order to sell a greater output
it may be necessary to reduce price, and a recognition of the
existence of price elasticity of demand implies that in many
cases the sales curve should be concave to the horizontal axis.
If price reductions are made in steps the sales curve should
take the form of a series of straight lines of decreasing slope,
each decrease in slope representing a reduction in sales revenue
per unit sold. Similarly it is not always realistic to depict the
variable cost line as a straight line; the existence of diminishing returns would produce a curve convex to the horizontal
axis.

A further limitation, implied in the preceding paragraph,
is that it is not possible to determine an optimum price-output
position from the break-even chart. Maximum profit is shown
in Figure 3.1 at 100 per cent capacity, but this begs the whole
question of the determination of capacity.

If the horizontal axis is measured in terms of units of output,

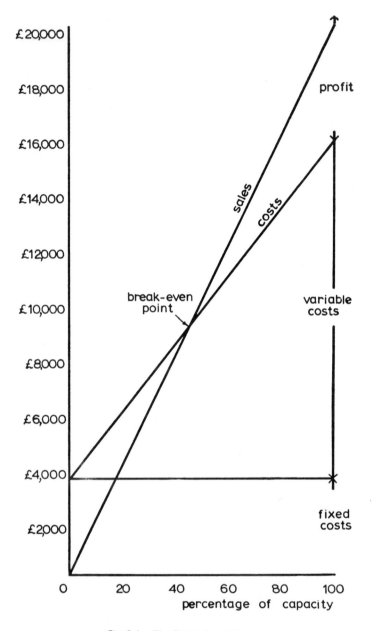

Fig. 3·1.   The Break-Even Chart

and sales curves and cost curves are drawn according to the principles discussed in the preceding paragraph, it is possible to determine the maximum profit position. This occurs in Figure 3.2 at the point where the vertical distance (AB) between the sales curve and the cost curve is greatest. In formal terms this point is where the first differentials (or tangents, or slopes) of the two curves are the same (this is equivalent to saying that marginal cost is equal to marginal revenue, since the slope of each curve measures the incremental, or marginal value of the curve at that point). It will be noted that there are two break even points (C and D) on Figure 3.2 (overleaf); these two points determine the range of profitable operation. The cost curves of Figure 3.2 are a representation in terms of total costs of the fixed, average and marginal costs of Figure 2.1 in the preceding chapter.

In the long run selling prices must cover fixed costs, and the success of a business which operated a marginal costing system would depend on maximizing the total 'contribution' to fixed costs over the whole range of products. In general, resources should be concentrated on those products which yield the greatest excess of selling price over variable (so-called marginal) cost; but there are so many possible exceptions to this rule that it is not necessarily so helpful as it may seem. It may be necessary to continue to supply special customers, or use certain lines as baits for other lines, and marketing policy rather than costs may dictate this approach, which may be in the long-run interests of the firm. Marginal costing itself does not provide information about this sort of thing, nor does it tell the businessman the effect of taking one order on other orders (there may be bottlenecks which may, for example, restrict the fulfilment of more than a limited number of orders using one group of machines). But this is the same thing as saying that a costing system does not tell a businessman everything about his firm; it is one useful tool, that is all.

Accounting information and technical information are useful, but they both suffer from the limitation that they do not explain relationships: the most useful approach, but the most expensive, is to try to find functional relationships between costs and the determinants of these costs as discussed in this chapter. Costs depend on the scale of output, fluctuations in output, the size of batch, changes in style, etc., and statistical cost analysis may be used to assess the relative importance of these and other factors.

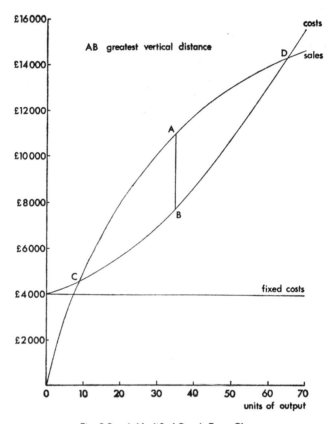

Fig. 3·2.   A Modified Break-Even Chart

Such analysis is useful for the empirical verification of economic theories; it is also of considerable practical value. One of the pioneers of this sort of analysis was Joel Dean.[3] In a study of the costs of a furniture factory he analysed direct labour costs and its determinants: larger lot sizes and increases in production tended to result in reduced unit costs, whilst on the other hand the introduction of new styles, increased labour

[3] Joel Dean, *Managerial Economics* (Prentice Hall, 1960). Chapter 5.

turnover and reductions in output all raised cost to different extents (to which it was possible to attach numerical values in place of mere statements that such might be expected to be the case).

A systematic analysis of the components of costs and the factors influencing costs can provide a basis for cost forecasting, cost control and for the making of business decisions.

PRODUCTIVITY

The work of cost accountants, efficiency experts and economists meet in making productivity comparisons.

Productivity measurements compare the output of a productive process with the inputs that are necessary for it to take place. This is not a simple operation. No productive process involves less than two forms of input; most employ at least three or four and the total number may rise to hundreds or even thousands. Output may be just as varied.

There are no absolute standards of efficiency in economics. Norms are constantly changing; what is good in one situation may be bad in another, standards of productivity that were revolutionary 30 years ago may be mediocre today; production methods suited to one set of prices may be quite inappropriate to others. There is very little that is analogous with efficiency in the sense that this term is used by engineers in relation to heat engines.

There will be few occasions when productivity comparisons can take into account all the possible relations that can be established between inputs and outputs. Fortunately quite crude comparisons can often put a new complexion on affairs; they are best confined to situations that have a good deal in common, for example, the same firm at different points of time, or firms with similar activities. It is often convenient to direct attention to certain principal products, particularly if these can be identified in physical terms such as tons of steel or yards of the same type of cloth.

Similar considerations apply to inputs. In the first instance it may be helpful to concentrate on the number of men employed or the number of man-hours worked, but labour is not a homogeneous unit and skilled labour may be expected to contribute more to output than unskilled labour.

It is usually preferable however to base comparisons on the *value* of outputs and inputs.

One widely used method of productivity comparison is to divide the net output or added value of a firm by the number of people employed. Such a measure may be misleading: firms may not be really comparable, one may use more capital than another, one may be a specialist producer experiencing a dearth of orders and the other in the full swing of mass production. But however crude the comparison it will set the ball rolling and suggest further comparisons. If the amount of capital used is thought to differ between the firms it may be possible to calculate the value of output per unit of capital employed; if the consumption of raw material is a widely variable factor it may be possible to do the same thing for raw materials and there are many other possibilities.

Profit as a proportion of value added is potentially one of the most useful measures of productivity and profitability; it is a guide to profit on the actual operations which produce the profits. In a comparison of two companies, the first may have a higher profit on sales and a lower profit on assets, which might be due to the fact that the second company had higher sales per unit of labour and capital, using these factors more profitably; comparison of profit on value added would be a more adequate basis in such cases. Few companies provide sufficient information to allow such comparisons to be made, but individual companies could well use such a measure for their own purpose.[4]

It may also be possible to make a more exhaustive comparison of the factors affecting productivity. A comparison of milling costs in four mills carried out by the *Centre D'études et de Mesures de Productivité*, provides a good illustration of what can be done by detailed comparisons. Table 3.1 shows costs per quintal produced in four mills. There are wide differences between the costs of the various operations that indicate differences in the performance of the four mills and it is clear that there are differences in productivity.

Inter-firm comparisons of this kind offer opportunities for

[4] See James Bates, *Some Problems in the interpretation of the accounts of unquoted companies, Business Ratios*, Summer 1969. and R. J. Ball, *The use of value added in measuring efficiency, Business Ratios*, Summer 1968.

improvement in performance. Low productivity is often unrecognized because those responsible for running a firm do not know what is possible. Productivity comparisons bring this to light, and, by stimulating interest in the whole subject, they indicate opportunities for further improvement in even the best practice. Best practices are rarely confined to one or two firms and an interchange of methods may be beneficial.

TABLE 3.1

COMPARISON OF MILLING COSTS IN FOUR MILLS

	Mill A	Mill B	Mill C	Mill D	Standard costs
1. Interest on employed capital	44.10	49.50	36.90	—	44.40
2. Financial charges	33.10	33.10	30.00	33.10	33.10
3. Taxes, rates, etc.	5.30	6.80	19.30	11.40	12.90
4. Insurance	13.90	12.20	9.80	7.40	11.80
5. Depreciation	63.50	69.00	60.50	—	63.90
6. Repairs and maintenance	35.50	95.50	67.20	40.70	49.20
7. Labour (production and storage)	115.90	134.70	94.00	—	85.90
8. Power	79.40	28.70	53.20	57.20	65.00
9. Sacks	14.80	19.70	13.50	—	18.60
10. Collecting of sacks	12.00	12.00	12.00	—	12.00
11. Charges calculated on output	2.40	4.00	4.00	—	4.00
12. Office overheads	54.40	25.10	51.80	—	50.70
13. Administrative overheads	37.30	68.50	52.60	—	41.80
14. Sundry sales overheads	46.90	49.30	45.70	—	42.20
TOTAL	558.50	608.10	550.50		535.50

It is not always possible to make detailed comparisons of efficiencies department by department as in the French study. Herbert Ingham and L. Taylor Harrington advocate making inter-firm comparisons on the basis of nine operating ratios.[5] These ratios are:

(1)—Profit after Tax to Capital Employed
(2)—Profit after Tax to Sales
(3)—Sales to Capital Employed
(4)—Cost of Production to Sales
(5)—Cost of Marketing to Sales
(6)—Cost of Administration to Sales
(7)—Fixed Assets to Total Assets
(8)—Sales to Average Stocks
(9)—Average of Outstanding Debts to Average Sales per Day

[5] *Inter-firm Comparison for Management* (British Institute of Management, 1958.)

Such comparisons may be expected to work only if the firms being compared are of reasonably similar size and engaged in the same kind of work. It requires considerable experience to assess the significance of such calculations and they may be misleading unless like is compared with like.

LINEAR PROGRAMMING

The use of linear programming in business may be regarded as a development of economic thinking, concerned with the allocation of scarce resources with alternative uses between different ends.

At any point of time a firm will find itself with certain production facilities such as machines. Some of them will be exactly interchangeable in use and others may be interchangeable to some extent, but many facilities are likely to exist which cannot be substituted for each other because the processes which they perform are quite different. A typical manufacturing unit will produce a variety of products which may make different demands on available production facilities. If any one product were manufactured to the exclusion of all others it might well be that parts of the production facilities would be underutilized and would not therefore contribute to the firm's earnings. Sometimes this can be eliminated, or at least reduced, by manufacturing a range of products which in combination enable a better balanced use of the plant to be made. In simple cases the best mix of product may be determined by trial and error or from previous experience; more complicated cases, however, require the kind of systematic analysis that is given by linear programming.

Consider a simple example. Suppose in a textile mill there are seventy-seven loom-hours and 100 finishing machine-hours available. Assume further that there is a market for two kinds of cloth, one requiring 2 weaving and 1 finishing hour per yard of cloth, and the other requiring 1 hour and 2 hours respectively. Suppose that after allowing for the costs of labour, materials and fuel used for each type of cloth, the profit made per yard of them is the same in each instance. How many yards of each type of cloth should be produced in order to maximize profit?

Graphically the solution can be reached in the following way (see Fig. 3.3).

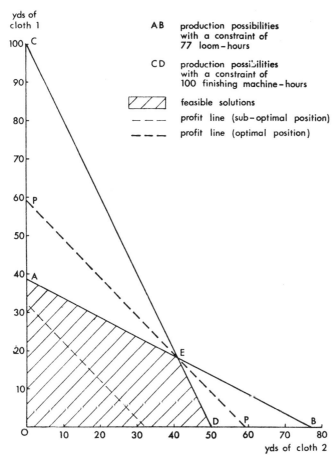

yds of
cloth 1

AB   production possibilities
      with a constraint of
      77 loom - hours

CD   production possibilities
      with a constraint of
      100 finishing machine - hours

⬚⬚⬚⬚ feasible solutions

_ _ _ profit line (sub - optimal position)

▬ ▬ ▬ profit line (optimal position)

yds of cloth 2

Fig. 3·3. Simple Linear Programming

Line AB shows how the limited weaving capacity affects production possibilities. With 77 loom-hours (and unlimited finishing machine-hours) we could produce $38\frac{1}{2}$ yards of the first type of cloth, represented by point A. The same number of loom-hours directed to weaving the second type of cloth would produce 77 yards. Any point on the line AB represents different combinations of the two types of cloth that can be woven with the 77 loom-hours available. Similarly, line CD represents different quantities of the two types of cloth that could be finished using the existing number of machine-hours, that is 100 yards and 50 yards for the first and second types respectively. We cannot produce quantities of cloth represented to the right of lines CD and AB on the diagram because we should not have either enough loom-hours (AB) or finishing machine-hours (CD). It follows that our production possibilities are limited and are to be found within the shaded area OAED. The choice within this area is large; it ranges from not producing anything (O) to producing as much as possible of the first cloth (A) and none of the second cloth, or producing the maximum quantity of the second cloth (B) and none of the first. There are also a great many combinations of the cloths that could be produced with the available machine-hours. Since in this example we have assumed the same profit per yard of cloth irrespective of the types of cloth we are producing, the problem is to produce as many yards of cloth in total as possible. If we were to produce OA yards of the first cloth we should find that finishing machinery was left unused; since the second cloth requires only 1 hour weaving hour per yard against the 2 needed for the first cloth it would pay us to cut down on the production of the first type of cloth and produce twice as much of the second type until all the finishing capacity was in use. Similarly, for the second type of cloth finishing capacity is the bottleneck. So long as looms are unused every yard of the second type of cloth forgone enables 2 yards of the first type of cloth to be produced. Thus whether we move from D to E or A to E we find that we produce more cloth in total. If E is superior to all points on the enclosing lines, points to the left of lines AE and ED must also be inferior, for in every case they offer less of at least one product than could be manufactured at a point on the enclosing lines. E is thus the point of maximum profit.

The solution can also be got by constructing equi-profit lines showing what combinations of output produce the same profit. In this case the same profit per yard is made on each cloth so that the profit lines run at 45 degrees to the axes. We can think of ourselves as drawing in such a line near to the origin and then pushing it outwards while maintaining its slope until it just touches the furthermost point of the feasible area. Such a line passing through E is PP and it indicates that it is possible to make a profit of 59 but no more, since pushing PP further to the right takes it outside the feasible area. At E we produce 18 yards of the first cloth and 41 of the second giving a total profit of 59.

Algebraically, a solution to the problem can be arrived at in the following fashion. The problem is to maximize the profit from the production of cloth subject to the conditions that there are only 77 loom-hours and 100 finishing machine-hours available. Let the number of yards of the first cloth which is produced be x_1 and the number of yards of the second cloth x_2. If the profit on each of them is the same, say one unit of money, the problem can be stated in these terms.

Maximise profits $P = x_1 \times 1 + x_2 \times 1$, subject to the constraints

$2x_1 + 1x_2 \leqslant 77$ (number of loom-hours available)

$1x_1 + 2x_2 \leqslant 100$ (number of finishing machine-hours available)

and subject to the inequalities $x \geqslant 0$, $x_2 \geqslant 0$ (negative quantities cannot be produced).

The problem is to maximise P, where P is the total profit arrived at by multiplying the quantities of each product made by the profit received per unit of product. The constraints simply record the fact that the product mix must not exceed the available capacity for performing various processes.

If for the moment we assume, as we know from the graphical solution, that all the loom-hours and all the finishing machine-hours can be used, we do not need to pay attention to the inequality signs in the equations expressing the constraints, mentally blocking them out and leaving the equality sign. We can then solve the equations for x_1 and x_2 and obtain the answer $x_1 = 18$ and $x_2 = 41$ which can be easily verified by substituting in the equations. Since neither x_1 nor x_2 are negative the other constraints are satisfied.

A problem of the same type involving more variables is set out in tabular form in Table 3.2.[6]

Expressed as a linear programming problem the mathematical representation is:

Maximise $P = 12x_1 + 8x_2 + 24x_3$ subject to:

[6] The table is taken from H. Harrison, Maximising Profits and Minimising Costs by Linear Programming, *Management*, Feb, 1968.

G

$6x_1 + 2x_2 + 4x_3 \leqslant 200$ (moulding production time limited to 200)

$2x_1 + 2x_2 + 12x_3 \leqslant 160$ (packaging production time limited to 160)

and $x_1, x_2, x_3 \geqslant 0$.

The answer to this problem is not intuitively obvious. The first step in solving it is to change the inequalities into equations by the device of introducing another variable called a slack variable. The slack variable makes the right hand side add up to the left hand. Thus we now write the two equations

$$6x_1 + 2x_2 + 4x_3 + x_4 = 200$$
$$2x_1 + 2x_2 + 12x_3 + x_5 = 160.$$

In effect the slack variables represent unused capacity and they will be zero only if production facilities are fully used.

TABLE 3.2

A LINEAR PROGRAMMING PROBLEM

Process	Production Time per Product			Daily available Production Time
	X_1	X_2	X_3	
Moulding	6 mins.	2 mins.	4 mins.	200 mins.
Packaging	2 mins.	2 mins.	12 mins.	160 mins.
Profit per Unit	12	8	24	

Many different values of the xs will satisfy the above equations; but only certain values will maximise P. A solution to the equations can be found using only two of the xs and if the correct ones are selected the introduction of other xs will not increase profit. The problem is which xs to choose. With an example as simple as the one under discussion no detailed procedures for selecting the xs need to be laid down; all possible pairs of xs can be investigated and the pair giving the highest profit selected. In cases involving more equations and variables this becomes impossible without efficient computational procedures, and computers are necessary for most problems. From the point of view of business procedures this is as far as it is really necessary to go. Provided the problem has been correctly formulated the data can be fed into a computer, which will produce the answer in a relatively short space of time. There may, however, be some interest in following a simple computational exercise applied to solving the problem outlined above if only to show the general nature of the approach used in problems of greater complexity. The explanation of why the computational procedures succeed is beyond the scope of this book.[7] For convenience the two equations concerned are set out and manipulated in a series of tables. Each column records the coefficients of the variables and constants. The rows and columns are numbered for ease of reference.

TABLE 3.3

INITIAL TABLEAU

Column Numbers		1	2	3	4	5	6	7	8
Row Numbers	1.			$C \rightarrow$	12	8	24	0	0
	2	Z	V	B	X_1	X_2	X_3	X_4	X_5
	3	0	X_4	200	6	2	4	1	0
	4	0	X_5	160	2	2	12*	0	1
	5	$Z_j - C_j$		0	-12	-8	-24	0	0

$$\left[\frac{160}{12} < \frac{200}{4}\right]$$

↑—————— largest negative

TABLE 3.4

1ST ITERATION

Column Numbers		1	2	3	4	5	6	7	8
Row Numbers	6			$C \rightarrow$	12	8	24	0	0
	7	Z	V	B	X_1	X_2	X_3	X_4	X_5
	8	0	X_4	$\frac{440}{3}$	$\frac{16^*}{3}$	$\frac{4}{3}$	0	1	$-\frac{1}{3}$
	9	24	X_3	$\frac{40}{3}$	$\frac{1}{6}$	$\frac{1}{6}$	1	0	$\frac{1}{12}$
	10	$Z_j - C_j$		320	-8	-4	0	0	2

$$\left[\frac{440}{3} \div \frac{16}{3} < \frac{40}{3} \div \frac{1}{6}\right]$$

↑————————— largest negative

[7] See *Linear Programming and Economic Analysis*, R. Dorfman, P. Samuelson, R. Solow, McGraw-Hill.

TABLE 3.5

2ND ITERATION

Column Numbers		1	2	3	4	5	6	7	8
Row Numbers	11			$C\rightarrow$	12	8	24	0	0
	12	Z	V	B	X_1	X_2	X_3	X_4	X_5
	13	12	X_1	$\dfrac{110}{4}$	1	$\dfrac{1}{4}$	0	$\dfrac{3}{16}$	$\dfrac{-1}{16}$
	14	24	X_3	$\dfrac{35}{4}$	0	$\dfrac{1^*}{8}$	1	$\dfrac{-1}{32}$	$\dfrac{3}{32}$
	15	$Z_j - C_j$		540	0	-2	0	$\dfrac{3}{2}$	$\dfrac{3}{2}$

$$\left[\frac{35}{4} \div \frac{1}{8} < \frac{110}{4} \div \frac{1}{4}\right]$$

↑_____ largest negative

TABLE 3.6

3RD ITERATION

Column Numbers		1	2	3	4	5	6	7	8
Row Numbers	16			$C\rightarrow$	12	8	24	0	0
	17	Z	V	B	X_1	X_2	X_3	X_4	X_5
	18	12	X_1	10	1	0	-2	$\dfrac{1}{4}$	$\dfrac{-1}{4}$
	19	8	X_2	70	0	1	8	$\dfrac{-1}{4}$	$\dfrac{3}{4}$
	20	$Z_j - C_j$		680	0	0	16	1	3

Optimal Solution as there are *no* negatives
in bottom row.

$$\begin{aligned} \text{Solution} \quad P &= \pounds 680 \\ X_1 &= 10 \\ X_2 &= 70 \\ X_3 &= 0 \end{aligned}$$

In Table 3.3 the coefficients of the *x*s in the equations are set out in columns 4 to 8 while column 3 shows the numerical value of the constraints. Row 3 gives the coefficients for the first equation and row 4 those for the second, and the equations can readily be re-constructed from the information in the table. The first row shows the profits made per unit of each *x*; they are indicated with the letter C. Column 1 repeats this information for x_4 and x_5 which are selected in the first instance as the pair of xs to be used to give a feasible solution; they are recorded in that role in column 2. All the other xs are excluded from the solution and assumed to be zero. We see at once that a solution of the equations is $x_4 = 200$ and $x_5 = 160$. Column 3 records this under B. x_4 and x_5, are the slack variables and the solution amounts to saying that the machines will be idle and that the profits referred to as Z_j, will be zero. This does not get us very far but it gets us started and provides a solution from which a better answer is derived (this is the essence of interative procedures). We do this by replacing one of the slack variables with either x_1, x_2 or x_3 making the choice in the following manner. First we take x_1 and multiply its coefficient given in row 3 by the pay-off for x_4; then we multiply its coefficient in row 4 by the pay-off for x_5 and add the results of these calculations together; because there is no pay-off from either x_4 or x_5 the total in this case happens to be zero. The next step is to subtract from this total the value of C given for x_1 in row 1. The result is recorded in row 5 under x_1 as -12. We do the same for x_2 and x_3 recording -8 and -24 respectively. The x showing the largest negative value is then chosen for insertion; in this case it is x_3.

The decision as to which variable to replace is taken automatically according to the following rule. First the value for x_4 under B is divided by the x_3 coefficient in the same line; i.e. $200/4$; the same procedure is followed for the value under B for x_5 i.e. $160/12$. The value $160/12$ is the smaller of the two and this indicates that x_5 should be dropped and replaced by x_3.

We can now proceed to the first iteration, that is finding a solution with the variable x_3 used in conjunction with x_4. The details of this are shown in Table 3.4. In this table all xs except x_4 and x_3 are assumed to be zero, but this does not prevent us from working out coefficients for the xs. These coefficients are arrived at first by eliminating x_3 and then x_4 from the equations setting out the constraints[1]

$$6x_1 + 2x_2 + 4x_3 + x_4 = 200$$
$$2x_1 + 2x_2 + 12x_3 + x_5 = 160$$

Using the standard procedures for solving simultaneous equations, multiply the top equation by 3 and then subtract the bottom one from it

$$16x_1 + 4x_2 + 3x_4 - x_5 = 440 \text{ or}$$

$$\frac{16}{3}x_1 + \frac{4}{3}x_2 + x_4 - \frac{x_5}{3} = \frac{440}{3}$$

The coefficients of the xs and the constant shown in the above equations can be quite readily identified in row 8 in Table 3.4 The coefficients in row 9 are arrived at similarly by eliminating x_4 from the equation. In effect this is already done in the equation expressing the second constraint, and we see after dividing throughout by 12 that

$$\frac{40}{3} = \frac{1}{6}x_2 + x_3 + 0x_4 + \frac{1}{12}x_5$$

If we now mentally block out the x_1 x_2 and x_5 terms on the grounds that they are given a zero value, we see that $x_3 = 40/3$ and $x_4 = 440/3$ (see rows 9 and 8). Profits with these values of x_3 and $x_4 = (40/3 \times 24) + (440/3 \times 0) = 320$ as given in row 10 under B.

We now consider whether replacing x_3 or x_4 with some other variable would increase profits. The rule is that the variable for which $Z_j - C_j$ is greatest is to be inserted in the next iteration. This is arrived at as before by multiplying the coefficient given for x_1 in row 8 by the value of Z given for x_4 in the same row and adding to this total the coefficient of x_1 in row 9 multiplied by the value of Z given for x_3, finally subtracting the value of C (profits per unit) for x_1 from the total. This works out as follows:

$$\frac{16}{3} \times 0 + \frac{1}{6} \times 24 - 12 = -8$$

Similarly for x_2 we have $\quad \frac{4}{3} \times 0 + \frac{1}{6} \times 24 - 8 = -4$

and for $x_5 \quad -\frac{1}{3} \times 0 + \frac{1}{12} \times 24 - 0 = 2$

The largest negative value is for x_1 and it is this variable that is to be inserted in the new solution. We decide whether it will replace x_4 or x_3 by dividing the coefficient for B in row 8 by the coefficient for x_1 in the same row and comparing the value of this $(440/3 \div 16/3)$ with the corresponding value for x_3, $(40/3 \div 1/6)$; the answer for x_4 is smaller that that for x_3 and this leads us to decide to eliminate $x4$.

The second iteration (Table 3.5) is now carried out using x_1 and x_3 along the lines already discussed for the first iteration and this leads to the conclusion that x_2 should be brought into the solution and x_3 eliminated. Table 3.6 carries out a similar operation for the third iteration.

It will be noticed that the successive iterations lead to progressively larger profits until the value of 680 is achieved, which is the maximum that can be attained. It is evident that the solution is an optimum because there are no negative values in row 20.

The solution is thus P = 680, $x_1 = 10$, $x_2 = 70$ and $x_3 = 0$. All the machine-hours will be used so that the slack variables also have the value zero.

It may seem improbable that an optimal solution should require that product x_3 should not be produced at all, particularly in view of the fact that x_3 earns a profit per unit of £24. A clue to the explanation in intuitive terms is that x_3 uses too much of the limited packaging facilities available; it requires 12 minutes of the time of the packaging machines and 4 minutes of the time of the moulding machines.

Table 3.7 restates the data of Table 3.2 in terms of percentages of available machine production time required for a unit of each of the three products x_1, x_2, and x_3. A unit of x_1 requires 3 per cent of total moulding time, and 1.25 per cent of packaging time; a unit of x_2 requires 1 per cent of moulding time, and 1.25 per cent of packaging time; a unit of x_3 requires 2 per cent of moulding time and 7.5 per cent of packaging time. A unit of x_3 is therefore too expensive in terms of the opportunity cost of using scarce packaging time, to justify its high profit.

TABLE 3.7

PERCENTAGES OF PRODUCTION TIME REQUIRED PER PRODUCT

Process	Percentage of Production time per product			Daily available production time
	x_1	x_2	x_3	
Moulding	3.0	1.0	2.0	200 mins
Packaging	1.25	1.25	7.5	160 mins.
Profit per unit	£12	£8	£24	—

This intuitive explanation also points to a factor which has been omitted from the calculation: the final answer depends to some extent on the relative costs of using the two types of machines and on the cost of installing new machinery (the latter would of course change the 'boundary' conditions which restrict the range of solutions).

Not all linear programming problems can be solved without further consideration, even by computers. It sometimes happens that degeneracy occurs and not one but an infinite number of solutions emerges. Resolution of this difficulty may be possible by the device of making small adjustments to the numbers involved, but further consideration of this and other problems would lead us too far afield.

Linear programming contributes nothing of itself to the meaning of the economic problems that it solves. It is a technique, not a form of economic analysis; nevertheless it does set off some interesting lines of thought. In the example discussed, profits were maximised by producing only two products although the possibility of producing three was stated in the problem. Full and most profitable use of equipment is made when no more products are manufactured than the number of constraints that are imposed; producing a wider range does not increase profits. This result follows from the way in which the problem was formulated and it may be an over-simplification of the business problem lying behind the data. The final decision about what to produce would be taken in practice only after considering the results of the linear programming exercise in relation to other factors not introduced explicitly into the problem. These might include the danger of becoming dependent on only two products or the need to supply subsidiary companies with particular components. Thus it might be possible to justify the manufacture of other products on more general grounds. Nevertheless the result is instructive in suggesting that maximum profits can be earned with a limited range of products and so gives some encouragement to specialization and to avoiding the administrative problems associated with great diversity of operations.

Linear programming also enables us to compute the returns earned by the types of machines in use. This involves reformulating the problem in the form of the 'dual' of the linear programming exercise. The dual is primarily a mathematical concept with its own properties and relations to the 'primal' which has just been considered, but it has significance and may be given an economic formulation. In effect we ask what prices should be assigned to the production facilities in use, thus allocating the profits to the facilities and so arriving at an imputed cost.

The primal problem is concerned with maximizing profits; the dual is concerned with minimising costs subject to the constraint that all profits are imputed. Suppose that in our example we impute a cost to moulding of Y_a units and to packaging of Y_b units. Then the cost of producing x_1 is $6Y_a +2Y_b$ since it takes 6 minutes of moulding and 2 minutes of packaging to produce a unit of the product. We impose the constraint that these costs must be at least equal to the profit made on the article, in this case 12 units. There are three such inequalities corresponding to the three products that the moulding and packaging machines might be used to produce.

$$6Y_a + 2Y_b \geqslant 12$$
$$2Y_a + 2Y_b \geqslant 8$$
$$4Y_a + 12Y_b \geqslant 24$$

These equations are subject to the requirement that total costs should be minimized i.e. minimization of

$$C = K_a Y_a + K_b Y_b$$

where K_a is the capacity of the moulding plant in minutes of usable time, and K_b the capacity of the packaging plant also in minutes of usable time. Y_a and Y_b must both be positive or zero ($Y_a \geqslant 0$, $Y_b \geqslant 0$). We do not need to go into all the niceties of solving the dual problem; its answer is in any case given in the process of solving the primal problem. It is sufficient for our purpose to note that only products x_1 and x_2 are made and that costs of production are equated to profits in total. This means that the imputed costs can be obtained by solving the equations:

$$6Y_a + 2Y_b = 12$$
$$2Y_a + 2Y_b = 8$$

The solution is $Y_a = 1$ and $Y_b = 3$. Available moulding time is 200 which multiplied by its cost of 1, gives 200; available packaging time gives a cost of $160 \times 3 = 480$. The two taken together are equal to the total profit of 680.

From the above exercise we see that one minute of packaging

time earns 3 units. This has implications for the investment decision because if packaging time can be installed and used at a cost of less than 3 units per minute it will pay to expand the plant.

Linear programming methods can be used to solve a wide range of business problems. One, almost classic application, that of determining combinations of feeding stuffs providing necessary quantities of nutrients at minimum cost has obvious applications in the rearing of animals. The problem presents itself in the form that an acceptable diet must contain so many calories, so many units of protein, calcium and so on. These are provided in various foodstuffs in differing proportions and the foodstuffs themselves are available at prices determined on the market. The specifications of the problem are shown in Table 3.8 which shows the amount of various elements included in unit quantities of foods F_1, F_2, F_3 etc.

TABLE 3.8

A FEED-MIX PROBLEM

Nutritional Element	Food F_1	F_2	F_3	F_4	Minimum requirements of elements
I	f_{11}	f_{12}	f_{13}	f_{14}	m_1
2	f_{21}	f_{22}	f_{23}	f_{24}	m_2
3	f_{31}	f_{32}	f_{33}	f_{34}	m_3
4		etc.			etc.

Suppose that quantities x_1, x_2, x_3 etc. are bought of the various foods. The amount of nutritional elements 1, 2, 3 . . . etc. contained therein are shown below together with the minimum quantity of nutrient that must be provided.

$$x_1 f_{11} + x_2 f_{12} + x_3 f_{13} \ldots \geqslant m_1$$
$$x_1 f_{21} + x_2 f_{22} + x_3 f_{23} \ldots \geqslant m_2$$
$$\text{etc.}$$

All the xs must be equal to or greater than zero, the usual inequality conditions. In addition the cost of purchasing the nutrients in the required quantity can be expressed in the form of an expression to be minimised. If the prices of the foods per unit are p_1 p_2 p_3 etc. this gives the total cost to be minimised as;

$$C = p_1 x_1 + p_2 x_2 + p_3 x_3 \ldots \text{etc.}$$

We now have all the elements of a linear programming

problem and the solution can be sought along the lines already indicated, if necessary by feeding the data into a computer.

Another classical application of linear programming lies in the transportation problem, the essence of which is that there are various geographically distinct sources of supply and various geographically distinct markets which have to be provided for at minimum transport cost.

A simple transportation problem is set out in Table 3.9

TABLE 3.9

A TRANSPORTATION PROBLEM*

Warehouse Factory	A	B	C	D	Factory Capacities (units)
No. 1	1.5	1.0	2.0	1.5	3500
No. 2	2.0	2.5	1.0	1.0	6000
No. 3	2.5	1.5	1.5	2.0	2500
Warehouse					12,000
Requirements	3000	4000	1000	2500	———
(units)					10,500

*This example was also provided by Mr. H. Harrison

The figures in the table give the cost of transporting a unit quantity of the product between the factory and warehouses corresponding to the entry. The problem is to supply the warehouses A to D with their requirements from the factories 1 to 3 while minimising transport costs. We can write the solution to the problem in symbolic form, as in Table 3.10.

TABLE 3.10

SYMBOLIC FORM OF TRANSPORTATION PROBLEM

Factory	Warehouse A	B	C	D	Factory capacity
1	a_{11}	a_{12}	a_{13}	a_{14}	3,500
2	a_{21}	a_{22}	a_{23}	a_{24}	6,000
3	a_{31}	a_{32}	a_{33}	a_{34}	2,500
	3000	4000	1000	2500	12,000

In this particular case there is excess factory capacity. The constraints of the problem take the form that each warehouse must be fully supplied and that the capacity of no factory may be exceeded.

The method of solving the problem is similar to that already discussed for other types of linear programming problems. A basic feasible solution is selected and improved systematically until (in this case) the cost of transportation is minimised. Note that the number of routes used for shipment will be limited to the number of variables needed to satisfy the constraints; by no means every factory will ship to every warehouse. The solution to this particular problem is shown in Table 3.11.

TABLE 3.11

SOLUTION OF TRANSPORTATION PROBLEM

Warehouse Factory	A	B	C	D	Cost
No. 1	2000	1500			4500
No. 2	1000		1000	2500	5500
No. 3		2500			3750
		TOTAL COST			13,750

It will be seen that factory No. 3 ships only to warehouse B and that there are blanks in the entries for the other factories as well.

Amongst applications of the transportation problem has been the allocation of cement from different factories to consuming areas, the allocation of the products of the pulp and paper industry in the same way and the transportation of coking coal from 154 collieries to 65 coke ovens in England and Scotland.[8]

The justification for using linear programming techniques lies in the fact that the solutions obtained are better than those derived from experience or rule of thumb. An interesting study by J. K. Wyatt compared the utilization of recovered metal in making up alloys to specification when decisions were taken on the basis of experience with those suggested by linear programming. It appeared that linear programming increased the use of recovered metal by 5 per cent and produced a worthwhile financial saving. At the same time the process of deciding on alloy specification was greatly simplified by being reduced to a routine and systematic procedure.[9] The study of the move-

---

[8] A. H. Land, *Journal of the Royal Statistical Society*, Series A, Part III, 1957, p. 300.
[9] *Operational Research Quarterly*, Vol. 9, No. 2, p. 154.

ment of coking coal showed that a saving of 10 per cent could be made in the transport of coking coal.

STOCK CONTROL

The purpose of holding stocks is to bridge the interval between the availability of a new supply of an article and an immediate requirement for it. But the average level of stocks must be related to the benefits to be derived from holding stocks balanced against the costs of holding them. Stock control can be regarded as an exercise in queueing theory, since queues for processing may form and machines may be kept waiting if stocks are exhausted.

The cost of holding stocks is often higher than is realized. It is not unusual for one-third or even one-half of the assets of a manufacturing business to be in the form of stocks or work in progress and exceptionally the proportion may be much higher, as in the tobacco industry. The cost of holding stocks includes the interest charged on money borrowed for the purpose (or the loss of profit involved in tying up the company's capital in financing them), warehouse and insurance charges, the cost of supervision and the risks that stocks will become obsolete or prove to be unsaleable. In some types of production the costs of holding stocks and the associated risks are so great that production is undertaken only to order; this is always the case when a product has to be tailored to the needs of specific customers, as with many capital goods. Although the cost of holding stocks is high the cost of running out of stock may also be considerable if the customer takes his business elsewhere.

The effect of running out of raw materials and components is almost always to cause a costly hold up in production. But this does not mean that excessive stocks should be held and it is necessary to establish some systematic way of verifying when stock levels are adequate but not excessive. Some compromise has to be effected between the size of orders and costs of holding stocks. Generally speaking, large quantities of goods can be purchased more cheaply than small quantities, and this points in the direction of ordering in large amounts; on the other hand, at any given rate of consumption the larger the orders placed the larger will be the average level of stock held. On certain assumptions it is possible to determine the optimum size of an order having regard to these conflicting considerations.

Let the cost of placing an order be C, irrespective of size of order; let N orders be placed each year; let the value of the material purchased and used each year be U; and the cost of holding stocks be a fraction R of their average value per year. Assume that consumption takes place perfectly evenly throughout the year and that deliveries are made just as stocks become exhausted. The average value of the inventory held will be U/2N since the quantity ordered will be U/N and stock levels will very between this and zero just before a new delivery is made.

The cost of holding this inventory will be UR/2N per year.

The cost of ordering will NC per year.

The quantity ordered will be U/N = Q.

Total costs per year (K) of holding inventory and ordering

$$K = \frac{UR}{2N} + NC = \frac{QR}{2} + \frac{CU}{Q} \text{ (substituting for N)}.$$

Differentiating with respect to Q and minimizing we have

$$\frac{dK}{dQ} = \frac{R}{2} - \frac{CU}{Q^2} \text{ and for } \frac{dK}{dQ} = 0$$

$$\frac{R}{2} = \frac{CU}{Q^2}$$

$$\text{or } Q = \sqrt{\frac{2CU}{R}}$$

Q is the optimum size of order. It will not matter very greatly however if there is some departure from the optimum. The cost of holding stocks will be altered if the order size is changed, but the cost of ordering will move in the opposite direction.

Uncertainty about consumption rates and delivery times adds a further complication. Suppose that the system of stock control used is to order a fresh supply of some component whenever stocks fall below some level. How should this level be fixed? In most cases, some time will elapse before the order can be delivered, and it will be necessary to have sufficient stock on hand to ensure that supplies of the components can be maintained until the new supplies arrive. Thus the level to which stocks can fall before a new order is placed must be related to the level of consumption that is anticipated, and the time to make delivery (the lead time). Both of these may fluctuate. It is often possible to appraise the extent of such variations from past experience, and to allow for alterations.

A simple statistical model illustrates the considerations involved. Consider the case where it is necessary to place orders for the 'season'. If demand cannot be met fully because stocks are exhausted, profit p per unit is lost; if stocks remain at the end of the season and have to be sold off, a loss of l is made. The question is how much to order. Suppose that past experience shows the following pattern of sales and that the goods are bought and sold in lots of 50.

TABLE 3.12

Units sold	Proportion of times indicated quantity was sold
50	1.00
100	.95
150	.80
200	.30
250	.10
300	.05
350	.00

The table indicates that it was exceptional to sell less than 100 and that at least 50 were always sold. Whether it is worth while buying more than 50 depends on balancing the chance of making an additional sale with its associated profit against the chance of failing to sell with its associated losses. Therefore at the margin the chance of sale x p must equal the chance of loss x l.

Suppose p equals 5 and l equals 10. Is it worthwhile to buy 150 rather than 100? The probability of selling 100 is 0.95; the probability of selling 150 is 0.80; the chance of failing to sell the additional 50 is thus 0.15 and correspondingly the chance of selling is 0.85. Actuarially the profit to be expected by purchasing an additional 50 units is 50 ($0.85 \times 5 - 0.15 \times 10$) = 137.5. It will pay to purchase 150, but will it pay to increase purchases still further to 200? The chance of failing to sell the additional 50 in this situation is 0.50 and the chance of selling is also 0.50. The profit to be expected on an actuarial basis is thus 50 (0.50 × 5 − 0.50 × 10), in fact a loss of 125. Clearly it is best to buy 150 units.

In practice questions of stock control will generally be much more complicated than the simple examples considered above, and elaborate systems of stock control may have to be devised. In practice it is wise to reflect on the degree and method of control that appears to be worth while for different components and raw materials. Study of the composition of inventories has shown that it is usual to find that about 15 per cent of the items held in stock account for about 85 per cent of the value of the raw materials and components consumed. This suggests that inventory control should pay most attention to the relatively few items that account for a large percentage of value and give much less attention to other items.

In one manufacturing concern it was found useful to group components and raw materials according to certain characteristics.

The first group was composed of items that represented an appreciable proportion of the value of components used and which were required in varying quantities. It was decided that the stock and future delivery position of these items would be kept-up-to-date at all times and in advance of assembly, so that supplies could be made available to meet requirements.

A second group included parts which represented a medium to high proportion of the value of components utilized but were consumed in reasonably constant quantities. It was decided in this case that the components should be manufactured, assembled, or purchased by schedule and that stock holdings should be no more than what was necessary to smooth out small irregularities in supply. No stock records would be kept but a strict watch would be kept on the floor stock at frequent intervals. Such a procedure is not without its dangers when it relates to goods that are purchased from outside for it means that continuity in production hinges on the ability of suppliers to maintain deliveries. Strikes at producers of motor accessories frequently make it impossible for car producers to finish cars in course of construction.

A third group of components consisted of items representing

a medium to high proportion of the value of components used, and which were subject to some fluctuation in use. The appropriate method of stock control for these items appeared to be that they should be ordered in 'economic order batches'.

The fourth group included parts that were much in demand but of small value. In this case the 'two-bin method of control' was used whereby immediately one of two bins or store locations was empty, a replacement order was put in hand. The effect of this decision was that supplies of these parts were assured at all times without it being necessary to pay particular attention to the stock position. Moreover, little supervision was exercised over the issue of the components.

One of the effects of the introduction of the method of stock control outlined above was that there was an appreciable reduction in stock levels, a considerable reduction in the chance of running out of stock of the various items in use and a saving in setting time needed for parts produced internally. The latter saving arose because it was not necessary to break production runs and reset machines to produce parts that had been used up unexpectedly.

The system of stock control just described is geared to production requirements. In some industries it is necessary to pay particular attention to the effects of price fluctuations on the business. It used to be said that the wool textile industry made most of its profits out of successful speculation on the course of wool prices rather than out of processing raw materials. It may be expedient in some cases to build up stocks when it is thought that prices will rise, and to live from hand to mouth when it is thought that a fall in prices is imminent. But not all producers take this view; many hold that the risk of running short of supplies or of misreading the market outweighs the chance of speculative gain.

The volume of work in progress depends largely on the effective planning of production. Minimum levels of work in progress in particular operations are determined by the technological requirements of the process, by the speed of a conveyor belt or by the time needed for paint to dry, and so on. The total inventory can be controlled by regulating the production of partially-finished products so that there is a smooth flow of production, and by relating the production programme closely to the delivery pattern or to the orders that are being received. Thus, the control of work in progress is much more likely to be a by-product of production control than anything in its own right.[10]

The considerations that affect stock control of finished goods are fairly similar to those affecting raw materials and components. If the product is always built to the order of customers the question of having a stock of finished products does not arise. It may be, however, that to some extent the finished product is a particular arrangement of components that are themselves standard, and in this case the problem of stock control appears at one remove. Where the firm is functioning as a supplier of components to another industry, the penalty of running out of stock is likely to be high. It may involve the loss of future custom, or taking emergency and costly measures which interrupt the production flow, dislocate other programmes and result in excessive amounts of overtime. The cost of such happenings must be weighed against the cost of holding inventories at a level designed to meet orders with little or no delay. There is also a dilemma in reconciling optimum rates of production (particularly where batch production is involved) with minimum stock levels and service to the customer. The simplest administrative solution to this kind of situation is to keep inventories on the high side, but this is unnecessarily expensive and may not be a solution at all if capacity is limited and the required inventory cannot be accumulated. In practice the problem may be resolved by laying down certain rules about the replenishment of stocks when they fall below certain levels, and control may be reduced to the automatic verification of stock levels. If this is done at regular intervals it may be adequate and an improvement on an unsystematic approach to the problem. But a more complete solution lies in a thorough investigation of the various cost functions that are involved; the costs of failing to make delivery to the customer on time, or being out of stock when he wishes to make an immediate purchase; the cost of stockholding, and the costs of operating alternative production programmes.[11]

---

[10] For an extreme example of this readers may care to consult Mark Spade, *How to Run a Bassoon Factory*, Chapter V.

[11] For a full discussion of these matters see Charles C. Holt, Franco Modigliani, John F. Muth and Herbert A. Simon, *Planning Production, Inventories and Work Force* (Prentice-Hall International, Inc. 1960)

For most firms refined methods of programming production and relating the control of stock levels to the programme will not be possible. The main form of control in such cases is making sure that the problem of stock control is not ignored. Automatic rules for the replenishment of stocks aid considerably in this and the indirect methods of budgetary control also come into their own. Deviations from expected or habitual stock levels may call for explanation, and such verification may be an effective check on stock levels if it is combined with periodic reviews of stock levels to assess whether circumstances have altered or new methods of production, or changes in market conditions, require alterations in accepted practice.

Control of stocks is an essential function of day-to-day management. Higher up the management tree, stock levels are likely to fall under broader scrutiny, such as the comparison of variations in figures of stocks with changes in production levels and comparisons with other firms. It might appear that when attention is paid to the regulation of stock along the lines we have been discussing nothing would remain to be done, and that little could be discerned from general considerations. But there is still room for the chairman of a large company to urge economy in stock accumulation on his various departments when credit is tight, or when money has to be husbanded for other purposes.

QUALITY CONTROL

From the point of view of production it is important to make sure that finished goods or components do not fall below certain measurable specifications. In a production run there are always some variations in the measurable characteristics of the product. The length of nails varies from one to the next, the strength of wire is not the same throughout its length, and the value of resistors is seldom that indicated by the nominal values shown on them. It is common in engineering to think of dimensions as being subject to tolerances. If the value assigned to some article falls within a certain range it will do for the job; if the value lies outside this range difficulty will be experienced and the article will have to be rejected. The function of quality control is to ensure that the production process is controlled in such a way as to minimize the number of articles that fall outside the tolerances that are prescribed. The advantages of quality control are that it reduces rejects, provides the customer with a more uniform and reliable product and avoids the waste of time, materials and effort that results from the incorporation of a faulty part in subsequent processes.

Statistical methods are used to control quality. The dimensions (whether length, strength, resistance or some other measure) of a series of similar articles can be regarded as varying about some central value.

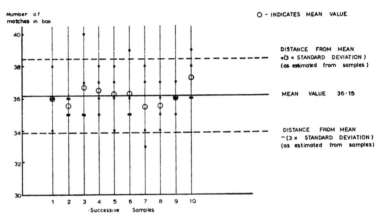

Fig. 3·4.   Numbers of Matches in a Box (Samples of Four)

Figure 3.4 shows the number of matches found in successive counts of samples of four boxes. It will be seen that the contents of the boxes vary from 33 to 40. Quality control operates by ensuring that the central value about which variations take place is that specified for the dimensions of the article and that the variations are kept within the prescribed tolerances. In order to do this it is necessary to be able to decide when the production process is really off-beam. Some deviations from the prescribed values are to be expected. When are they so great that they indicate that something is not as it should be? And how many measurements have to be made to detect this? In many cases it is too costly to test all the components coming off the production line because the tests require a long time to perform. In other cases universal testing may be impracticable; if, for example, the longevity of a component is in question and this can be established only by using it until breakdown or disintegration occurs, universal testing would leave no components for subsequent use.

It is possible to provide statistical answers to all these questions. It is known, for example, that it is uncommon for the mean value of a small sample taken from the production line to differ from the mean of all the articles that are being produced by more than a certain amount. On the chart these limits are shown by the two dotted lines.[12] If the average number of matches in the samples exceed these limits, the process is technically out of control. Similar rules can be used to judge whether samples indicate greater variability in the value of the articles than is specified, even though their average is about right.

For many purposes this kind of test will give adequate results but it suffers from the defect of being comparatively insensitive, and a change in performance may pass undetected for some time because the readings taken continue to fall within the limits set, even if they occur predominantly on one side or other of the mean, indicating an incipient change in standard. If the deviations from the mean are cumulated they become readily noticeable.

Setting up these tests calls for some specialized knowledge, particularly about the nature of the statistical distributions involved, but the use of them can be reduced to routine. All that is needed is to take sample measurements at appropriate intervals and to plot these on a chart. If the values fall outside the control limits marked on the chart it is evident that something is wrong. The next step is naturally to try to bring the process into line and to repeat the cycle of tests and adjustments until results are satisfactory. Like so many administrative devices

---

[12] The filling machinery is adjusted in the first place to attain the standard of performance desired and to give no more than an acceptable number of rejects. The process of control is to ensure that these results are maintained subsequently. Statistically this is a question of making sure that the numbers contained in the sample could have been drawn by chance from a population of the characteristics originally laid down. One test of this is whether the means of the samples differ from the mean of the population by more than three times the standard deviation of the means of repeated samples drawn from the population (or three times the standard deviation of the population divided by the square root of the numbers included in the sample). This is, of course, a rather wide range and the percentage of cases falling outside it by chance is very small. In practice twice the standard deviation is frequently used.

this is not entirely costless. But one reason for the success of the Volkswagen is said to have been the fact that its components were produced to closer tolerances than those of rival makes and that this conferred greater reliability in performance. Quality control can be well worthwhile if its results in an improved and more reliable product.

QUEUEING THEORY

In business it is frequently difficult to decide the proportions in which productive facilities should be provided. The problem would be simple if there were no uncertainty. But in real life uncertainty is present. Consider the operation of doffing spinning machines, which consists of removing the full bobbins and replacing them with empty reels. The machines stop when the bobbins are full, at intervals that are not predetermined. If a large number of machines stop within a short period of each other it will not be possible to service them at once unless the doffing team is very large, in which case there may be long periods when the doffing team is underemployed. On the one hand there will be a queue of machines waiting to be serviced; on the other, there will be a queue of doffers waiting for work.[13]

The same type of problem arises in getting a taxi at a station; there may either be taxis on the rank waiting for fares or would-be passengers waiting for transport. It rarely happens that the flow of taxis corresponds with the arrival of passengers so that neither one nor the other is kept waiting. Other examples of queueing problems include the flow of traffic at traffic lights, the stacking of aircraft for landing or take-off, service at cash desks or in shops, and the arrival of ore-carriers at ports with limited unloading facilities.

The lack of balance between the provision of some service, such as checking-in at an airport, and the demand for the service arises because one or other is unpredictable or intermittent in some way. Thus, passengers arrive at varying times to be checked-in and take varying times to be serviced. The provision of additional check-in points reduces the waiting time for passengers but it increases the cost of the clerical labour needed for the purpose. The problem of the airport officials

<hr>

[13] See A. W. Swan, 'Operational Research in Industry'. *Productivity Measurement Review*, 1960.

is to provide an acceptable service at minimum cost. In order to do this it may be necessary to consider such factors as the number of clerks to be employed; the system of check-in to be adopted, whether to have different desks for different flights or the same desks for all flights or some combination of the two; the time that passengers must report before take-off; and so on. Acceptable service from the point of view of the passenger depends on how long he is kept waiting before being attended to, how long he has to report before the departure of his flight, and the chance that even if he does report on time the queue will be so long that registration will not be completed in time for him to catch the flight before closing-out time. Acceptable service from the point of view of the airline depends on the number of clerks that have to be employed, the risk that delays in registrations due to queues will hold up the departure of flights, and on the danger that customer goodwill will be lost if the wait for the service is protracted.[14]

The ratio of the mean (average) service-time of a single customer to the mean interval between arrival of successive individual customers is known as the utilization factor or the traffic intensity (ρ). This is important in determining how many customers will be in the queue on the average and the proportion of time for which the server will be unoccupied. It takes a little time for the pattern of queueing to settle down; if a queue forms only after opening time the first customer is sure of being serviced without delay; similarly the second arrival cannot have more than one customer in front of him. But as the day goes on the queue assumes its characteristic pattern, summarised by the utilization factor. If we assume that the arrivals of customers are random and that service times are exponentially distributed, it is possible to relate traffic density to the mean size of the queue and the probability that the server will be free. Table 3.13 shows the relationship.

There are a number of features of this kind of relationship. It shows that if the traffic intensity is low (short service times, long intervals between arrivals) there is a good chance that the server will be free and the average number of people in the queue will be small. The reverse is also true. The proportion of

---

[14] For a discussion of the whole of this problem see A. M. Lee and P. A. Longton 'Queueing Processes', *Operational Research Quarterly*, Vol. 10, p. 56.

time the server is occupied is $1-\rho$, the rest of the time he is idle. If on the average there is to be no more than one person in the queue the server will be idle for half the time. The more irregular are the arrivals of customers the greater is the length of the queue likely to be.

TABLE 3.13*

DEPENDENCE OF VARIOUS CHARACTERISTICS OF THE QUEUE UPON THE TRAFFIC INTENSITY; SINGLE SERVER WITH RANDOM ARRIVALS AND EXPONENTIAL SERVICE-TIMES.

Traffic intensity ρ	Probability server free $1-\rho$	Mean queue size $\rho/(1-\rho)$	Probability of more than four customers in queue ρ^5
0.1	0.9	0.111	0.00001
0.2	0.8	0.250	0.0003
0.3	0.7	0.429	0.002
0.4	0.6	0.667	0.010
0.5	0.5	1.000	0.031
0.6	0.4	1.500	0.078
0.7	0.3	2.333	0.168
0.8	0.2	4.000	0.328
0.9	0.1	9.000	0.590

*Taken from D. R. Cox and Walter L. Smith, *Queues*, Methuen, 1961.

Notes: The exponential distribution takes the form $e^{-\alpha t}$ where e is the natural logarithmic base with the value 2.718. In saying that service times follow an exponential law we mean that the expression $e^{-\alpha t}$ gives the chance that the time taken to service any customer will be greater than t. Thus if $\alpha = 1/20$ and $t = 20$ mins the expression $e^{-\alpha t}$ becomes $e^{-1/20 \times 20} = e^{-1} = 1/e = 0.37$. This means that in 37 cases out of 100 the time taken to service the customer will be greater than 20 mins. The exponential distribution is a fairly simple one; fortunately it has a wide range of applicability to queueing problems.

As ρ approaches 1 the length of the queue increases sharply and values greater than 1 mean that the queue will build up to infinite length. Figure 3.5 shows for a case where all service times are equal, how the ratio of 'mean waiting' time to mean service time builds up as ρ increases. When $\rho = \frac{1}{2}$, the time spent waiting is only half the time being served. When $\rho = 0.9$ the ratio increases to 4.5 and to $9\frac{1}{2}$ for $\rho = 0.95$, while with $\rho = .99$ the ratio is nearly 50.

The conclusions set out above apply to queues and service times of the simplest form, but in practice the pattern may be disturbed. Customers will leave a queue long before it becomes infinite in length and most managers will take steps to prevent this happening even when the queue concerns not people but machines rooted to the spot. The speed of service may also be affected by the size of the queue, decreasing when the queue is less pressing. Even if the average number of customers queueing is low there will be times when a sizable queue will form. The sudden arrival of a number of individuals to be checked in at an air terminal, whilst passengers already in the queue are taking a long time to complete their business, may result in a queue which will take some time to disappear.

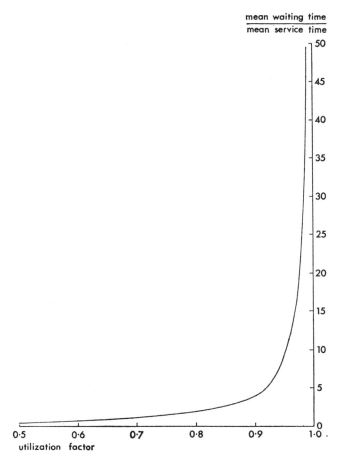

Fig. 3·5. Variation in Quality of Service with Utilization Factor (service times assumed to be equal)

Simple changes in queueing procedures may result in a marked reduction in average waiting time. The quick checkouts of supermarkets which allow customers wishing to purchase few articles precedence over those more heavily burdened, reduces average queueing times because those who can check out quickly do not hold the others up for long and are not kept waiting.

It is also of interest that doubling the number of servers, while at the same time doubling the number of persons to be served, will have the effect of reducing the size of the queue and the duration of the wait. In fact the effect can be so great that the number of customers queueing changes very little. The reason for this is essentially statistical; it results in a smoothing out of the irregularities of arrivals and service times and gives economies of scale. Systems introducing appointments may also help, and in some cases a more thorough-going re-organization of service facilities or increased mechanization may be needed.

Such improvements are likely to be carried out in the interests of the organization responsible for service. There will be an incentive to improve the service if the return to the organization is improved; but few organizations attempt to balance the gains from better service against the costs incurred by the organization. If, however, queues and servers belong to the same organization as for example, when machines are awaiting repair by a company's maintenance engineer, service procedures may be adjusted to minimise costs. In the study of doffing spinning machines it was found that a team of five was the best choice.

The first step in queueing problems consists of observing what happens and measuring such things as arrival rates, service times and queueing times. The next step is to consider alternative arrangements, and if these hold out promise of success to try them on a small scale before finally deciding on an acceptable system. The whole of this procedure might be conducted on a trial-and error-basis. But it is not always possible to proceed in this way, when, for example, the modifications proposed may be costly on even a small scale, or when it may be too complicated to conduct experiments, such as re-scheduling the arrival times of aircraft. The use of a mathematical model, along the lines discussed above, may enable

good operating procedures to be devised without the difficulty
of experimenting. It is not always possible to handle queueing
problems in this way; the mathematical solution may be difficult or impossible and it may be easier to carry out a kind of
paper experiment. This is known as simulation.
Table 3.14 illustrates what this means. We take the case of
patients queueing for a consultation and assume that patients
arrive for appointment exactly on time at the rate of one every
five minutes. Suppose, however, that the time taken for a
consultation is variable and may last for any number of minutes,
1, 2, 3, etc., up to 10 minutes with equal probability. We
could decide the length of consultations for the purposes of our
experiment by throwing a ten-sided dice.

TABLE 3.14

SIMULATION OF A QUEUEING PROBLEM

Patient's number	Time of patient's arrival	Numbers in queue on arrival including patient in consultation	Length of time in queue (min)	Length of time of consultation (min)
1	0	0	0	7
2	5	1	2	4
3	10	1	1	2
4	15	0	0	4
5	20	0	0	7
6	25	1	2	9
7	30	1	6	5
8	35	2	6	6
9	40	2	7	8
10	45	2	10	1
11	50	2	6	1
12	55	0	5	4
13	60	2	4	5

In this simulation the length of the queue was quite short,
averaging 1.2 persons, the average waiting time being 3.8
minutes. For most of the period the consultant was fully occupied, but patients four and five arrived to find no one ahead
of them in the queue and the consultant waiting. The maximum length of time spent waiting was 10 minutes.
    The intervals between the arrivals of patients and the average
length of a consultation were the same. The reason that a
queue developed was that the time for a consultation varied
and that for a period the consultant was not occupied. It is

clear from the previous discussion that the simulation set out in the table is too short to show that in a long series of consultations the queue could become very large ($\rho = 1$).

Development of a queue can be justified on the ground that the provision of the service is relatively expensive in relation to the cost of the time spent waiting by a patient. There is no reason to suppose that this always applies, however; the time of a business magnate may be worth more than that of the consultant and the services that he employs. In the case of a consultant with a number of wealthy patients it could be argued that it was economical to keep the consultant waiting rather than the patients, though a consultant in this position might find it possible to charge fees such that the value of his services exceeded those of his patient!

For the reason we have seen it might prove impracticable to have patients arriving every five minutes. If it were not possible to reduce the time needed for consultations a new system for making appointments would have to be devised or the system modified in other ways.

A practical example of the use of simulation techniques is given in a study carried out by Andrew L. Wood, Management Sciences Unit of Radio Telefis Eireann in Dublin. R.T.E. had decided to instal a central dictating system in order to improve executive efficiency; the problem was to decide how many machines were required to handle the load if: (a) a 'Successful Connection', defined as a person being immediately connected to a dictating machine, was to be obtained in 95 per cent of cases; (b) the time a caller had to wait for a machine was not to exceed 5 minutes.

The first step was to examine the daily logs of the dictating room secretaries and select the record of the busiest day for examination. Three basic tables were compiled from the information. Table 3.15 shows inter-arrival times in the form of a frequency distribution of the time between one request for service and the next following request. Requests for service may come singly or one, two or more may be made simultaneously in the sense that they all occur within the time unit of 5 minutes (maximum waiting time) used for the simulation.

Table 3.16 shows a frequency distribution of the number of persons requesting service during a time interval. In 10 cases all requests were made singly, but in one time interval 4 persons asked to dictate.

TABLE 3.15

FREQUENCY DISTRIBUTION OF TIMES BETWEEN ARRIVALS

Interval between arrival	No. of times occurring	Probability of occurrence	Cumulative probability	Associated band of numbers
0	0			
1	0			
2	2	0.1538	0.1538	0000 to 1537
3	3	0.2308	0.3846	1538 to 3845
4	2	0.1538	0.5384	3846 to 5383
5	0			
6	0			
7	0			
8	0			
9	3	0.2308	0.7692	5384 to 7691
10	2	0.1538	0.9230	7692 to 9229
11	1	0.0769	0.9999	9230 to 9998
TOTAL	13	0.9999		

TABLE 3.16

NUMBERS OF ARRIVALS

No. of arrivals	No. of times occurring	Probability of occurrence	Cumulative probability	Associated band of numbers
1	10	0.7692	0.7692	0000 to 7691
2	2	0.1538	0.9230	7692 to 9229
3	0	0		
4	1	0.0769	0.9999	9230 to 9998

Table 3.17 shows to the nearest five minutes how long dictation took; in most cases this was half an hour or less but in one instance dictation took 125 minutes.

The next step in the analysis is to prepare the tables for the use of random numbers in the simulation. This is shown for Table 3.15 and Table 3.16 but it is omitted in Table 3.17 in order to save space. The procedure is first to calculate the proportion of cases falling into the various divisions. In Table 3.15, 2 cases out of 13 had a time interval of 2, the proportion or probability is thus 0.1538, and similarly for the other divisions. The probabilities are then cumulated and each division is allocated a corresponding band of numbers; the numbers 0000 to 1537 represent the range assigned to the interval 2, the numbers 1538 to 3845 to the interval 3, and so on. The use of the number 0000 leads to the range for 2 terminating at 1537 rather than 1538, and similarly for the other ranges. Table 3.16 is treated similarly and Table 3.17 can be treated in the same way.

TABLE 3.17

DICTATION LENGTH AND FREQUENCY

Dictation length (Mins)	Frequency	Dictation length cont'd.	Frequency
5	49	70	1
10	54	75	3
15	42	80	2
20	36	85	0
25	24	90	2
30	15	95	1
35	24	100	1
40	11	105	1
45	5	110	0
50	11	115	0
55	0	120	0
60	5	125	1
65	4		

It is now possible to start the simulation by selecting random numbers from tables compiled for the purpose. The first four figure random number is taken to represent the time between arrivals, the second the number of arrivals, and the third the length of dictation. The first number selected was in fact 7881 and this indicates (Table 3.15) 10 intervals or 50 minutes. This represents a situation in which the first call for dictation comes 50 minutes after the start of the working day. The second number selected was 6209. From Table 3.16 it may be seen that this represents a single call for service (only numbers over 7691 represent multiple calls). Similarly selections of a further random number can be made to show the time that dictation lasts. In the actual simulation the time was 30 minutes.

In the first simulation the assumption was made that three dictating machines would be available. When all three were in use a queue would form. As the simulation was continued it happened that a queue formed very soon because 4 calls on the service were made after about 3 hours. The process of simulation was continued until the frequency distribution of the items in Tables 3.15, 3.16 and 3.17 corresponded closely with those observed initially for the worst day, indicating that a stable pattern had been reached.

It was then possible to assess the results of the simulation. It was found that queues developed frequently and that out of 175 requests for dictation 14 were relegated to a queue showing that a successful connection to a machine were made in only 92 per cent of the cases. Two requests were delayed for as long as 20 minutes and the average waiting time was 9.3 minutes while the machines were utilized for only 30.8 per cent of the time. This performance was clearly inadequate in relation to the standards laid down and it was therefore decided to repeat the simulation, using four machines. In this case only one request for service out of 175 failed, resulting in a wait of only 5 minutes; this system thus fell well within the standard of service presented. Machine utilization, however, was reduced to 23.1 per cent of the time.

This particular simulation has the added interest that subsequent results obtained with a system of four machines closely corroborated the conclusions of the study. In fact the success level was 99.52 against a calculated level of 99.4 and the utilization rate was 23.8.

CHAPTER IV

DEMAND

FEW businessmen would manufacture a product unless they thought that there was a demand for it; but frequently the decision to produce is taken without any proper analysis of the market. Economic theory can illuminate several of the major practical problems in this field.

There are three significant managerial aspects of demand; first is the analysis and forecasting of demand; second is the effect of demand on the organization and activities of the firm; third is marketing, or the positive approach to the meeting of demand. The first and second may be called the passive managerial aspects of demand because they represent factors which influence the firm; the third is active and represents factors which the firm itself can influence.

Forecasting implies knowledge of the factors likely to affect demand in any given situation. In a general way, many of these factors are fairly obvious—incomes and tastes of buyers, prices, the availability of substitutes, credit facilities, advertising—all of these clearly have some influence on demand, and even an intuitive 'hunch' about the market for a product contains an implicit consideration of these factors.

THE DETERMINANTS OF DEMAND

In practice demand is determined simultaneously by a whole complex of variables, but it is convenient for purposes of analysis to simplify the problem by considering each main factor in isolation, assuming that the others remain constant. The purpose of this procedure is to identify the effect of each factor in isolation: there is no logical difficulty, though there are frequently several practical difficulties, in generalizing the arguments to include more variables than one. Most demand forecasts, whether verbally or numerically expressed, take account of several variables, even though in practice the significant ones may be few.

PRICES AND THE DEMAND CURVE
In a discussion of factors affecting demand, the price of a commodity is usually the first to come to mind. The simplest expression of a demand relationship is the Demand Curve, which portrays the relation between the price of a commodity and the quantity bought in the form of a simple graph derived from a demand schedule, as in Fig. 4.1 and Table 4.1. On the vertical axis is shown the price of the commodity, and on the horizontal axis the quantities of the commodity bought at the various prices.

TABLE 4.1

DEMAND SCHEDULE FOR TEA*

Price per lb (pence)	Quantity consumed (000 cwt)
20	4000
21	3865
22	3775
23	3700
24	3650
25	3600
26	3550
27	3510
28	3475
29	3438
30	3405
31	3380
32	3356
33	3332
34	3315
35	3300

* This demand schedule covers approximately the same range of prices and quantities consumed as those in an empirical study of demand discussed later (R. Stone, *The Measurement of Consumers' Expenditure and Behaviour in the United Kingdom, 1920–1938* (Cambridge University Press, 1954)). This lends verisimilitude to the data, but it must be stressed that the observations themselves are not those of Stone's study.

Typically the demand curve slopes downwards to the right, indicating that the lower the price the more of a commodity is bought. There are cases, as of luxury, or 'conspicuous consumption' goods, where demand falls as prices fall, and other unusual cases, but these are exceptions and are easily accounted for; in general the downward sloping demand curve portrays

I

reality for most practical purposes, and is the form normally used as a tool of analysis.

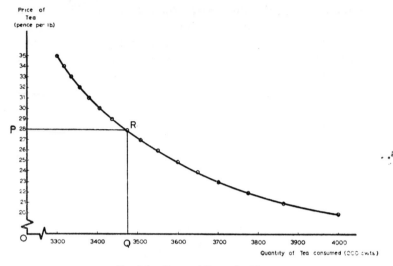

Fig. 4·1.   Demand Curve for Tea

By demand economists always mean effective demand, or demand backed by the ability to pay as distinct from a vague desire to possess a commodity. The demand curve therefore represents the curve of average revenue per unit sold by the producers of the commodity; the price paid per unit of the commodity is the revenue received per unit of the commodity. Total revenue (or total consumers' outlay) from the purchase of a number of units of a commodity appears on the diagram as the rectangle subtended under the demand curve at the price at which the goods are bought. In Fig. 3.1, at price OP, when OQ units are bought, total revenue (price multiplied by number of units) is the rectangle OPRQ. (3,475,000 cwt. at 2s. 4d. per lb., or approximately £45,400,000).

ELASTICITY OF DEMAND

More of a commodity will usually be bought the lower the price of the commodity, but this fact alone is not of much help to the businessman, who wants to know how much more will be bought, and whether more money will be spent: he wants to know what effect a change in price will have on the revenue which he receives. The elasticity of demand of the commodity, which represents the responsiveness of demand to change in price, will tell him this.

More precisely, price elasticity of demand[1] represents the proportionate change in demand resulting from a small change in price, and is measured by the formula:

$$\text{elasticity of demand} = \frac{\text{relative change in quantity purchased}}{\text{corresponding relative change in price}}$$

$$\text{or, symbolically;} \quad e = \frac{\dfrac{dq}{q}}{\dfrac{dp}{p}} = \frac{dq.p}{dp.q}$$

where q = quantity purchased
p = price of commodity
dq = small change in quantity purchased
dp = small change in price

The response of demand for a commodity to a change in the price of the commodity involves two steps. The first (the 'income effect') is due to what may be thought of as a change in the real income of the consumer: if money income remains constant and the price of a commodity is reduced, the real income or purchasing power of the consumer is thereby increased, because his money goes further. The income effect may be positive or negative: if negative, demand for a commodity falls as its price rises; if it is positive the demand for a commodity will increase as the price of it rises. A positive 'income effect' may occur in the case of so-called 'inferior' goods: a large proportion of the income of peasants in the Far East is spent on rice, which is cheap and filling, and there is little left for other food-stuffs; if the price of rice increases the peasant may become so poor that he cannot afford any of the other foods and will buy even more rice simply in order to fill his stomach. The second step (the 'substitution effect') is due to the substitution which takes place between one commodity and other commodities

---

[1] This concept—usually referred to as 'point' elasticity of demand—applies only to small changes round a defined point on the demand curve, although the point may be located anywhere on the curve.

when the price of the first commodity changes; this is always negative and a fall in the relative price of a commodity leads to an increase in the demand for it. Normally the substitution effect dominates and the demand for a commodity increases as its price falls.

Thus the numerical value of price elasticity of demand is usually negative; it is fairly common practice however to ignore the sign and to speak in terms of positive values.

Five interesting cases of elasticity may be distinguished: the first two are limiting cases, which it would be difficult to imagine in real life; the third is also rather unlikely, but conceivable; the fourth and fifth are typical of the whole range of possibilities within these limits.

1. Completely inelastic demand ($e = 0$)

This is the case where, regardless of changes in price, there is no change in quantity demanded and consumed, and total revenue changes solely in accordance with and in direct proportion to price. A completely inelastic demand curve may be represented diagrammatically as a vertical straight line. This is most unlikely to be found in practice, but it is possible to conceive of a case in a very primitive society with one staple food (e.g. rice or bread) where over a very wide range of prices the demand for the staple food remained constant.

2. Completely elastic demand ($e = \infty$)

A completely elastic demand, represented diagrammatically by a horizontal straight line, is the case where any increase in price, however small, causes demand for the product to cease entirely. Although this is unlikely in practice for any commodity in total, many firms are in practice faced with something like a perfectly elastic demand for their product: they produce goods in the knowledge that there is in the market a ruling price for their product which may be fixed by custom, competition or possibly even by government regulation, to which they must conform if they are to sell anything. This may well occur in the case of easily standardized agricultural goods, such as eggs or milk, and in real life the producers of such goods are frequently faced with a completely elastic demand. If they raised their price above the ruling price, no one would buy from them and demand for their product would cease entirely; if they reduced their price they would attract the whole of the demand to them (though they would be unable to satisfy it).

3. Unitary elasticity of demand $(e = 1)$

An elasticity of demand equal to unity is most easily conceived of as the case where, for any change in price, total revenue remains constant and demand changes absolutely in proportion to the change in price. To meet this precise case in real life, though perfectly possible, is improbable, because it represents merely one of an infinite number of possible cases between the two extremes of cases 1 and 2; many observed elasticities of demand do however approximate to it.[2]

4. Relatively elastic demand $(1 < e < \infty)$

When the proportionate change in quantity of a commodity consumed is greater than the proportionate change in price, demand is relatively elastic. There is a whole range of possibilities and the shape of the demand curve may be anywhere between those for cases 2 and 3; but typically, an elastic demand is one in which total revenue increases with a fall and decreases with an increase in price, and the amount by which revenue changes is an indication, though not a measure, of elasticity of demand. Thus, in the case of a highly elastic demand, a small fall in price would produce a large increase in quantity consumed.

5. Relatively inelastic demand $(0 < e < 1)$

Demand is inelastic when the proportionate change in quantity consumed is smaller than the proportionate change in price, and when total revenue decreases with a fall in price and increases with an increase in price. This situation is typical of most so-called necessities.

The most straightforward expression of elasticity of demand is in terms of total revenue. If as a result of a reduction in price total revenue rises, demand is elastic and the bigger the increase in total revenue the more elastic is demand; if total revenue falls demand is inelastic. In practice this may, of course, be difficult to determine, because some other factors may also affect demand at the same time as the price change; but it is the change in total revenue which interests the businessman.

[2] See Tables 4.2 and 4.3.

THE IMPORTANCE OF ELASTICITY OF DEMAND

The examples given above are all simplified,[3] but are useful in that they indicate what economists mean when they talk about elasticity of demand. All businessmen would be expected to know something about the likely effect of price changes on the demand for their product, even though they would rarely express their knowledge in terms of elasticity of demand; but it is noticeable to the outside observer that several business decisions pay insufficient attention to the elasticity of demand for the product. When costs are rising, it is tempting to try to pass on the cost increases by increasing price to the consumer, and if demand for the product is relatively inelastic, this measure may well succeed; but when, as for example in the case of rail transport, there are many substitutes and the demand is relatively elastic, increasing prices may well lead to a reduction of total revenue rather than an increase.

It is not necessary to labour this point further; most businessmen intuitively know something about the elasticity of demand for the goods which they make, and base their pricing policy on some notion of elasticity. It is desirable to go beyond this and to try to form as precise an idea as possible of the degree of elasticity of demand. The concept of elasticity of demand is useful because it is a convenient shorthand way of expressing the effects of price changes on the demand for a commodity and as such it is relevant to price fixing.

Estimation of the demand curve and measurement of elasticity of demand are by no means easy, but they are feasible, and the more that is known about elasticity of demand the easier it is to take decisions about pricing and other aspects of policy.

[3] Strictly it is not permissible to speak of the demand for any product as elastic or inelastic in total: at very low prices the demand for most products, even for luxury goods, is inelastic: at very high prices the demand for most goods, including necessities, is elastic. Formally elasticity of demand is different at each part of the demand curve.

The most that can usually be said of the demand for a commodity is that its demand is elastic or inelastic at prices around those which have been general in the market; but since it is in this range of prices that most decisions will be made, and very large price variations are not common features of business policy it is usually sufficiently accurate for practical purposes to talk of elasticity of demand without specifying the price range to which the statement refers.

But prices are not the only things which affect demand. The demand curve is an apparently simple device, and price elasticity of demand is an indispensable concept; but a great deal underlies both of them. When other things alter the demand curve may change, either in shape or location, and the entrepreneur is faced with a new situation. This is because other determinants of demand are having their effect; this may be due either to the actions of the firm itself (as in the case of advertising) or to outside causes (such as changes in tastes, incomes of consumers, etc.).

INCOMES AND INCOME ELASTICITY OF DEMAND

Demand for a commodity is also affected by the incomes of the people likely to buy it. At times of general prosperity, when incomes are high and unemployment is low, the demand for such commodities as motor cars is likely to be high, but to fall off rapidly, regardless of price changes, when incomes fall. For such commodities income elasticity of demand, which represents the responsiveness of demand to changes in income is more important than price elasticity.

The formula is similar to that for price elasticity of demand:

$$e_y = \frac{\dfrac{dq}{q}}{\dfrac{dy}{y}} = \frac{dq.y}{dy.q}$$

where y = income
dy = small change in income.

Income elasticity of demand is high for most consumer durable goods which have the character of luxuries. In times of restraint, credit squeezes and other periods when the Government has been trying to reduce the level of activity, demand for such goods has frequently fallen, even though prices have not risen; indeed, one of the objects of such credit restraint is to reduce the size of disposable incomes and hence to reduce the demand for commodities which have a high income elasticity of demand. The demand for many British exports (motor vehicles, whisky, capital goods, etc.) is income elastic, and the volume of British exports depends very much on prosperity overseas.

Income elasticity of demand is frequently more important than price elasticity of demand in determining the volume of goods sold. The relationship between demand and income variations is not always straightforward: much will depend on the suddenness or permanence of a change in income, and there is frequently a lag between changes in income and changes in demand; the demand for many goods is readily postponable when incomes fall; it takes time to plan changes, some commitments, such as hire purchase repayments, may remain fixed, and old consumption habits tend to die hard, particularly if a change in income is only expected to be temporary.

SUBSTITUTES AND CROSS ELASTICITY OF DEMAND

The existence of substitutes is another important factor affecting demand, and in fact price elasticity of demand may be looked on to some extent as an indication of the existence or otherwise of satisfactory substitutes for the commodity. If satisfactory substitutes exist, and price is raised, demand will be transferred to the substitutes: commodities with many substitutes are usually found to have a rather high price elasticity of demand. Thus the demand for margarine depends very much on the price of butter, for which margarine is a close substitute in many uses; the demand for chocolates as a whole may be rather inelastic, but the demand for a particular brand may be very elastic simply because there are several close substitutes. The substitutes need not be obvious: for example, gardening may well be a substitute for the ownership of a motor car, and the demand for more cars may, within certain limits, be affected by the availability of houses with gardens; most substitutes are more easily recognized than that however, and the substitutes with which many business decisions are concerned are the products of competitors. Cross elasticity of demand is a useful measure of the relationship between the demands for two commodities, or their substitutability, and may be defined as:

$$\text{cross elasticity of demand} = \frac{\text{relative change in quantity of X}}{\text{relative change in price of Y}}$$

where X and Y are commodities, and where the price of commodity X is kept constant. The formula is:

$$\frac{\dfrac{dq_x}{q_x}}{\dfrac{dp_y}{p_y}} = \frac{dq_x \cdot p_y}{dp_y \cdot q_x}$$

A similar concept is that of 'share elasticity'[4] or 'market share' elasticity of demand, which relates an individual firm's share of the total market sales of a commodity to the difference between its prices and general market prices. Sales of detergent X, for example, are likely to fall if the price of detergent Y in the same market falls. Other factors affecting demand, such as incomes, advertising, tastes, etc., may also have their relevant 'share' elasticities.

Since the businessman is not merely concerned with total market demand for his product, but also with how much he can expect to sell, the relationships between the demand for his product and that for its substitutes is clearly of some importance to him.

In general, the demand relationship between two commodities may be of two kinds: competing or complementary. If the demand for two commodities is competing, which is to say they are substitutes (e.g. lamb and beef), if one (lamb) falls in price, this will lead to a decrease in the demand or a fall or shift to the left in the demand curve for the other (beef); and, in general, demand for any commodity will move in the same direction as the price of its substitutes. Complementary goods, such as motor cars and petrol, are in the opposite relationship—if the demand for one falls, so will the demand for the other—and if the price of motor cars rises there will be a reduction in the demand for petrol. In general, the demand for a commodity moves in the opposite direction to the price of its complementary goods.

[4] See, for example, Joel Dean, *Managerial Economics* (Prentice Hall, 1957). The only real difference between the two concepts is that cross elasticity refers to the response of total demand (or absolute sales) to a change in the price of a substitute whereas share elasticity refers to the response of one firm's share of the market.

TASTES AND PREFERENCES

One of the fundamental determinants of demand for most non-necessary goods is the taste or preference of the consumer. There are certain basic needs, such as a certain calorie intake of food, some warmth, some clothing, some shelter, but there are several ways of satisfying these needs, and given his income the consumer's preferences or tastes frequently determine in what form he will buy the goods to meet these needs. These tastes are usually shaped by the kind of society in which we live, and in which part of that society: housing 'needs', for example, depend very much on professional and 'class' status, clothing needs usually far exceed the minimum necessary for warmth. One of the tasks of market research must be to find out something about this society and the effects which it has on demand. Further, the businessman can influence tastes and preferences, mainly by advertising, and later we look more closely at ways in which tastes and demand may be affected by the actions of the businessman.

SOME EMPIRICAL FINDINGS

To sum up the discussion so far, the main factors likely to influence demand in a given situation are: the price of the commodity, the price of its substitutes, the price of complementary goods, the incomes of consumers, and the tastes and preferences of consumers. Demand will change as one or any combination of these factors changes or is expected to change.[5]

Attempts have been made to quantify many of the basic relationships affecting demand.

The most comprehensive survey in Britain was undertaken by the Department of Applied Economics of Cambridge

---

[5] Theoretical economists have evolved neat ways of expressing the logic underlying demand theory, by the use of 'indifference curve' analysis and 'revealed preference' analysis. This sort of analysis conveniently summarizes the fact that, with a limited income and known prices, a consumer's demand is limited: he must, therefore, make a choice and he will have a system of preferences between commodites (these may be subconscious and not formalized in any way). He may substitute one commodity for another (if he is indifferent between them) and what he is in effect doing is maximizing the satisfaction which he receives from the expenditure of his income. All of the factors influencing demand can be consistently analysed by the use of this sort of technique; but the analysis is more of theoretical than practical interest and has been omitted from the present discussion. The interested reader will find this sort of analysis conveniently summarized in W. J. Baumol, *Economic Theory and Operations Analysis* (Prentice Hall, 1965) Chapter 9.

University.[6] For a whole range of commodities (broadly food, drink, tobacco and fuels) it was possible to calculate three categories of elasticity of demand: income elasticity of demand; price elasticity of demand (or, more accurately, the substitution effect of a change in price[7]); and two main cross-elasticities of demand (elasticity with respect to the price of certain related commodities, and with respect to all other prices). Table 4.2 gives an example.

TABLE 4.2

SOME CALCULATIONS OF THE ELASTICITY OF DEMAND FOR BUTTER, 1921–38.

Income elasticity	0.37
Own price elasticity	−0.43
Substitution Elasticity with respect to:	
Flour price	−.023
Margarine price	0.10
Cakes and biscuits price	0.59
Carcass meat price	0.56
All other prices	−0.58
Residual trend coefficient	0.04

Notes: This table gives the results of only one out of a number of sets of calculations made. On the calculations as a whole the author comments:
> 'A small but positive income elasticity is found. The own-price (substitution) elasticity is of a similar absolute magnitude and is significant as also is the considerable upward trend. The use of butter in home cake making is reflected in the relationship of supplementarity with flour and of substitution with cakes and biscuits. Both coefficients are significant. A significant relationship of substitution with carcass meat is also found. There is evidence of a relationship of substitution with margarine, but the elasticity is small and it is not significant. This result is not surprising in view of the size of the substitution elasticity with respect to butter in the analysis of margarine and the smallness of the expenditure on margarine relative to that on butter.'

Source: op. cit., p. 334 and Table 106.

Significant relationships were obtained from individual foods or food groups, which are summarized in Table 4.3.

An older study[8] of the price elasticity of demand for agricultural products in the U.S.A. between 1915 and 1929 yielded the following measurements: sugar, 0.31; corn, 0.49; cotton, 0.12; hay, 0.43; wheat, 0.08; potatoes, 0.31; oats, 0.56; barley, 0.39; rye, 2.44; buckwheat, 0.99.

[6] See R. Stone, *Measurement of Consumers Expenditure and Behaviour in the United Kingdom, 1920–1938* (Cambridge University Press, 1954).
[7] See p. 115.
[8] See H. Schultz, *Theory and Measurement of Demand* (University of Chicago Press, 1938), especially Table 49.

Another interesting study was made of the factors affecting the ownership of durable goods (specifically motor cars, television sets, washing machines, and refrigerators) in the United Kingdom.[9] Three non-economic factors were considered —size of household, age of head of household and habitat (rural or urban)—and these affected ownership in different degrees. Washing machine ownership is related to size of family,

TABLE 4.3

DISTRIBUTION OF FOOD ELASTICITIES, 1920–1938

	Frequency of elasticities with respect to		
Range of elasticity	Income	Own price (substitution)	Other specific prices (substitution)
-2 to $-1\frac{1}{2}$	—	2	1
$-1\frac{1}{2}$ to -1	—	5	4
-1 to $-\frac{1}{2}$	1	16	5
$-\frac{1}{2}$ to 0	4	10	7
0 to $\frac{1}{2}$	$10\frac{1}{2}$	3	$15\frac{1}{2}$
$\frac{1}{2}$ to 1	$12\frac{1}{2}$	—	$13\frac{1}{2}$
1 to $1\frac{1}{2}$	2	—	7
$1\frac{1}{2}$ to 2	2	—	5
2 to $2\frac{1}{2}$	—	—	2
$2\frac{1}{2}$ to 3	—	—	1
3 to $3\frac{1}{2}$	—	—	1
Total	32	36	62

Note: The author comments:
'This table show that the income elasticities for foodstuffs are predominantly positive and largely concentrated in the range 0–1. Of the thirty-two income elasticities in the table only five are negative and twenty-three lie in the range 0–1. In the case of the own-price (substitution) elasticities three, which are not significant, are positive and the remaining thirty-three are negative as in theory they should be. Of these no less than twenty-six lie in the range —1 to 0. The cross (substitution) elasticities shown in the last column of the table are spread, as might be expected, over a wide range. Relationships of substitution are more frequently observed than relationships of complementarity, since there are forty-five positive as against seventeen negative values. No less than twenty-nine values are found in the range 0 to 1. Thus food demand responses appear to be predominantly inelastic. Elastic responses both positive and negative are found, but they are comparatively infrequent'.

Source: Stone, op.cit., pp. 339–40 and Table 108.

motor car ownership to age and habitat, television to size of family and habitat, but refrigerator ownership is not influenced by any of these factors. Two economic factors were also consid-

[9] J. S. Cramer, The Ownership of Major Consumer Durables, University of Cambridge Department of Applied Economics, Monograph No. 7 (Cambridge University Press, 1962).

ered—income and net worth (or capital)[10]—and were found to have an effect on ownership, conveniently summarized respectively as income elasticity of demand (as defined earlier) and net worth elasticity of demand (which measures the responsiveness of demand to a change in net worth). Table 4.4 shows these two elasticities.

TABLE 4.4

THE DEMAND FOR CONSUMER DURABLE GOODS

Ownership of	Income Elasticity	Net worth Elasticity
Refrigerators	0.96	0.93
Washing machines	0.74	0.54
Motor cars	0.69	0.86
Television sets	0.50	0.33

Source: Cramer, *The Ownership of Major Consumer Durables* (Cambridge University Press, 1962).

Such analyses as these are full of pitfalls and require the use of sophisticated statistical techniques if they are to overcome the difficulty that all other things cannot be held to have been constant during the period of the observations.

To take a simple example which typifies a fairly common sort of error, one could take the data of Table 4.5 and plot it on a graph as in Fig. 4.2. It would be tempting to say, then, that the line of best fit (AB—fitted freehand) represented the demand curve for this commodity: it may possibly do so, but equally the series of points on the graph, being observations for different years, may each be on different demand curves (for example CD, EF, GH, etc.), which represent the different conditions of individual years and may reflect (for example) changes in incomes, tastes, increasing number of substitutes, etc., which have caused the curves to shift. This is an example of what is known as the identification problem.

But controlled experiments have been carried out which have yielded excellent results. Perhaps the best known of these was a

---

[10] Defined as the difference between the assets of a household (liquid assets, securities, house and property, unincorporated business value, car and loans) and its liabilities (overdraft, mortgage, hire purchase debt and personal debts). Ibid., pp. 20–1.

study[11] of the short-term relationship between prices and sales of certain staple products over a period of $2\frac{1}{2}$ months in a large American store. The details of this study are not needed here, but what is interesting is that the author of the study was able to draw demand curves for the products; he chose demand equations representing curves of constant elasticity which, when plotted on a graph with logarithmic scales on both axes, appear as straight lines.

TABLE 4.5

ESTIMATED PRICES AND QUANTITIES CONSUMED OF TEA,
UNITED KINGDOM, 1920–38

Year	Estimated average price (d. per lb)	Estimated quantity purchased (ooo cwt)
1920	34.50	3297
1921	31.00	3455
1922	28.75	3467
1923	30.50	3406
1924	28.75	3531
1925	29.25	3560
1926	29.25	3599
1927	28.75	3661
1928	29.00	3727
1929	25.75	3761
1930	23.75	3922
1931	22.25	3963
1932	21.00	3968
1933	21.50	3887
1934	23.25	3844
1935	23.50	3942
1936	24.75	3913
1937	26.00	3880
1938	27.50	3855

Source: Stone, op. cit., p. 151, Table 49.

A field experiment to determine elasticity of demand for a product of a manufacturer selling in competition with other producers is likely to be expensive. Such an experiment was conducted on behalf of Cadbury Bros. and was reported in the Financial Times.[12] The experiment consisted of raising the price of one item from 6d. to 7d. for a trial period in one area and comparing sales in that area with a control area which had been closely matched for similarity. From the control area it was possible to predict what sales would have

[11] R. H. Whitman, 'Demand Functions for Merchandise at Retail', in *Studies in Mathematical Economics and Econometrics*, edited by O. Lange (University of Chicago Press, 1924), pp. 210, 214.
[12] Feb. 1, 1968, p. 13.

been had the price been maintained. Two methods of measuring the fall in sales were used and, although there was some appreciable divergence between them, it appeared that sales fell by at least 17 to 18 per cent and possibly by as much as 30 per cent. These figures would give an elasticity of roughly 1 to 2, indicating a high value of elasticity of demand.

The experiment was related to an attempt to measure elasticity of demand by questioning a representative sample of

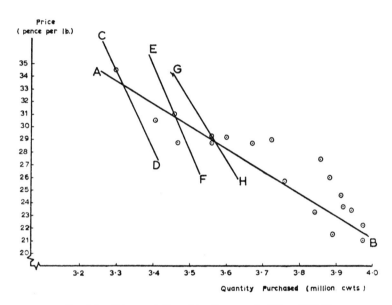

Fig. 4·2. Prices and Quantities Consumed of Tea, 1920-38

regular confectionery buyers. They were asked to make a series of value judgements to establish the theoretical price above which they were unlikely to consider buying the product. From the replies it was possible to construct a fairly crude demand curve to represent the theoretical demand for the product over a predetermined range of prices. While it is obvious that such techniques can produce unreliable responses the elasticity of demand calculated in this case was close to the lower estimate of 1 arrived at from the experiment of actually increasing prices in one district.

MARKETS

For the specialized purposes of economic theory, economists have adopted rigorous definitions of markets. For example:

'Economists understand by the term Market, not any particular market place in which things are bought and sold, but the whole of any region in which buyers and sellers are in such free intercourse with one another that the prices of the same goods tend to equality easily and quickly.'[13]

Such a market would not be readily found in real life, and in practice it is rare to find markets in which prices of the same goods tend to equality easily and quickly. Imperfections, caused by geographical factors, imperfect communications, transport costs, imperfect knowledge of buyers and sellers, monopolistic tendencies, advertising and product differentiation, etc., all militate against the easy functioning of the market. For present purposes it is preferable to speak of the market as the area in which producers, both manufacturers and distributors, compete and in which buyers seek to satisfy their wants.

The nature of the market for a product will depend to some extent on whether the commodity is durable or perishable (or 'single-use'): sales of durable goods are the subject of much more complex decisions by the buyer. The demand for most consumer durable goods is postponable and, in total, very volatile and dependent on fashion and changes in income.[14] Much of this sort of demand (particularly, for example, for motor cars) is a replacement demand, and the rate of replacement or depreciation depends on changes in fashion, the number of new models and so on. Technological change can produce sweeping changes in the demand for durables: the advent of the motor car fundamentally changed the whole demand for transport and transport facilities in all developed countries, the invention of television had far-reaching effects on the demand for radio, cinemas, public houses and other forms of entertainment outside the home. The demand for durable goods is also influenced by the credit facilities available. A high proportion

[13] Cournot, *Recherches sur les Principes Mathématiques de la Théorie des Richesses,* Chapter IV, quoted by Alfred Marshall, *Principles of Economics* (8th edn.) (Macmillan, 1920), p. 324.

[14] See pp. 119–122.

of consumer durable goods are bought on hire purchase: it has been estimated that about 25 per cent of new cars and two-thirds of second-hand cars are bought on hire purchase; almost half of the sales of furniture and radio shops, and a quarter of the sales of cycle shops are on hire purchase terms.[15]

An analysis of the users of hire purchase provides a convenient illustration of some of the factors affecting the demand for this class of goods. Surveys carried out by the Oxford University Institute of Statistics provide some such information.[16] In 1953 22.5 per cent of all income units in a Savings Survey sample purchased durable goods costing £25 or more, and of these 43 per cent actually used hire purchase; in 1954 a quarter of all income units had hire purchase outstanding. The average amount of hire purchase outstanding was quite small (about £10 in 1955), but this amount has probably doubled since then. In 1953 70 per cent of total hire purchase in the consumers' sector of the economy was held by people in the income range £400-£800, but such debt is nowadays more widely used by consumers in higher income ranges. Hire purchase is commonest in the age range 25-44 and is used most commonly by relatively young married couples with children. People living in rented accommodation accounted for over a quarter of the debt outstanding in 1953 but more and more people who are buying their houses on mortgage are contracting hire purchase debts. As would be expected, people with small liquid assets, bank deposits, saving certificates, etc., and with small wealth and capital were also the commonest users. Similar factors were found to be dominant in their influence on hire purchase in the U.S.A.[17] but there nearly half of the total number of families owe money on hire purchase.

The importance of hire purchase is such that any changes in the regulations affecting hire purchase credit will radically affect the demand for consumer durable goods.[18] Similarly

---

[15] The *Board of Trade Journal* publishes monthly statistics of hire purchase debt; the proportions quoted here are fairly typical of the 1950's and 1960's.
[16] K. H. Straw, 'Hire Purchase in the Consumer Sector', *The Bankers' Magazine* (February and March, 1957).
[17] J. Lansing, S. Maynes and M. Kreinin, 'Factors Associated with the Use of Consumer Credit', *Federal Reserve Board on Consumer Instalment Credit* (Federal Reserve Board, Washington, D.C., 1957). See also *Federal Reserve Bulletin* (July, 1957).
[18] See F. R. Oliver, *The Control of Hire Purchase* (Allen & Unwin, 1961).

changes in the rates of purchase tax (or effectively in the selling price of the goods) will have a considerable effect, the extent of which will depend on the price elasticity of demand; and other credit restrictions (such as reduction of bank advances) will also have a large impact, acting as they do on the disposable incomes of consumers. The motor car industry is particularly sensitive to such changes in Government policy, but so, too, are the radio, electrical and furniture industries.

The distinction between derived and autonomous demand is of some importance, autonomous demand being demand for a commodity in its own right, derived demand being derived from the demand for something else (a large part of the demand for coal, for example, is derived from the demand for steel). Derived demand is usually more price inelastic than autonomous demand, partly because the cost of the producers' good usually only represents a small proportion of the price of the final product. The demand for steel for motor cars, which probably only accounts for about 10 per cent of the final cost of motor cars, would be little affected by, say, a 5 per cent increase in the price of steel, since this should only cause a 0.5 per cent increase in the cost of manufacturing motor cars. The distinction between derived and autonomous demand is often arbitrary—is the consumption of potato crisps partly derived from the consumption of beer?—but the assessment of demand in practice implies a recognition of the fact that it may be influenced by much more complex factors than are apparent at first sight.

There is also a distinction to be drawn between producers' and consumers' demand, though again, in practice, the distinction is not always easy to draw (is a salesman's car a producers' good or a consumers' good?) The demand for most producers' goods is derived from the demand for something else, and a demand forecast has to look more at the final product than the intermediate product. The demand for car headlamps and other motor vehicle accessories is obviously closely related to the demand for motor cars, and the manufacturer of components must look at the final demand when planning his production. It is often claimed that the demand for producers' goods is more rational that the demand for consumers' goods, since the buyers are usually more expert and the motives for purchase are purely economic, products being bought for profit prospects, not for themselves alone. But it would not be difficult to make an impressive list of pieces of machinery which have been bought because of some fashion fad, some gimmick, 'keeping up with the Joneses', or high-pressure salesmanship (it is often argued that electronic computers come into this category); although there is a lot of truth in this proposition it is by no means self-evident. It is usually true, however, that the demand for producers' goods (both for capital and current use) fluctuates more violently than the demand for consumers' goods :[19] this is partly because such demand is derived from final demand and is subject to the lags between production and consumption, and partly because capital goods last for a long time.

The consumer has both rational and irrational motives for choosing a particular product from the available range. Rational motives might be defined as those which are influenced by the quality and price of the product and include considerations of durability, economy in operation, dependability of after-sales service, the desire to take advantage of low prices and so on (the so-called motives of 'economic man'). Irrational motives include 'keeping up with the Joneses', impulse buying, etc., and the term might even be stretched to include various emotional factors such as pride in appearance, fear of monotony and desire for individuality (the sort of motive which induces people to put fancy and operationally useless trimmings on their cars). These motives may well conflict; the successful businessman understands and caters for them.

Consumers also have their reasons, rational or irrational, for buying from particular suppliers: many housewives, for example, prefer to buy their groceries from the corner shop rather than from the supermarket because they enjoy a chat with the local grocer or their neighbours. Buying habits, too, may influence demand: much buying of books, for example, is on impulse by people who happen to be in the shop, and the successful bookseller may well be the one who attracts the casual buyer by his display; successful marketing by the publisher may also involve choice of those sellers who cater for the impulse buyer. The railway bookstall, for example, caters almost entirely

[19] See G. Haberler, *Prosperity and Depression*, p. 180, and W. Beveridge, *Full Employment in a Free Society* (Allen & Unwin, 1944) pp. 287–94.

for the impulse and casual buyers, particularly for the lighter sorts of reading; the specialist, stock-holding bookseller caters for a different public but, like a supermarket, his sales may depend a great deal on having a wide variety of books on display to attract the casual purchaser.

These habits may change with time : the increase in the number of married women who go out to work has led to an increase in all types of buying by men, who now have to help with the shopping, and the best approach to selling to men is usually different from that needed for selling to women; urban and suburban populations have different buying habits from the population of villages, and the growth of the former group has brought about changes in marketing methods.

Structural or institutional factors may also have their effect. In Britain we have not yet approached the American level of supermarket selling, but the trend has been established,[20] and there are several differences between marketing via the small seller and the big supermarket. The lower costs of bulk distribution from the manufacturer or wholesaler to the supermarket are usually offset to a large extent by the demand of the latter for bigger discounts for bulk purchase, but these in turn are frequently compensated by bigger sales and economies of scale for the manufacturer. It has been estimated[21] that in the food trade it is possible for the supermarket to save one-third of the wage-bill of a counter grocery shop, and that it would be possible for supermarkets to do over two-thirds of a country's food trade. The small manufacturer, however, is frequently in a disadvantageous position in such circumstances since he has to accept the terms dictated by the big seller, who may be his sole customer: several large chain stores in Britain owe their success in large part to the fact that they have been able to dictate terms to several manufacturers. It has been argued on the other hand, however, that 'Supermarkets, with their concentrated buying power, their competitive situations and their price flexibility, can be an important power on the side of the consumer, countervailing the power of the manufacturer, which is widely judged to be not only

---

[20] W. G. McLelland, 'Economics of The Supermarket', *Economic Journal* (March, 1962). There were eighty supermarkets in Britain in 1957, and 572 in 1961.
[21] Ibid.

excessive but overweening ... they could do for the food shop-
per what Marks and Spencer have done for the clothes shop-
per'.[22] The attempts by groups of smaller retailers to achieve
co-operatively what the supermarkets have achieved unilaterally
in the purchasing field is another move in the direction of
changing the structure of the retail trade.

Customs of the trade frequently determine the structure
of markets, but these can be, and indeed often are, changed
by a progressive approach to marketing.

To some extent also the nature of the marketing problem
depends on the product itself; we have already noted the
distinction between producers' and consumers' goods, but there
is another distinction which cuts across these divisions. Some
firms work entirely to specifications from other firms (who may
be retailers or other manufacturers) and their marketing
problem is very largely a matter of securing a contract from
customers; others concentrate on producing fairly standardized
commodities (either for producers or consumers) which they
then put on the market for sale after manufacture. In a report
on the survey of small manufacturing firms carried out by
the Oxford University Institute of Statistics, H. F. Lydall[23]
commented on the differences between the two types of firm,
which he called respectively 'jobbers' and 'marketers', depending on whether they were predominantly engaged in the
former or the latter activity. He found that, in the sample
analysed, about half of the firms were jobbers, and half marketers; jobbers predominated in metal manufacture, engineering,
wood products, and paper and printing; marketers predominated in bricks, concrete and glass, chemicals, textiles, clothing,
and food and drink; there was also a tendency for the proportion of jobbers to be less amongst larger firms than smaller.

The nomenclature of the distinction is not particularly helpful in the present context, since it obscures the fact that both
types of firms, in fact, have a marketing problem (a problem of
getting their goods to buyers in the shape which they want);
what does matter, however, is the timing of the marketing, and
the effect which this has on the marketing decision. The jobber

[22] Ibid.
[23] H. F. Lydall, 'Aspects of Competition in Manufacturing Industry', *Bulletin
of the Oxford University Institute of Statistics* (November, 1958).

can to some extent adapt his productive process after he has received the order; the marketer has to find out about the market first (or take a guess). The market analysis of the jobber is of a different nature from that of the marketer: one waits for the order before starting production, though he may stock up in anticipation of the renewal of an order; the other produces in advance of the order. If the marketer finds out about his market first in an intelligent way there is little difference in the final analysis, since he knows what he has to make in much the same way as does the jobber, and, since he usually standardizes his product and production processes, he may have fewer production problems into the bargain. All that happens is that the proper assessment of demand replaces the firm order from someone else; one function of market analysis is to minimize the difference between the two methods.

TABLE 4.6

GEOGRAPHICAL DISTRIBUTION OF THE POPULATION OF THE UNITED KINGDOM, 1911 and 1965

Region	1911		1965	
	No. (000)	*Per cent of total*	*No. (000)*	*Per cent of total*
Standard Regions of England and Wales				
North	2,815	6.7	3,309	6.1
East and West Ridings	3,564	8.5	4,264	7.8
North-West	5,793	13.8	6,704	12.3
North Midland	2,623	6.2	3,800	6.9
Midland	3,277	7.3	4,975	9.1
Eastern	2,106	5.0	4,044	7.3
London and South-Eastern	9,100	21.7	11,297	20.7
Southern	1,864	4.4	3,092	5.7
South West	2,507	6.0	3,585	6.6
Wales	2,421	5.6	2,693	4.9
Scotland	4,760	11.3	5,204	9.5
Northern Ireland	1,251	3.0	1,469	2.7
TOTAL	42,082	100.0	54,436	100.0

Source: *Annual Abstracts of Statistics* 1957 and 1967, H.M.S.O. (1965 figures are mid-year estimates of *de facto* home population).

The nature of the marketing problem also depends to some extent on the geographical distribution of markets and incomes. In Britain there is a tendency to concentrate intensive marketing in the large concentrations of population around London and in the Midlands (though the advent of television advertising has spread the net a little further). Table 4.6 highlights the tendency for population to concentrate in these areas; one of the more frequently discussed problems of Britain in the present century (and particularly in the 1950s and 1960s) has been the drift of population and industry to the Midlands and south-east of England. To some extent the table underestimates the shift in demand: since these are the prosperous areas of Britain, incomes and spending power are higher there than elsewhere.

Patterns of consumption also differ locally—haggis is rarely eaten and the kilt rarely worn outside Scotland, tripe and onions is still very much a north country dish—but these differences are tending to disappear in much the same way as dialects are tending to die out, largely because of the 'success' of mass media of communication.

Markets and consumers are never static. They may change because of changes in prosperity or incomes, or changes in tastes or preferences, or increasing competition.

TABLE 4.7

AGE AND SEX DISTRIBUTION OF POPULATION OF THE UNITED KINGDOM, 1901 AND 1966

Sex/Age	1901		1966	
	No. (000)	Per cent of total	No. (000)	Per cent of total
Male	18,492	48.4	26,602	48.6
Female	19,745	51.6	28,142	51.4
Age Groups				
under 5	4,382	11.5	4,809	8.8
5— 9	4,105	10.7	4,231	7.7
10—19	7,762	20.3	8,069	14.7
20—29	6,981	18.2	7,148	13.1
30—39	5,328	13.9	6,691	12.2
40—49	4,002	10.5	7,063	12.9
50—59	2,801	7.3	6,997	12.8
60—69	1,808	4.8	5,521	10.1
70 and over	1,066	2.8	4,215	7.7
TOTAL	38,237	100.0	54,744	100.0

Source: *Annual Abstracts of Statistics* 1957 and 1967 (1966 figures are mid-year estimates).

The changes may be more fundamental and due to changes in population, birth rates, marriage rates, age structure of the population, its geographical distribution and so on. Table 4.7 illustrates some of these changes: it shows that total population in the United Kingdom has increased by approximately one-third since the beginning of the present century, the proportion of males and females remaining approximately the same; but the age distribution has changed considerably : 30.6 per cent of the population were over 50 years old in 1966, compared with 14.9 per cent in 1901; 31.2 per cent were under 20 in 1966 compared with 42.5 per cent in 1901. Marital conditions have changed as well : in 1901 there were about 11 million single males in the United Kingdom and 6½ million married males; in 1966 there were 10.5 million single males and over 12 million married ones.[24]

[24] Annual Abstract of Statistics, 1967.

CHAPTER V

MARKETING

MARKETING is that part of business activity which is concerned with the assessment, manipulation and fulfilment of demand. The borderline between production and marketing is indistinct[1] and in the final analysis both are concerned with meeting demand; it is frequently convenient however to separate them for purposes of analysis.

Marketing orientation is the feature which identifies the mature business enterprise. The majority of businesses in the past have started with a distinct product orientation, typified by concentration on manufacturing the product; at a later stage management consciously identifies consumer wants and does something about meeting them; the next phase may come with a realisation that the facilities of the firm are capable of producing new products, or with recognition of the fact that the market may suggest profitable opportunities; eventually marketing becomes the basic motivating force of the business and is integrated with top management decision making. The ultimate stage of development, which few firms have yet reached, is that in which the enterprise is viewed as an integrated business-cum-technological system, the whole of which is aimed at the profitable satisfaction of the needs of the consumer.

In most firms therefore the marketing management problem is to develop an integrated marketing programme through the co-ordination of its resources in the attempt to achieve the objectives of the enterprise.

It is sometimes argued that marketing is unproductive and

[1] One of the major problems of many firms in real life is that of integration of the production and marketing functions, and frequently these two 'sides' of a firm pursue mutually inconsistent objectives to the detriment of the efficiency of the firm. For an example of such a process at work in a large British manufacturing company see James Bates and A. J. M. Sykes, 'Aspects of Managerial Efficiency'. *Journal of Industrial Economics* (July 1962) and same authors 'A Study of Conflict Between Formal Company Policy and the Interests of Informal Groups'. *Sociological Review* (November, 1962).

wasteful, because it adds nothing tangible to the product. It is true that much marketing activity is inefficient, that distribution is often carried out wastefully, and that much of the effort and resources put into the manipulation of demand could be put to better use, but the same is true of much manufacturing activity. A certain amount of marketing activity is necessary to get goods to the consumers at all, and the creation of a market for goods is just as necessary as the production of them. Marketing adds value (or utility) to goods in the sense that it puts the goods where they are wanted when they are wanted; it is analagous to the addition of value in production. Efficient marketing adds no more to the cost of goods than is necessary for the fulfilment of these functions.

An estimate of the cost of marketing was made in the U.S.A. in 1948.[2] In mining, quarrying, agriculture, manufacturing and construction, the value added by production was 37.7 per cent of sales. For the American economy as a whole (including retailing, wholesaling and transport) value added by production was 16.4 per cent of sales, value added by marketing was 15.2 per cent of sales. The marketing process as a whole accounted for about half the total value added.

Gross margins (or value added) in retailing in the United Kingdom was about 22 per cent of total receipts; in wholesaling they account for between 12 and 13 per cent.[3] Margins differ from trade to trade and by size of firm: firms with working proprietors and sales of over £100,000 in 'bread and flour confectionery with baking' have gross margins of almost 50 per cent of total sales; tobacconists have gross margins of about 9 per cent of total sales. The former have a large manufacturing element in their sales, the latter are largely stockholders.

The biggest gross margins are in the service trades, in which purchases are a relatively small proportion of total costs, whilst wages and salaries are a high proportion; wholesale margins are lower on average than retail margins, largely because pur-

---

[2] Calculated from data in P. D. Converse, H. W. Huegy and R. V. Mitchell, *Elements of Marketing* (6th Edition) (Pitman 1958), Appendix A.

[3] The *Census of Distribution*, from which this information is taken, analyses the retailing and wholesaling trades in considerable detail, giving among other information size and ownership patterns in individual trades, and dispersions of gross margins around the mean. It is a mine of useful information about wholesale and retail outlets.

chases are a high proportion of total costs and value added by processing and services is small.

MARKETING PRACTICES AND POLICIES

Marketing is part of the competitive process; the various policies and practices are judged by their effectiveness as weapons of overall marketing policy. The *marketing mix* is the combination of resources required in a marketing programme in order to fulfil the company's marketing objectives. Each element in the mix is interdependent and a coherent policy requires programmes for market research, promotion, product development, distribution and pricing.

MARKET RESEARCH

Marketing decisions depend on the acquisition and interpretation of information. Market research is the scientific assessment of demand, which is closely analagous to the intelligence service of the armed forces.

The major uses of market research are:[4] to tell management of the position of the firm in the industry and its share of the market; to provide information about present and possible future trends of the industry; to help in the introduction of new products and the improvement of old ones; and to provide for the appraisal and improvement of the effectiveness of sales management.

Market research is a tool of management, but it cannot by itself solve marketing or other problems; it can narrow the range of uncertainty and help to make decisions more intelligent and less of a guess. The ultimate value of market research depends on how the results are used. It is not a method of formulating decisions, but of providing a guide for this; in the last analysis the evaluation of results and the formulation of policy are the job of the manager.

There is a tendency to think of market research in terms of surveys of a cross-section of the population by interview and questionnaire, but market research is much more comprehensive than this. Having decided to embark on market research management still has to decide how to do it, and there are

---

[4] See R. D. Crisp, *Company Practices in Marketing Research*, American Management Association, New York, 1953, pp. 28–29.

several possibilities. Some firms employ outside agencies, some do their own, but most do a bit of both.

Whether or not to perform a particular piece of market research oneself is a straightforward decision, similar in nature to the decision to manufacture or to sub-contract; the answer depends very much on the scale of operation of the company. The costs of the market research must be weighed against the returns expected from it; almost all market research expenditure is overhead cost, and whether or not to use a particular method depends on whether the firm can work on a large enough scale to justify the expenditure involved. Small firms can rarely afford the specialized staff for field research, and indeed most big firms prefer to have such work done outside by specialized agencies.

The cost of field research, surveys, etc., is rather high, and this sort of work involves a great deal of specialized knowledge and planning which is rarely possible even in very large firms. Firms which have their own market research departments frequently buy regular, specialized services, such as the products of Retail Audits, in addition to their own work. But most firms can do a great deal of intelligent market research on their own at relatively little expense.

However the research is done, few firms can afford to do without some market research,[5] carried out independently of the Sales Department. In a firm manufacturing electrical components, the production and sales side of the firm had for several years worked on the assumption that their trade was seasonal (largely because everyone said so). A statistician was engaged by the company, and, in order to determine the magnitude of the seasonal fluctuations, he did some research into the sales of the firm over a period of years; there was no seasonal pattern whatever. In the same firm, the Production Department had relied for several years on the sales forecasts provided

---

[5] A study of the preparation of sales forecasts by 297 American companies examined the principal factors considered in the preparation of the forecasts. The most important factors, listed in order of importance, were: (1) past sales trend of firm: (2) sales department estimates: (3) judgement and hunch: (4) general economic indicators; (5) economic data on own industry; (6) salesmen's field reports; (7) new product plans; (8) competitors' activity; (9) production capacity; (10) market surveys; (11) promotion plans; (12) other sources, *Sales Forecasting, Uses, Techniques and Trends*, American Management Association, Special Report, No. 16.

by the Sales Department, with some adjustments in the light of past experience. These forecasts were becoming increasingly unreliable; since the scale of operation of the company was increasing and more accurate predictions were needed, the statistician was asked to make a demand forecast. This turned out to be much more accurate and has since superseded the forecasts of the Sales Department. All of this was done internally by one man, at very little cost to the company.

One of the main objectives of market research is to establish a market profile for the products of the organization; such a profile is nothing more than a detailed practical analysis of the factors considered in the previous chapter. Table 5.1 outlines the main factors and provides a convenient checklist.

TABLE 5.1

THE ELEMENTS OF A MARKET PROFILE

The Consumer
Total number of consumers
Regional distribution
Total income
The effect of income and wealth, measures of elasticity
Income per household
Distribution of income
Consumers tastes
Behaviour characteristics, where do consumers buy, when do they buy etc.?
The effect of design

The business itself
Current level of sales
Current stocks
Trends in sales and stocks
Share of the market
Seasonal fluctuations
Trends in research and development
Company strengths and weaknesses
New product possibilities

The Market
The effect of price, measures of price elasticity etc.
Unique characteristics of products
Identification of competitive products
Number and nature of competitors
Institutional arrangements, channels of distribution etc.
Forms of competition (price, advertising, brand policy etc.,)
Expected technological changes
General price levels
Prices of similar commodities

General considerations
The economic climate, level of activity, employment etc.,
Government policy
Taxation

Possibilities in the field of market research can be enumerated briefly. Even the vaguest hunches can be improved by a quick look at some of the mass of published information now available; the *Monthly Digest of Statistics,* the *Trade and Navigation Accounts,* the *Trade and Industry Journal,* the *Census of Production and Distribution,* the *National Income Blue Book,* the various publications of trade associations, and several other sources quickly yield useful quantitative information to the intelligent searcher. Even in its raw form such information is useful, but its utility can be increased enormously by intelligent statistical analysis.

In the field of capital goods, for example, there are several series of statistics which provide good indicators of demand. The Confederation of British Industries conducts periodic surveys of the intentions of manufacturers to spend money on capital equipment and buildings; the Department of Trade and Industry publishes tables showing quarterly estimates of planned industrial building; the Royal Institute of British Architects surveys and publishes details of new commissions of private architects; the Cubitt Index[6] of construction activity provides a guide to about half of total investment in the economy. There is also a large variety of published information in trade journals, the financial press, company reports and several other sources.

Similarly, still within the firm, the analysis of the firm's own sales patterns can give useful clues to markets; it is frequently possible to find out with little trouble the patterns of distribution (does the firm sell, for example, mainly to small corner shops or to large chain stores?), and from this to deduce an intelligent sales policy. Masses of such information comes into most firms daily and is frequently ignored, or treated unsystematically.

Even so, there are usually important gaps in the information required for policy making, and there are many forms of market research which the typical firm cannot conduct for itself, for which it needs to employ a specialized agency. External market research is usually carried out on a basis of sample surveys, either by interviewers, through the mail, on the telephone (a method rarely employed in Britain, where telephone ownership is not widespread), by consumer panels and so on.

[6] Published quarterly by Holland & Hannen & Cubitts Ltd.

Such surveys cover a wide field and there is a range of altern-atives: they may concentrate on past sales, on the buying inten-tions of consumers, or they may approach the problem from a psychological standpoint.

Surveys of past sales are useful, partly because they give an indication of the firm's share of the market, and partly because the proper statistical analysis of past trends is necessary for forecasting.[7]

Ascertainment of a firm's share of the market is an indispens-able function of market research; it can often best be carried out by an external agency which can, as part of its normal activities and at small extra cost, collect a great deal of the available information about the market, much of which is in-accessible to the firm without considerable expense. One such method is the Retail Audit, effectively developed by the A. C. Neilsen Co., which consists of regular periodic visits to a selected sample of retail shops, during which checks are made of stocks and purchases of the commodities under review, enab-ling sales of brands to be computed. Another method is the Consumer Panel, members of which keep diaries of products purchased. The information which can be obtained from Consumer Panels[8] is extensive : it includes the extent of the market, market structure (geographical distribution, habitat, household composition, etc.); from this data it is possible to make studies of consumer buying habits, such as frequency of purchases, quantities bought, brand loyalty, seasonal pattern, patterns of distribution and types of outlet; they may also help in the assessment of the effectiveness of advertising.

Useful information about shares of the market may also be obtained without the use of an external agency. In some indus-tries members report their sales to a trade association or similar body which provides members with a total figure. The growth in the number of trade associations which publish such informa-tion means that much of this type of market research is possible within the firm at relatively small cost.[9]

---

[7] See Chapter IX.
[8] See *The Consumer Panel* (Technical Leaflet of the Belgian Distribution Com-mittee, Brussels) summarized in *Digests of Marketing and Distribution Publications* (O.E.E.C.), No. 5. 1961.
[9] The Society of Motor Manufacturers and Traders, for example, regularly publishes analyses of sales and stocks of all types of motor vehicles.

Surveys of consumer buying intentions are useful, within broad limits, as guides to market expansion, and they may help to narrow the range of error of forecasts. In Britain, with the exception of a small range of capital goods, such surveys are usually available only from specialized agencies. A danger of relying on such surveys is that people do not always act in accordance with their expressed intentions, however honest they may try to be; there is a similar difficulty with public opinion polls. But experience allows intentions to be checked against realizations, and some correction of estimates is possible.

Motivational research is another possibility. This has been defined as '. . . a phase of marketing research which attempts to answer the question "Why?" . . . (and which) seeks to relate behaviour to underlying processes, such as people's desires, emotions and intentions'.[10] The rationale of motivational research is that if one knows why people buy things, one can not only predict how they will behave in given conditions, but one can also decide on ways on which they can be influenced, which form of advertising or other promotional method to use. Its main usefulness to date has been in the second sphere, and much advertising, many styling 'gimmicks' and so on owe their existence to motivational research.

Whatever the type of market research used, if it is competently carried out, it can provide useful information for decision making. The more and the better the information which a firm has about the market and the demand for its products, the better it is able to formulate marketing, production and financial policy.

Despite advances since the Second World War, market research is surprisingly little used in Britain. According to a survey[11] carried out in 1960, external expenditure (outside the firm) on market research was about £7 million, total expenditure about £18 million (less than 0.1 per cent of total industrial turnover).

Market research for capital goods in particular is a sadly neglected field. In the B.I.M. survey twenty-nine out of thirty-

[10] G. H. Smith, *Motivation Research in Advertising and Marketing* (McGraw Hill, 1954.) p. 3.
[11] *A Survey of Marketing Research in Great Britain* (British Institute of Management, 1962).

six manufacturers of industrial products possessed market research departments (and spent less than £600,000), compared with twenty-five out of twenty-six manufacturers of consumer goods, who spent more than £500,000. This is rather surprising in view of the facts that the market for capital goods is generally much more sensitive to trade fluctuations than the market for consumer goods and that, since buyers are few and orders usually relatively large, a mistake can be even more expensive than in the consumer goods field. Market research for capital goods is usually aimed at end products, since the demand for capital goods is a derived demand, and this does tend to make the research more difficult. Some capital goods, of which steel is a good example, are the raw materials of a wide variety of finished products, so that the problem is one of building a complex model of a very large part of the economy (though experience may suggest that certain key indicators may be sufficient for planning and predictive purposes in many circumstances).

Changes in tastes, incomes, substitutes, etc., are often sudden, and frequently when it is found out that such changes have taken place it is too late to have much effect on goods in the pipeline and for which production plans and investment decisions have been made. The invention of a commercial process of seamless nylon stockings (which are not prone to 'laddering') brought severe competition in the American industry to get the new product on to the market first; several new processes and patents were involved, all expensive. A review of the market reported: 'The seamless fad itself had already caught the manufacturers flat footed and with them the manufacturers of stocking-making machinery. But by this spring (1962) some fifteen makers of seamless machinery were competing. If now the lock-stitched seamless and ladderless stocking makes the new machinery obsolete, there will be carnage in the stocking industry.'[12]

The analysis of distribution costs is another important field of market research. Not only does the entrepreneur want to know how much his distribution is costing him in total, he also wants to be able to allocate his costs to products, areas, salesmen, customers and so on. By so doing he can decide, for

[12] *The Economist* (June 2nd, 1962), p. 897.

L

example, whether concentration on a few outlets would yield better results than a wide spread. A full analysis of distribution costs and profits may often reveal that products are sold at a loss to some customers; this may well be desirable in certain cases, for prestige reasons or for future relations, but these are exceptional cases, and in general it is preferable to avoid losses on individual products wherever possible.

AN EXAMPLE OF MARKET RESEARCH IN PRACTICE[13]

The Edison Group, which produces most of the electric power used in Northern Italy, carried out a survey of domestic refrigerators.

The survey was in two phases. The first, in May and June of 1957, was devoted to ascertaining the distribution of refrigerators in the areas served by the group, and the effect of four major factors : (1) area (divided into the Riviera, the plains, hills, mountains, urban centres); (2) demographic size of the areas; (3) number of family members and (4) occupation of the family's wage earner. A 5 per cent sample was drawn from the total of 1.9 million customers for house lighting.

The second phase, from January to April 1958, consisted of analyses of owners and non-owners of refrigerators in an attempt to identify the characteristics of the present and potential market.

The results of the first phase showed that : (1) only 11.8 per cent of customers had a refrigerator; (2) the market was concentrated in Milan and Genoa (41 per cent of the refrigerator owners, 20 per cent of customers); (3) ownership is directly connected with standard of living (71.6 per cent of professional families had refrigerators compared with 1.2 per cent of rural families); (4) ownership was also connected with size of family.

The results of the second phase were divided into two groups. Among refrigerator owners : (1) 88 per cent of refrigerators were of the compressor type, 49 per cent had a capacity of 100-150 litres, 26 per cent had a capacity of 150-200 litres; (2) 64 per cent of refrigerators were less than 3 years old, 78 per cent less than 5 years old; (3) 61 per cent had been purchased from shops, 14 per cent from manufacturers; (4) the

[13] Thea Gelsomini, 'Market Research on Domestic Refrigerators among Customers of the Edison Industrial Group', *Studio di Mercato* (Rome, April 1960).

advertising media most frequently remembered were magazine advertisements and television; (5) 70 per cent of owners used the refrigerator throughout the year; (6) 70 per cent thought that meat, dairy products and vegetables are best suited to refrigerators; (7) for 44.9 per cent the major advantage of refrigerator ownership was preservation of foodstuffs, for 13.6 per cent it was the saving of shopping time which was thought to be most important; (8) only 19.6 per cent found inconveniences in the use of refrigerators; (9) the automatic light and inner door shelves were thought to be useful, the locking key was little used; (10) only 9 per cent planned to replace the refrigerator within 2 years.

Among non-owners: (1) 55 per cent had food preservation problems; (2) 26.5 per cent intended to buy a refrigerator within 2 years (95 per cent of these preferred the compressor type, 82 per cent the ordinary model, 76 per cent a 100-175 litre capacity, 94 per cent a white refrigerator); (3) the probable sales channels would be household appliance stores (53 per cent), manufacturers (15 per cent), electric companies (11 per cent); (4) the basic sales appeals of a refrigerator were a well-known brand (21 per cent) and a guaranteed motor (17 per cent); (5) as regards questions of the usefulness of accessories and best advertising media, the answers were the same as those of the non-owners.

The reader might care to consider the policy implications of this survey.

THE MANIPULATION OF DEMAND

There are three broad ways in which management may attempt to manipulate demand: by advertising (and its corollary of product differentiation); by product development and design; and by price policy. In formal terms, the first two of these policies attempt to bring about a shift in the demand curve, or to substitute a new demand curve for the existing one; although the third policy cannot strictly be considered separately from the other two it may be regarded as an attempt to select an appropriate price, given the demand curve.

ADVERTISING

The principal function of advertising is to bring about a change in the tastes and preferences of the consumer and hence to bring about an expansion of the market; but it has other useful roles as a marketing tool. Advertising can be used to prepare the market and help in the introduction of new products, and similarly it prepares the way for the sales force; by making it easier to sell the product it increases the number of dealers prepared to stock it. It is sometimes claimed that advertising performs a useful service in the provision of information to the public. This is not a primary aim, and in any case the selective information provided is not of much direct help to the public in choosing between products, but at least advertising does tell the public what products are available.

That much advertising is irresponsible and even mischievous is undeniable, and management has something of a social responsibility to minimize these undesirable aspects, but it is not the task of this book to pronounce on these aspects so much as to evaluate the usefulness of advertising as an aid to marketing, and a way of improving the overall efficiency of the firm.

One big advantage of advertising is its relatively low cost per contact: one newspaper advertisement frequently places the product before the eyes of many more prospective buyers than the equivalent expenditure on salesmen. But it is usually only a preliminary part of the operation of selling; its weakness lies in the fact that advertising rarely closes a sale, though mail-order selling relies almost entirely on advertisements plus the offer of credit facilities.

The opportunities for advertising depend on the nature of the business and the market. Firms selling mainly 'within the trade' have to restrict their advertising largely to trade journals and catalogues, and a nationwide television advertising campaign would be inappropriate. In highly competitive markets such as those for cigarettes and motor cars there is little prospect of success for a new product without large expenditure on advertising in mass media.

Advertising may be used to create new demands, to arouse latent demands and to bring about 'psychological obsolescence'[14] Much of this sort of advertising is socially undesirable and economically wasteful, but some of it is reasonable and

---

[14] Vance Packard's book, *The Hidden Persuaders* (Penguin) is an entertaining though eclectic description of some of the less favourable features of advertising.

acceptable and achieves the aim of expanding sales and efficiency.

Advertising has its limitations and some businessmen expect far too much of it. Expensive advertising cannot compensate for poor quality, poor service, excessively high price, poorly selected channels of distribution; and it is rarely effective if only used for a short period. It is but one tool of marketing, and it cannot do the job alone.

A study[15] enumerated a series of conditions favourable to advertising.

1.—The product should be identifiable (by means of a brand).
2.—It should be possible to differentiate the product.
3.—The consumer should be able to judge, or notice the characteristics of the product.
4.—It should be possible to give the product 'subjective' values, which should be of some importance to the consumer.
5.—The product should be readily available on the market.
6.—The product should be bought regularly.
7.—The consumer should be able to choose the product without the help of the retailer (it should, in the jargon of the trade, be of the 'self-selection' type).
8.—There should be a trend of increasing demand for the product group as a whole.
9.—The product should be acceptable to the consumer (it is pointed out that too novel products often create unfavourable reactions among consumers).
10.—The product should have a certain share (undefined in the report) of the market.

Goods identified in the study as suitable for advertising included cosmetics, branded foods and such consumer durable goods as television sets and washing machines; most producers' goods bought by professional buyers according to specification, and individually tailored consumer goods were regarded as unsuitable.

Successful advertising has a number of basic requirements:

[15] Bo Wickström, *About Measures to Measure the Effectiveness of Advertising* (European Productivity Agency, Organization for European Economic Co-operation. 1961).

1.—The definition of objectives (at whom the advertising is to be directed, how much the firm wants to sell, etc.).

2.—The identification of constraints (size of the market, etc.).

3.—Determination of the direction of advertising (the main consumer groups, the principal existing and potential markets).

4.—The choice of media (which depends partly on the market, partly on the potential of the media, and partly on cost; the main categories are television, the press, catalogues and display, but there are many alternatives in practice).

5.—The nature of the advertisements (the arguments or appeals to be employed, etc.).

6.—The advertising budget or appropriation.

7.—The timing of the campaign.

8.—Testing.

Most advertising involving more than use of trade journals and classified advertisements in the press can be carried out most efficiently by specialized agencies. Such agencies have expert knowledge, contacts and specialized services which may be too expensive for the individual firm because they depend on large-scale operation for their most efficient use.

The aims of advertising and production may conflict; advertising and production programmes need to be co-ordinated. An advertising campaign may be too successful and the firm may lack the productive capacity needed to meet the demands placed on it. In the early 1950's a large British manufacturer of cosmetics and allied products undertook a large-scale advertising and marketing campaign, and found that its production and distribution facilities were unable to cope with the success of the campaign. Such a selling campaign is probably worse than none at all.

The cost of advertising and the advertising appropriation depend on the nature of the product and market. The budgeting process should be designed to ensure that expenditure on advertising is related to the increase in sales that is expected to result from it.

In highly competitive fields, where real distinctions between products are small, advertising usually represents a high proportion of total costs; such fields are medicines (37 per cent), cosmetics (34 per cent), shampoos (50 per cent), toothpaste (28 per cent) and some foods.[16]

Testing is also necessary if the firm is to know whether the money spent on advertising has had a significant effect or whether it would have been better spent in other ways. Table 5.2 summarises methods of testing, and shows what effects the tests might have on the advertising decision.

TABLE 5.2

MEASURES OF THE EFFECTIVENESS OF ADVERTISING

Method of Measurement	Timing (A)	Effects on (B) Decisions	(C) Consumers
INTERVIEW METHODS			
(1) *Judgement*			
(a) Expert	Before		Information
(b) Consumer	Before	4	Influence
(2) *Indirect methods*			
(a) Product, brand image	} Before or after	2, 4	Influence
(b) Attitude			
(3) *Memory methods*			
(a) Brand awareness	After	1	Information
(b) Audience, readership value	After	2, 3, 4	Information
OBSERVATION METHODS			
(4) Purchase studies	After	1, 3, 4	Behaviour
EXPERIMENTAL METHODS, ETC.			
(5) Time series analysis	After	1	Behaviour
(6) District analysis	After	1, 2	Behaviour
(7) Campaign analysis	Before or after	1, 2, 3, 4	Behaviour
(8) Coupon analysis (D)	Before or after	2, 3, 4	Behaviour
(9) Retail index studies	After	1, 2	Behaviour
(10) Consumer index studies	After	1, 2	Behaviour

Notes: (A) Time of measurement in relation to actual advertising campaign.
(B) Effect within the company on:
(1) Advertising versus other marketing activities.
(2) The allocation of advertising between media.
(3) The allocation of advertising within media.
(4) The qualitative design of advertising.
(C) The effect of advertising on the consumer:
Information—the transmittal of information to the consumer.
Influence—influence on consumers' scales of values.
Behaviour—influence on consumer behaviour.
(D) The analysis of the effect of 'coupon' schemes (e.g. for soaps, detergents, etc.) on sales.

Source: Adapted from Wickström, op. cit., p. 63.

Useful information may be obtained about the actual and potential audience of various media; surveys of television

[16] Packard, *The Hidden Persuaders*

audiences and readership of newspapers are readily available. But the firm needs to know more than the size of its audience; it must assess the likely effectiveness of projected campaigns and the success of those that have been undertaken.

Pre-testing is attractive because it can prevent wasteful expenditure in advance; its major disadvantage is that it does not accurately produce the conditions under which the actual campaign will be carried out. This is a snag of all experimental assessments, but in advertising the effect is cumulative and the existence of the campaign is an influence in itself.

The ultimate test of the success of an advertising campaign lies in its effect on sales and profits. It may be difficult to disentangle the effect of advertising from other factors affecting sales, and the cumulative effect may not be readily apparent. Statistical and econometric techniques may be required for analysis.

In 1956 the U.S. Department of Agriculture[17] made a study of a promotion campaign aimed at increasing the consumption of lamb carried out in Cleveland, Ohio, in July and August 1956. Advertising was carried out mainly through newspapers and radio plus some display material for shops and visits to retailers, and cost about $20,000.

Analysis yielded the following regression equation

$$x_1 = -37.2 - 7.1x_2 + 3.4x_3 + 8.7x_4 + 9.4x_5 + 7.4x_6$$

Where

x_1 = estimated sales of lamb per month in 000 lb   (712.2)

x_2 = weighted retail price of lamb in cents   (68.1)

x_3 = weighted retail price of other meat, etc., in cents (63.1)

x_4 = total consumer income in Cleveland in $m   (27.4)

x_5 = regular advertising for lamb in per cent of total

advertising (4.2)

x_6 = seasonal index per cent   (100)

(Figures in parenthesis indicate mean values for the preceding 40 months)

Using this equation predictions of actual sales were made for July, August, September and October. In July actual sales were somewhat below predicted sales (but within the range

[17] *Promotion of Lamb, Results of a Campaign in Cleveland, Ohio, U.S.* (Department of Agriculture, Washington, D.C., 1958).

of error); in August sales were 14 per cent higher than expected; in September (after the campaign finished) sales were again below the expected value. The study showed that in the short run advertising and other methods had an effect, and that it was possible to sell a surplus of lamb with the aid of a short, intensive campaign, but to do so was expensive (the cost was 20 cents per lb, the average price of lamb was 17 cents during the period).

Operational research techniques may also be used to test the effectiveness of advertising. Figure 5.1 draws on an article by Benjamin and Maitland to illustrate how expenditure on advertising and the response it provokes may be related.[18] In this case the response to advertisements for radio equipment in newspapers is shown on the vertical axis and the amount of advertising is shown along the horizontal axis. It will be noted that the amount of advertising is plotted on a logarithmic scale, where proportional increases are given the same distance along the axis. Thus, the distance from 100 to 200 is the same as the distance from 1,000 to 2,000. The relationship between the amount of advertising and the response follows a straight line. In effect, in order to get equal *absolute* increases in sales, says from S *to* S+*a* and then to S+2*a*, expenditure on advertising has to be increased in the same proportions from *e to er* and from *er to er*². This means that in order to keep on increasing sales, advertising expenditure will have to be increased by rather large amounts after a time. If the relationship between advertising expenditure and sales is known and if the marginal cost of producing the article that is being sold is constant, it is a comparatively easy matter to decide at what point advertising no longer pays at the price that is being charged. The fact that sales appear to be related to advertising in the way we have described is consistent with other reactions to stimuli. For example, it is known that the intensity of a sound to a listener increases in proportion to the logarithm of its intensity as measured by instruments; this is why the volume controls of wireless sets are designed to fit a logarithmic law. In practice, it might be possible to predict the effects of an advertising campaign from the initial reactions shown to it.

[18] B. Benjamin and J. Maitland 'Operational Research and Advertising', *Operational Research Quarterly*, Vol. 9, No. 3, p. 207.

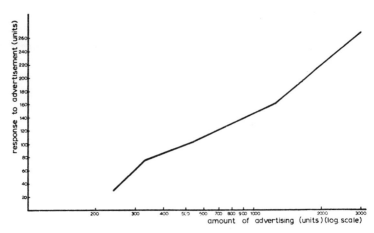

Fig. 5·1.   Sales of Radio Equipment in Relation to Advertising

Whilst it is true that successful advertising campaigns can be conducted for homogeneous products, these are usually carried out in terms of the whole market and by co-operative endeavour: examples are the Drinka Pinta Milka Day campaign, advertising by the Egg Marketing Board, by other national boards and some trade associations. Detergent and soap manufacturers claim that what they try to sell through their campaigns is the 'concept of cleanliness'; cosmetic manufacturers sell 'charm' and so on; it is claimed that by increasing the total market for these 'commodities', all manufacturers gain. There may be some truth in these claims, but generally the aim is more competitive, and individual manufacturers try to maintain their share of the market, or to increase it by advertising.

Most advertising is competitive, and the competition takes place between firms in the same, or closely related industries; in these circumstances some differences, real or imaginary, between the products of the firms, are an essential pre-requisite of the advertising campaign.

PRODUCT DIFFERENTIATION AND DEVELOPMENT

'A general class of product is differentiated if any significant basis arises for distinguishing the goods (or services) of one seller from those of another. Such a basis may be real or fancied, so long as it is of any importance whatever to buyers, and leads to a preference for one variety of the product over another'.[19]

Classic examples of product differentiation are motor vehicles, detergents, cosmetics, petrol and petroleum products, breakfast foods, confectionery and so on.

A study of product differentiation in the United States classified a sample of industries according to the basis of differentiation as follows:[20]

(1) Advertising; (2) product quality; (3) product design; (4) consumer service; (5) controlled distributive outlets.

The industries were ranked as:

(a) *Those with 'great' differentiation:*
Cigarettes (1); distilled liquor (1,2); automobiles (3, 4, 5); heavy farm machinery and tractors (3, 4, 5); high-quality fountain pens (1, 3); typewriters (1, 3, 4).

(b) *Those with moderate differentiation:*
Petroleum refining (1, 4, 5); rubber tyres (1, 3, 4, 5); high-quality men's shoes (1, 5); tin cans (4, 3); flour (1, 4).

(c) *Those with 'slight' differentiation:*
Steel (4); meat packing (1, 2); low-priced fountain pens (1, 3); low-priced men's shoes (1, 5) and

(d) *Those with 'negligible' product differentiation:*
Copper; cement; rayon yarn and fibre; tinned fruits and vegetables; flour (commercial); fresh meats.

Products may be differentiated in a variety of ways—by exclusive patent features and trade marks, brand policy, packaging, design, or by advertising—and it is possible to extend the notion to include such factors as reputation (of manufacturer or distributor), location of distribution (e.g. in a 'high-class' district) and a whole host of intangible and personal factors which may bind a consumer to a seller. The wider definition really covers the whole field of marketing, but it is possible to

---

[19] E. Chamberlin, *The Theory of Monopolistic Competition* (Harvard U.P. 1935).
[20] The data is adapted from Joe S. Bain, *Industrial Organization* (Wiley & Sons, Second edition 1968. pp. 239–40. The basis of differentiation is in parenthesis after each industry.

pick on certain factors connected exclusively with the product itself, which are usually referred to under the heading of product development and design.

Product Development is a positive managerial function, and may be defined as the effort to improve or add to the variety of the products of the firm. All too frequently this function is performed accidentally; but the haphazard approach of leaving this to free-lance inventors and brain-waves is giving way, at least in the bigger firms and the newer and more progressive industries, to systematic programmes of research and development. The returns from comparatively small expenditure on research and development may be large and striking; as a proportion of total costs this sort of expenditure is usually small. Research and development is still very much a matter of chance; major discoveries are often made in small sheds in back yards at relatively small expense, but steady if unspectacular developments stream constantly from the systematic expenditure of large corporations on this important aspect of their activities, and the National Research Development Corporation makes a contribution on the national scale.[21] Research can be directed to any of a number of ends, from the reduction of production costs and genuine improvements of the product to the development of new lines, new uses for by-products or the improvement of sales appeal.

Other methods of product development are less direct, and the aim may be achieved *inter alia* by integration with other firms, manufacturing different ranges of products, by re-organization of the production or marketing sides of the company in order to increase its own range of products, or through market research aimed at finding out what people want. The directions of development of most products follow well-defined patterns, which include the addition of refinements in operation or style and design, the improvement and standardization of quality, the provision of services, use of new materials and methods and packaging. Product development has come to be one of the major methods of marketing most mass consumer goods such as motor cars, detergents, electrical goods and furniture.

It is only in recent years that design has come to be accepted

21 See K. Grossfield, 'Inventions as Business', *Economic Journal* (March 1962).

as of fundamental importance in the selling of a product. In Britain we still tend to lag in improvements of design. The Scandinavians are far ahead in the design of furniture, household goods and buildings and can price accordingly; for many years the European manufacturers of motor vehicles were more prepared to experiment with the technological aspects of design. There is a growing realization of the importance of design, for functional as well as aesthetic reasons: some of it comes about at the initiative of consumers, but good design policy anticipates and forms their preferences.

Brand Policy is another aspect of product development, the success of marketing policies depends very much on the identification by the consumer of certain standards of quality with a particular product or source of supply. The building up of a 'brand image' underlies much effort in sales promotion and product development: it has led to advertising wars between rival manufacturers but, outside the rather weird world of detergents, aspirin and cosmetics it has brought benefits. Brand policy really implies some acceptance of responsibility for standards and service, and this is part of the price paid for the gains from brand policy. The advantages of branding by manufacturers are many: it simplifies and aids advertising and other methods of sales promotion; if successful it encourages later repeat sales; a sound brand image helps with the introduction of new items; and branding is some protection against competition. In addition many wholesalers and retailers prefer to handle branded goods.

It is possible to make too many claims for brand policy, and many firms are obsessively concerned with 'brand images' and brand loyalty, which they may not be able to demonstrate. Brand awareness does tend to be closely associated with recent advertising campaigns, and housewives buying toothpaste and detergents frquently tend to buy that brand which has been most recently advertised on television. It is frequently claimed that motor cars have a brand image to which patrons tend to be loyal through the years, and the brand policy of the British Motor Corporation, with its range of Austins, Morris, Wolseleys, Rileys, and M.G.s which differ in little but trimmings, appeared to be based on some such concept.

Some interesting results of brand awareness for men's and

women's wear came from an investigation made in 1954-55 by the Swedish Institute for Marketing and Management Research.[22] 1813 consumers were the basis of the study, 1170 of whom were men; observations and interviews were made in fifty-eight shops in twelve Swedish cities. Table 5.3 shows that between a third and a quarter of those interviewed could mention no brand for different types of garments.

TABLE 5.3

AWARENESS OF BRANDS

Type of Garment	Knows one or more brands %	Knows no brands %	Total %
Men			
Suit	58	42	100
Jacket	75	25	100
Trousers	68	32	100
Heavy coat	55	45	100
Light coat	27	73	100
Suit	51	49	100
Women			
Dress	67	33	100
Suit	45	55	100
Heavy coat	60	40	100
Light coat	70	30	100

Source: Wickstrom, op. cit. p. 23.

Packaging Policy is a further development of brand policy, aimed broadly at making the product more immediately attractive to the consumer. A certain minimum of packaging is necessary for the protection of the product, or for hygienic reasons and general cleanliness; beyond this it is doubtful whether heavy expenditure on packaging fulfils its purpose of attracting the purchaser. Much packaging policy would not stand up to rigorous *costs versus returns* analysis. As a method of competition it is merely an extension of product differentiation, and it is open to the same snags and advantages.

THE MARKETING PROCESS AND SELECTION OF CHANNELS OF DISTRIBUTION

Many firms have no consciously formulated policy about channels of distribution. Standardized procedures save time and trouble and make control, prediction and evaluation of

[22] Quoted by Wickström, op. cit., p. 23.

success much easier; co-ordination within the firm is easier; and the firm's channels of distribution themselves find advantages in standardized policies. A possible danger is that competitors, too, will find prediction easier, but reasonable flexibility reduces the risk of this. Channels should be subject to frequent review and reappraisal.

The simplest channel of distribution is from producer direct to consumer; goods may pass through middlemen (wholesalers, retailers, agents), and the commonest arrangement for consumer goods, is a chain of producer, wholesaler, retailer, and consumer. Generally the less complex the links the better, and, since price mark-ups are charged at every stage, the lower the price to the consumer; but the solution to any particular problem is rarely as simple as that. Wholesalers may be necessary because the cost to the manufacturer of providing specialized storage facilities at widely dispersed points may be excessive (much depends on the scale of operation of the firm), and the whole-saler provides useful services to the retailer by maintaining large and usually varied stocks from which choice is possible. There are very few consumer goods which can be sold direct to the consumer without a retailer. The growth of discount houses in the U.S.A. and in the U.K. with their own warehousing, trans-port and retailing facilities or special bulk agreements with suppliers, has tended to reduce the number of links in some circumstances and the growth of large retail chains and super-markets, which can often afford their own warehousing, oper-ates in the same direction; but customs of the trade, and restrictive practices of one kind or another, tend to restrict possibilities in this direction.

The choice of channels of distribution depends partly on the nature of the product, partly on the nature of the market and partly on the sort of consumer at whom the product is aimed; it may also depend on the existing structure of distribution, although it is frequently possible to change this. The final selection of the channel will depend on the sales expected from the use of the channel balanced against the costs of using it. Frequently the most costly methods are those which involve selling direct to final buyers but there are cases where this may be cheaper.

Co-operation with the distributor is part of marketing policy.

It may be necessary to supply display material, to guarantee rapid delivery, to provide financial aid in the form of extended credit, to be prepared to offer after-sales service and so on. The co-operation may be mutual, and the distributor may be prepared to offer long-term contracts and special facilities. Much depends on the customs of the trade, particularly in the case of credit and discounts.

The sole agency is one such form of co-operation, which has mutual benefits. These accrue to the retailer in the form of a degree of local monopoly, advertising by the producer, elimination of duplicate brands and lower stock costs. The producer gains by having a semi-guaranteed and regular outlet, he can concentrate his promotional effort, and he benefits from the fact that the distributor can carry complete stocks of his range of goods and provide after-sales service and repairs. For some goods, particularly those bought on impulse, sole agencies offer fewer advantages. One of the arguments, that sole agencies help in resale price maintenance and price stability is likely to be of decreasing force in the U.K. in future.

Another aspect of the marketing process is the decision about number of outlets. Complete coverage may be desirable, as in the case of detergents and many foodstuffs; but selective distribution through a limited number of outlets is often preferable, as in the case of products sold largely to a few income groups or to specialized sectors of the economy, where large-scale distribution would be wasteful. In general, expensive durable goods such as refrigerators and motor cars, which usually have to be maintained in fairly large stocks at the outlet, with relatively infrequent turnover, are best distributed selectively; goods such as foodstuffs, groceries, cosmetics, detergents, etc., manufactured on a large scale, are best distributed through as many outlets as possible. With selective distribution care is necessary in selecting outlets; with large-scale distribution such care is neither possible nor in most cases necessary. Many goods are sold by grocers, chemists, confectioners and multiple stores, and have to be distributed through the appropriate wholesale channels for each type of shop.

The growth of the supermarket, large chain stores and other organizations with near monopolistic powers have tended to take the marketing initiative away from the producer and to give it to the distributor. There have been big changes in both the scale and technology of distribution. In the U.K., Marks & Spencer are renowned for the fact that they employ their power over manufacturers in the interests of securing cheap goods of consistent quality for the consumer. The economic principles underlying such situations are quite clear; the balance of power depends on the relative share (of output or market respectively) of the manufacturer and distributor. The power of Marks & Spencer depends largely on the fact that they buy from many dispersed and independent producers; the power of the British Match Corporation and the British Oxygen Company is due to their domination of the sources of supply. The large distributor is tending to win this battle at present. Small distributors are being forced to band together to achieve some of the economies of scale and bargaining power of the large concerns.

Manufacturers are therefore having to think much more deeply about marketing policy than in the past because the choice of distribution channels is narrower and distributors have more power. Effective marketing in the future may involve a larger share of the market, co-operation with other producers or the ownership of channels of distribution. New approaches to marketing may widen outlets: books for example, are now sold in shops which would never have considered such merchandise 30 years ago; the book club idea has spread to gramophone records, reproductions of paintings, wines, travel and even some foodstuffs.

An operations research approach may also be adopted. In a mail order firm an analysis was carried out of merchandise rejected by customers, it was found that 30 per cent of goods sent cash-on-delivery were being returned. The analysis showed that when merchandise was dispatched on the day the order was received, only 20 per cent of the merchandise was returned; when there was a delay of 10 days the percentage of rejections reached 60 per cent. The implications of this conclusion for policy decisions was clear: it was worth while incurring extra expense on production, stocking and dispatch in order to reduce the percentage of rejections.[23]

[23] See Horace C. Levinson, 'Experience in Commercial Operations Research', *Operations Research for Management*, p. 265.

M

An interesting example of the choice of a channel of distribution is provided by the Olivetti Company[24] in the case of its portable typewriter 'Lettera 22'.

Traditionally in Italy the distribution pattern for office machinery was one of direct sales through branch offices and sole concessionaires. This was justifiable for several reasons: the market was concentrated mainly on industrialists and commercial undertakings; most office machinery sales are made by personal salesmen; it is necessary to provide technical assistance and repairs, which are best operated under the direct control of the manufacturer; and the system allowed direct contact between producer and market.

But in 1950 the company introduced a new portable typewriter, and was faced with the question whether the existing policy was adequate or whether some new sales policy would have to be adopted. The company believed that it would be possible to create a large market for portable typewriters in private households; it was also hoped that this would be good advertisement for the bigger machines, and would help their sales in offices.

In order to achieve this result, sales price should be rigidly controlled, and kept below the monthly salary of a clerk; advertising was needed to stress the usefulness of typewriters; a wider knowledge of typewriters should be fostered; and lastly, distribution arrangements should be tightened up in such a way as to bring the machine to the notice and within the reach of passers-by.

The company conducted an experiment in Trieste and Milan with retailers of household electrical equipment with encouraging results; sales were mainly to clerks, artisans, students and women, and sales of the company's own branches were not affected. Electrical goods shops were chosen because they were numerous; even in small towns, they have good display windows, they have regular customers, with high purchasing power, and they are organized for hire purchase sales.

There were objections from concessionaires and from office

---

[24] U. Galassi, 'The Case of the Portable Typewriter 'Lettera 22'' published in *Marketing by Manufacturers* (Organization for European Economic Co-operation, 1957).

machinery dealers, but the company managed to overcome these.

In the light of experience the policy of sales through these outlets was adopted, and was bolstered by other measures such as advertising, the formation of typing schools and so on.

In 5 years the volume of sales of this model was increased to a figure four times higher than that of the previous model.

SALES MANAGEMENT AND PERSONAL SELLING

The term 'Sales Management' means different things in different firms. In some firms the sales manager or director is responsible for all aspects of marketing; in others he is merely responsible for the management of the sales force; in others he may be the man responsible for personal selling, or for price policy, or for any other aspects of marketing. It is defensible, if not completely logical, to think of sales management as the function of organizing the sales force and personal selling, and that is the sense in which the term will be used in this chapter.

Supervision of sales personnel is largely an administrative task: the manager will want to know how well his men are doing their work, their problems, and what assistance is necessary; and this means that he must have the necessary information. Much of this comes from records in his own department; some comes from other departments, occasionally in the form of rebukes. Volume of sales is not necessarily the best measure of performance, since this will depend on the size and complexity of the sales area, the number of calls and the number of other tasks which the salesman has to perform; against these the personal selling ability of the salesman may have little chance. 'Super-salesmen', though frequently successful in the short run, often antagonize customers and work against the long-term interests of the firm. Experience and research can usually help management to set and maintain reasonable performance standards.

Personal selling by the sales force of manufacturers and distributors is the oldest marketing method, and is the most effective in many circumstances. The term embraces over-the-counter selling, house-to-house selling, the calls of salesmen on wholesalers and retailers, and specialist salesmen and executives calling on important customers. More often than not it is the method used to close the sale. Effective personal selling, though it is frequently left to inferior personnel, depends on a knowledge of the market and the products, on locating the buyers, on concluding the sale and on the maintenance of good will. A whole industry has grown up based on the training of salesmen, and training courses of this sort usually ring the changes on a few basic ways of being a good salesman; these include finding out the customer's needs, presenting goods as effectively as possible, meeting objections, and ways of closing the sale. But effective personal selling depends much more on the representative just being there than on tactics or gimmicks. Contact above anything else is the essence of salesmanship.

Personal selling usually has a high cost per contact, but it is also, as a rule, more effective than other methods. How many salesman to use and where to concentrate them is an integral part of the whole marketing decision, and has to be seen as part of the *promotional mix,* but the personal salesman remains a key part of the marketing process.

CONCLUSIONS

It is possible to sum up the main elements of the marketing decision. Three managerial aspects of demand were outlined at the beginning of Chapter IV. These are interdependent but the classification provides a framework for the examination of market decisions.

The first aspect is analysis and forecasting. This is the function of market research. The second aspect, the effect which demand may have on the organization and activities of the firm is partly a production problem and partly an administrative problem; it concerns the fields of product development and design, organization of the marketing department, adaptation of the productive process to meet the conditions of the market, and policy with regard to stocks.

The third aspect is the positive approach to meeting demand, or marketing; it includes the choice of channels of distribution, problems of transport and storage, of finance, the provision of services before and after sale, co-operation with distributors, and pricing policy.

Policy decisions are necessary about all of these, and they have to be made in the light of the firm's assessment of the factors affecting markets; this includes consideration of factors within the firm itself, general consideration affecting the market, and specific consideration of consumers and distributors.

Within the firm itself marketing largely determines overall policy, which is affected by production capacity, its flexibility and projected changes, the production time lag (which determines the length of forecast necessary), research, development and design, the storability of the product, the number of suppliers and the flexibility of supplies.

In the market in general, the main points to consider are: the size and structure of the market; transport facilities; distance from the main parts of the market and main centres of demand; credit possibilities, the seasonality of demand, the number of competitors, their share of the market, and the forms of competition; the number and type of substitutes; prices; prospects for various types of sales promotion; and the relative powers of producers and distributors.

Coming to *the consumers,* the main factors affecting policy are: the number of consumers and the number of economic units (such as households); their incomes, tastes and preferences; their demand patterns; their consumption capacity over a period of time; the storage capacity of the household or other unit; and the time lag of consumption (the increasing number of refrigerators and freezers, for example, tends to impose new time patterns on consumption).

The main considerations relating to *distributors* are: the structure of distribution and the variety of channels; the number of distributors and their power; the ability of distributors to handle products; the attitudes of distributors; warehousing facilities; the customs and the traditions of trade; trade association policies; discount and credit possibilities; the possibilities of mutual co-operation; and the costs of distribution.

The reconciliation of all these factors and individual decisions forms the marketing policy of the firm, which must be consistent with its overall objectives.

CHAPTER VI

PRICING

THE PRICING decision is an integral part of marketing policy. Not all firms are able to set prices for their products; they are *price takers* rather than *price makers* and under the pressure of competition must accept what they can get for their products. Sellers of rubber, cotton and tea are in this category and their prices are determined by supply and demand; sellers of many other commodities have to accept prices fixed by government or international agencies. Sometimes the opportunity to charge a higher price than that ruling in the market may be made by producing a superior grade of product or one that is specially adapted for its market, but in many industries short-run market conditions approximate to what the economist refers to as perfect competition. The characteristics of such markets are the presence of large numbers of buyers and sellers dealing in a homogeneous product with full knowledge of the market; firms are free to enter or leave the industry and all factors of production are fully employed. In these conditions price is market determined and firms are price takers.

In sharp distinction to conditions of perfect competition are those of monopoly with one seller dominating the market for a clearly differentiated product with no close substitutes. A monopolist is not at the mercy of his competitors, but what he can sell at any price depends on what the consumer is prepared to buy at that price; he cannot fix both prices and sales.

Manufacturing industry does not operate in conditions either of perfect competition or monopoly. Many firms, in agriculture and distribution, as well as in manufacturing industry, sell in a market in competition with a small number of other firms. Economists refer to this state of affairs as oligopoly; its essence is that the actions of any firm greatly affect the others. Another economist's term, monopolistic competition, describes a market situation involving more producers, all of whom are affected to some degree by the actions of the others. Nevertheless they have some scope for independent action without experiencing serious retaliation from their competitors. In monopolistic competition firms are able to differentiate their products from those of their competitors by advertising, design, trade marks, selection of location etc.; price however remains a vital element in the strategy and tactics of the firm. When there is only a small number of buyers the market condition is referred to as oligopsony and where there is a single buyer the term monopsony is used. Oligopolists may sell to oligopsonists or monopsonists or to a multitude of buyers, and buyers and sellers may be matched in a variety of other ways

Important though pricing is, it must not be looked at in isolation from the other activities of business. Since price is a determinant of sales it must be related to output and production costs and in turn to decisions to invest. The ability to sell at particular prices is quite likely to determine what can be spent in making the product and how good it can be; production may have to be tailored to a price as often as a price has to be fixed to cover production costs.

The need to relate these elements of business decisions applies to all firms whatever the precise ends they set themselves. But the way they fix prices is likely to reflect the objectives they are pursuing: we might, for example, expect some firms concentrating on expanding their turnover to set lower prices than those concerned with maximising profits in the short term and so on.

Opinions differ as to what is characteristic in these respects. Professor Galbraith assumes that modern industry is characterized by giant companies controlled by professional managers who have their particular empires and dynasties to preserve.[1] Modern industry is constantly changing; periods of gestation are long and effective planning of industrial operations for years ahead is unavoidable. Planners attempt to reduce the uncertainties inherent in long time horizons and try to plan for the comparative stability of certain elements over which they can exercise control. One of these elements is price, which can fluctuate much more than production costs if price determination is left to the market. Such fluctuations can be reduced either by achieving close relationships with suppliers or by

[1] See *The New Industrial State*, Hamish Hamilton, 1967.

extending control to earlier or later production processes by vertical integration. Price is thus reduced to a secondary role in planning decisions. This assumes, however, that the ultimate prices charged to consumers can be controlled so as to maintain the profitability of companies and provide them with the resources needed to expand their businesses.

The Galbraithian thesis is exaggerated, but oligopoly is becoming increasingly common in industry. Oligopolists are unlikely to indulge in price-cutting or raising prices ahead of their competitors; they fully recognize that they have a common interest in maintaining prices, as retaliation is bound to follow a price cut; they also know that if they attempt to increase prices individually their competitors may not follow suit, preferring to gain a larger share of the market. In such circumstances price leaders emerge and their decisions about price levels are tacitly followed by competitors.

If it can be assumed that all firms effectively operate in collusion and attempt to maximise their pooled profits, the theoretical analysis is fairly simple. It is in fact the case of monopoly, and output may be determined in conditions of complete knowledge in such a way as to maximise profits. The basic postulate is that of the falling demand curve, which expresses the fact that demand will be greater at a lower than at a higher price. Every increase in sales necessitates a reduction in price and this means that the additional (marginal) revenue from increasing sales by one unit is less than the price at which the unit is sold because *all* units are sold at the same, lower, price. We can represent this state of affairs by Figure 6.1 (p. 190). The average revenue line represents the price at which various levels of output can be sold; the marginal revenue line (which is always less than this) represents the increase in revenue that results from selling an additional unit after allowing for the fact that the price of all units, and not just the marginal unit, have to be reduced. The lines relating to costs show both marginal (additional) costs incurred in producing an additional unit and the average cost of producing the number of units under consideration.[2]

If the intention is to maximise profits, that output for which marginal cost equals marginal revenue should be produced.

[2] See Chapters II and III.

The logic of this is quite simple. If marginal costs exceed marginal revenue, an expansion in output means that each successive unit of output adds more to costs than to revenue, with the result that both incremental and total profits fall; it would be pointless to expand output in these conditions and it would pay to reduce output. If marginal revenue exceeds marginal costs, an expansion in output results in the addition of more to revenue than to costs, and further expansion is therefore justified. It follows that the equilibrium condition, in which it pays neither to expand nor to reduce output, is where marginal costs equals marginal revenue. It should be noted however that in formal terms this is a profit-maximising model, and the conditions do not apply if the firm has some objective other than maximization of profit.

It is always open to a firm not to maximize profits and in this case it will produce more or less than the output for which marginal costs and revenues are equal, decreasing its profits below the maximum attainable, but achieving other objectives such as good will or charging a 'fair' price. Thus the firm that is at a sub-optimal profit position at any moment has scope for increasing profits if it needs to do so in order to plough back more resources into investment, as the Galbraithian view would necessitate.

The description of the behaviour of firms in terms of the selection of a price-output combination is sound enough so far as it goes but it is not always easy to fit it to actual conditions, and it is certainly an over-simplified model of what happens, whether or not competition is experienced. Fitting the product to the price is as important as selecting the price for a given product. Also in many consumer markets it would be unwise to act on the assumption either that the prices set by apparent price leaders should be followed invariably, or that consumers are loyal (or so ignorant) that their purchases will not be affected by the price set or by that charged by competitors.

Although prices of consumer goods must not be seen in isolation from other factors which make the product appeal to consumers, there is strong evidence that the housewife is more price sensitive and more responsive to price as an indicator of quality and cheapness than is commonly assumed. A

survey conducted by Gabor and Granger[3] of the price cons-
ciousnesss of consumers in the Nottingham area confirms results
from previous investigations. Out of 5,276 purchases made by
housewives within seven days of the survey it appeared that
in 82 per cent of cases the housewife was able to name the
price at which she had bought. Using this as a measure it
appeared that all social groups were price conscious, although
those in the upper groups were somewhat less price conscious
than others. Further examination to see whether those housewives who named the price for their purchases were correct,
according to a fairly rigorous standard, showed that this was
so in almost 60 per cent of cases. Price is thus undeniably
important in the minds of housewives and conditions their
purchases; the study of how they react to prices is therefore
worthwhile.

Gabor and Granger[4] have conducted investigations to test
the view of Stoetze and Adam, two French workers in this
field, that a typical consumer feels that low prices indicate
poor quality and high prices indicate high quality. They found
from the results of a questionnaire that the housewife had in
mind a range of price which indicated acceptable quality
without extravagance. From their enquiry it was possible to
gauge the percentage of consumers who would buy nylon
stockings at particular prices and to draw curves to represent
this. Some such curves of potential customers tend to be fairly
strongly peaked, indicating that if the size of the potential
market is to be made as large as possible the choice of sales
price is critical; other curves, however, were found to have a
fairly wide plateau at the top with critical prices at each end,
indicating a fairly wide range of acceptable prices.

The information obtained by this kind of enquiry is valuable
but it requires careful interpretation. It may be of considerable help if it indicates that no brand is being sold at or near
some price at which a high proportion of the consumers appears
willing to buy, or if it reveals that the proposed price lies outside the range in which consumers are at present interested; it
is not necessarily impossible to persuade consumers to extend

[3] A. Gabor and C. W. J. Granger, 'Price as an Indicator of Quality', *Economica*,
February 1966.
[4] loc. cit.

their range but it can be very costly, and it is often safest to launch a new product with a price which is inside it. If the enquiry indicates several promising prices, there will be room for discussion as to the best part of the market to attack. Fewer customers at a higher price may be profitable even after allowing for the cost of producing a higher quality article. Strong competition may be experienced in particular price ranges and this may make it desirable to concentrate on other sectors of the market by appropriate product differentiation.

The curve of potential customers must not be confused with a demand curve: it shows only the proportion of customers willing to buy at each price and not the frequency of purchase. It cannot be used to predict how competitors would react to price changes or to the introduction of a new product, and the reactions of competitors might result in changes in consumer attitudes that would invalidate the curve. What it does show, however, is that reducing prices beyond a certain point will result in fewer, not more, sales.

It is one thing, as we have emphasised, to assess the general characteristics of a market and quite another to assess the characteristics of that segment of it that particular manufacturers hope to serve. The market demand for a product can be quite price-inelastic, but the demand for the same product sold by a particular manufacturer may be highly elastic because by cutting prices he can attract customers from his competitors, and because he will tend to lose them if he raises his prices above those characteristic of the market. The determination of prices of consumer goods by manufacturers was very common before legislation was introduced to give retailers the opportunity to fix prices themselves.

Price determination in the retail trade presents its own problems. W. G. McClelland lists the level of marginal costs, the range of stock carried, the service given and the competitive situation as key factors. Prices and standard of service are closely interrelated; there are many new forms of retailing each with a characteristic mix of overhead and variable costs and standard of service, so that marginal costs can range from high to low and prices charged can vary correspondingly. Complementarity between sales means that the demand for a particular good and the price charged for it must be seen in relation to the effect that it will have on other goods sold in the same store. The case of a product priced as a loss leader must be understood in this connection: the loss on the product is more than made up by the additional demand generated for other goods. Price cutting is also affected by complementarity. Those goods that are subject to price cuts need to have a low elasticity of demand, so that the cuts will not be too costly, and there is little point in selecting products where the consumer is not 'price aware'. If competitors cut prices it may sometimes be necessary to match cuts exactly unless customers are to be diverted to other stores, but if the main reason for cutting is to get customers to shop in the store, cuts on other articles may often be as effective.

Complementarity is also important as a means of generating interrelated economies of scale between various facets of the operation of a retail store. As Holdren[5] has put it: '.... it pays the multi-product firm to do more advertising, and it pays the large advertiser to become a multi-product firm.'

Gabor and Granger also comment on the problem of spacing prices of a limited range of similar articles filling more or less the same purpose (for example cars or radio sets). Many human reactions are related to proportionate rather than absolute changes and consumers probably react in this way to prices; Gabor and Granger argue that the prices of models within a range should increase in geometrical rather arithmetical progression.

The approach to price fixing described above is directed towards consumers and is often described as backward costing because the article is built to fit a sales price related to quality and consumer spending patterns; design and manufacturing decisions will follow from this having regard to the expected share of the total market that can be secured in the face of competition.

This process may also dictate the terms on which businesses deal with each other. Marks and Spencer appear to follow the practice of specifying the product and negotiating with suppliers to secure the quantities needed at the price which they

---

[5] *The Structure of a Retail Market and the Market Behaviour of Retail Units*, New Jersey 1960.

have in mind. If necessary, Marks and Spencer will advise suppliers on how to meet their requirements at the appropriate price. Quite often this means changing production methods in response to the market situation rather than adjusting price and output to meet the cost of production. Marks and Spencer are able to negotiate with a full knowledge of the cost of many manufacturing processes, although they are retailers rather than manufacturers themselves.

The essential ingredients of price determination along these lines is a knowledge of efficient manufacturing procedures, a knowledge of costs and some understanding as to how profits are to be determined. Such knowledge is often lacking. One of the difficulties faced by the Central Electricity Generating Board when placing orders with a limited number of suppliers of generating equipment is that it is not really in a position to determine what prices are acceptable, because it has no experience of the cost of manufacturing such equipment using the best available methods. Even for those that have such knowledge pricing is not an easy matter. Technology has been changing rapidly and it is not easy to estimate the cost of producing new designs of equipment with attendant technical snags and teething troubles.

In such cases price determination becomes a matter for negotiation; there is little in the way of a competitive market situation to give a guide, and costs may become the starting point for deciding appropriate prices. Nevertheless it is necessary to prevent such arrangements leading to a lack of concern with costs in the knowledge that the purchaser will meet them. Cost-plus pricing was common during the war and is still applied to many government contracts. Contracts at set prices are not necessarily a good substitute for cost-plus pricing if the knowledge of the parties is uncertain. Ferranti, for example found itself having to repay large sums to the Government in respect of a contract which had been negotiated at a price which, as it transpired, was regarded as unreasonable. The best answer in some circumstances, particularly for government contracts let for public works, may be to select a limited number of suitable contractors and ask them to tender competitively for an initial contract with the prospect that they may be awarded additional contracts on the basis of the standard costs estimated in the original tender. This is known as serial tendering;[6] it offers the advantage of providing a check on costs without the necessity of incurring the expense involved in the preparation of a large number of detailed tenders; it also gives successful contractors some assurance of continuing employment and more effective and economical use of heavy plant needed for such contracts as the construction of motorways. Once again the basis for the determination of prices is costs plus an acceptable profit margin as determined through a process of partial competition. The ultimate check exercised by government on the reasonableness of the cost of subsequent contracts depends very much on familiarity of its quantity surveyors with changes in costs due to the introduction of better methods or changes in raw material prices and wages.

Competitive bidding lends itself to analysis on the part of a bidder. If records exist of bids submitted on previous occasions for similar classes of work, it may be possible to estimate the probability that rivals' bids will fall above or below the estimated cost by various percentages, and to work out the chances of success of a particular bid. It would then be possible to work out on the basis of probability how much profit might be expected from any particular bid. Thus a bid which would give a profit of 5 per cent and have a 20 per cent chance of acceptance would not on the average yield as much as one with only a 15 per cent chance of acceptance at a 10 per cent rate of profit. Strategies of this kind are likely to work only so long as a reasonable number of contracts is coming forward; there is a danger that if few but large contracts are placed and the bidder is unsuccessful in most tenders it will be difficult to meet overhead costs. The whole basis of the analysis and the strategy would have to be changed if competitors adjusted their tactics in response.[7]

Between the extremes of fitting products to prices accepted by consumers and making a once-and-for-all bid, there remains a large area of transactions between businesses in which higgling and haggling play a part when both buyers and sellers have imperfect knowledge. It is generally assumed that the

[6] It was strongly advocated by the Banwell Committee, *The Placing and Management of Contracts for Building and Civil Engineering Work*, H.M.S.O. 1964.
[7] For a discussion of some aspects of the subject see Oxenfeldt *et al.*, Pricing in Competitive Bidding, in *Insights into Pricing*, Wadsworth 1965.

degree of imperfection of knowledge in transactions between professional buyers and sellers will be less than that between consumers and suppliers, but knowledge may be limited because a purchaser may have little direct information about production costs, and can often judge the reasonableness of a price only against the prices being quoted by other suppliers in the market. The price that it is reasonable to pay also depends on adherence to delivery dates, quality and the value of a long-term association between purchaser and supplier. Thus in all such transactions there is likely to be a range of prices which either buyer or seller might regard as reasonably satisfactory. This element of uncertainty and arbitrariness makes it difficult to lay down hard and fast rules about how prices should be determined by sellers.

It is all the more difficult to determine the price at which products should be sold when the pricing policies of competitors are in doubt. To set prices and then to find that competitors fix lower prices, perhaps by producing an inferior model, may require consequential adjustments. To some extent costs limit the prices at which competitors sell, unless they have some special know-how, but there are circumstances in which costs may be rather far removed from selling prices. For example, a manufacturer may launch a new product for which competition is not expected immediately but at some time in the future; the intensity of the competition will be partly determined by the price set by the innovator. A choice may have to be made between attempting to cash in on the new product by skimming the cream and attempting to secure a more lasting return by setting a price which will encourage the growth of the market and make possible savings in production costs through economies of scale. Much depends in these cases on the extent of potential demand, the speed with which it can be exploited, the responsiveness of purchasers to prices and the extent to which competition is to be feared. High potential demand combined with a strong competitive threat might lead to a decision to go for a large share of the market by setting low prices. In other circumstances a different approach might be followed. Price fixing must be seen in relation to the whole strategy of making and selling the product over a long period. The problem is to acquire sufficient knowledge and make good enough projections to calculate the probable results of alternative policies. Decision theory may be of some help in setting out the various alternatives that could occur with different 'states of nature', so enabling these to be considered systematically.[8]

Costs and prices may also diverge appreciably in industries where prime costs are small in relation to total costs (capital-intensive industries) and in industries producing joint products where production costs may have little clear relation to market prices. In the first case, there is scope for price cutting by competitors whenever there is excess capacity; so long as prime costs are more than met some marginal profit will be made but it is likely to be insufficient to meet all costs.

The manufacture of joint products is typical of the chemical industry, in which price determination is complicated. Large chemical companies manufacture a wide range of products; some are produced in large quantities and are sold in highly competitive markets, others are specialities, sometimes newly introduced on the market. It is difficult to assign production costs to joint products or by-products, or to allot overhead costs, including research costs. It is scarcely surprising that in such an industry 'prices cannot be reduced to mathematical formulas (although) an understanding of the forces which influence them is of vital concern to a company'.[9] Some price policy must, however, be formulated, for prices in the chemical industry are set by company officials rather than determined by the market, and guidance must be given to them so that the 'administered' prices will be consistent with the company's aims.

We have already discussed the relationship between the objectives of companies and the pricing policies that are likely to be consistent with the attainment of these objectives. We are concerned at this point with the way in which these objectives are linked administratively to individual prices and incidentally with the light that this throws on company objectives.

Some interesting work has been done in this field by R. V. Lanzillotti.[10] Table 6.1 summarises some of the information.

[8] See Chapter I.
[9] Jules Bachman, *Chemical Prices, Productivity, Wages and Profits*, Washington 1964, p. 2.
[10] 'Pricing Objectives in Large Companies', *American Economic Review*, 1958, page 921.

The principal goals vary but they can be grouped in a limited number of categories. Several companies relate prices to the return that they wish to get on their investment; this return might relate only to money put up by shareholders or to all money used in the business irrespective of the source from which it came. Other companies lay stress on maintaining their market share as the criterion for price fixing; those who state that they aim to match prices may be implicitly following a similar objective.

The collateral pricing goals associated with the principal goal may not always be consistent. A 'promotive' policy on new products may not conflict with a target return on capital, but price stabilization could well be inconsistent with the latter objective in the short run. A target of maintaining market share could be consistent with obtaining a required rate of return on capital if the policies of competing companies were broadly similar.

The right approach to such questions is to regard pricing goals as guide lines rather than inviolable rules. Instructing managers to plan for some return on capital is a different thing from telling them to maximize profits; but it is just possible that the instruction to obtain a given return on capital may be the best way of getting managers to maximize profits. Conversely an inappropriate instruction may not always lead to an inappropriate action as Professor Pearce brought out;[11] he was concerned to investigate whether a firm was following a stated policy of adding a pre-determined mark up to costs in order to arrive at prices. The policy turned out to be no more than a guide line: it was departed from on occasions when there was a favourable opportunity to increase the margin or when it was necessary to meet competition. Thus modified, the principle of fixing prices in relation to costs need not operate very differently from the economist's view that selling prices should be determined so as to equate marginal cost and marginal revenue.

Some costs of production vary closely with output;[12] other costs vary intermittently, some of them increasing only when it is necessary to install new plant. So long as capacity is

---

[11] I. F. Pearce, A Study in Price Policy, *Economica*, May 1956.
[12] See Chapter II.

N

TABLE 6.1

PRICING GOALS OF TWENTY LARGE INDUSTRIAL CORPORATIONS

Company	Principal Pricing Goal	Collateral Pricing Goals	Rate of Return on Investment (After Taxes) 1947–55		Average Market Share
			Average	Range	
Alcoa	20% on investment (before taxes) higher on new products (about 10% effective rate after taxes)	(a) 'Poromotive' policy on new products (b) Prices abilization	13.8	7.8–18.7	Pig and ingot, 37%; Sheet, 46%; other fabrications, 62%
American Can	Maintenance of market share	(a) 'Meeting' competition (using cost of substitute product to determine price) (b) Price stabilization	11.6	9.6–14.7	Approximately 55% of all types of cans
A. & P.	Increasing market share	'General promotive' (low-margin policy)	13.0	9.7–18.8	n.a.
Du Pont	Target return on investment—no specific figure given	(a) Charging what traffic will bear over long run (b) Maximum return for new products—"life cycle" pricing	25.9	19.6–34.1	n.a.
Esso	'Fair-return' target—no specific figure given	(a) Maintenance market share (b) Price stabilization	16.0	12.9–18.9	n.a.
General Electric	20% on investment (after taxes) 7% on sales (after taxes)	a) Promotive policy on new products (b) Price stabilization on nationally advertised products	21.4	18.4–26.6	—
General Foods	33⅓ gross margin: ('⅓ to make ⅓ to sell and ⅓ for profit') expectation of realizing target only on new products	(a) Full line of food products and novelties (b) Maintaining market share	12.2	8.9–15.7	n.a.
General Motors	20% on investment (after taxes)	Maintaining market share	26.0	19.9–37.0	50% of passenger automobiles
Goodyear	'Meeting competitors'	(a) Maintain 'position' (b) Price stabilization	13.3	9.2–16.1	n.a.

Gulf	Follow price of most important market in each area.	(a) Maintain market share (b) Price stabilization	12.6	10.7–16.7	n.a.
International Harvester	10% on investment (after taxes)	Market share: ceiling of "less than a dominant share of any market"	8.9	4.9–11.9	Farm tractors, 28–30% combines, corn pickers, tractor plows, cultivators, mowers, 20–30%; cotton pickers, 65%; light and light-heavy trucks, 5–18%; medium heavy to heavy-heavy 12–30%
Johns-Manville	Return on investment greater than last, 15-year average (about 15% after taxes); higher target for new products	(a) Market share not greater than 20% (b) Stabilization of prices	14.9	10.7–19.6	n.a.
Kennecott	Stabilization of prices		16.0	9.3–20.9	n.a.
Kroger	Maintaining market share	Target return of 20% on investment before taxes	12.1	9.7–16.1	n.a.
National Steel	Matching the market—price follower	Increase market share	12.1	7.0–17.4	5%
Sears-Roebuck	Increasing market share (8-10% regarded as satisfactory share)	(a) Realization of traditional return on investment of 10–15% (after taxes) (b) General promotive (low margin) policy	5.4	1.6–10.7	5–10% average (twice as large a share in hard goods vs. soft goods)
Standard Oil (Ind.)	Maintain market share	(a) Stabilize prices (b) Target return on investmen (none specified)	10.4	7.9–14.4	n.a.
Swift	Maintenance of market share in live-stock buying and meat packing		6.9	3.9–11.1	Approximately 10% nationally
Union Carbide	Target return on investment	Promotive policy on new products; 'life cycle' pricing on chemicals generally	19.2	13.5–24.3	
U.S. Steel	8% on investment (after taxes)	(a) Target market share of 30% (b) Stable price (c) Stable margin	10.3	7.6–14.8	Ingots and steel, 30% blast furnaces, 34%; finished hot rolled products, 35%; other steel mill products, 37%

Source: R. V. Lanzillotti, Pricing Objectives in Large Companies

adequate, the marginal cost of production approximates to the direct costs of materials, labour etc. incurred in increasing output by a single unit. It is to the consumer's advantage to buy additional units of output if he is prepared to pay more than the marginal cost of production; this would also benefit the producer because he would make a profit on his marginal output. If there is excess capacity the marginal cost of producing additional output can be assumed to be less than the average cost; only if we were getting close to the capacity of the plant would it be at all likely that marginal costs would exceed average costs. But if a price very little in excess of marginal cost is charged (and it has been shown that this would be in the interest of both consumer and producer for this to be done) insufficient revenue will be raised to cover fixed costs as well as marginal costs, and the enterprise would operate at a loss.

Private enterprise is unlikely to fix prices in this way if it has any choice in the matter. Sometimes it may be forced to do so by competitive pressures when any contribution to overheads is welcome even if it does not cover full costs; it will not do so in the long run because if it cannot provide for renewal of its capital equipment it will go out of business.

Although private enterprise cannot be expected to equate price to marginal cost when this results in its making a loss, it has been suggested at times that this might be the right approach for public enterprise.[13]

PRICING METHODS IN PRACTICE

All firms need a pricing policy. The most commonly adopted method is *cost-plus* or *full-cost* pricing, which consists of adding some mark up to costs to cover overheads and profit. It is necessary to define the costs to which the mark up is to be added and to select an appropriate margin for the mark up: it is common to use standard costs as the basis for estimation and the margin is frequently related to a target return on capital or based on some judgement as to what is fair and reasonable.

The main advantage of cost plus pricing is that it is simple to operate, particularly when little is known about demand condi-

---

[13] This case is dealt with in the discussion of the pricing of electricity, Appendix I to this chapter, pp. 182 ff.

tions. With this system prices respond to changes in production costs and not to demand. Although this may be acceptable to customers, who understand the logic of a price increase based on cost increases, its failure to emphasis the importance of demand and competitive conditions is a major weakness. The effectiveness of the method depends partly on having the right definitions and accurate measurement of costs; ideally the measure should reflect opportunity costs and be concentrated on marginal or incremental rather than average costs.

Flexible mark up pricing is a slightly more sophisticated variant which permits the firm to adapt its mark up to market changes to some extent; administratively it may be expensive if frequent demand estimates are required, and many firms restrict the use of flexible mark ups to products sold to customers whom they know well. The emphasis is likely to be on what the market will bear, which many firms think is disreputable.

Intuitive pricing is fairly common; it is normally based on some such vague notion as the 'feel of the market' or on hunches and guesses. Although the method may be made to work by people with a great deal of experience, it suffers from the drawback of inadequate analysis.

Experimental pricing is difficult to operate in practice, but it may be particularly useful in the market testing of new products.

In appropriate demand and cost conditions a variety of other methods may be used: these include *product line pricing, loss leader* pricing, and following *price leadership*. Prices may also be used as part of the tactics employed to make *tie-in* sales, when for example buyers are expected to take materials and machines as part of a co-ordinated deal. *Price discrimination* requires separated markets each with its own price elasticity of demand; it may take the form of geographical differentials, two-part tariffs or discrimination between consumers.

Ideally the firm which wishes to maximise profits should fix price and sales at the level which equates marginal cost and marginal revenue; this is difficult but *incremental* or *marginal-cost* pricing frequently approaches this ideal in practice.[14] This approach has the virtue that it gets away from prices based on average costs plus some mark up and makes an attempt to take account of demand conditions.

[14] See Chapter III.

CHAPTER VI, APPENDIX I

PRICING ELECTRICITY[1]

THE economist's rule that output and price should be determined so that marginal cost and marginal revenue are equated is more complicated than appears at first sight. In its simplest form it was applied to private firms concerned to maximise profits, and as it was developed it gave an adequate picture of the operation of an economy directed by market forces. Nationalisation of industry raised the question of how pricing principles should be applied in the case of statutory monopolies and an examination of this led to the development of more refined price theory capable of application in such cases. The sector of industry concerned is now large and it is worthwhile, therefore, to examine some of the considerations that are relevant to pricing in nationalised industry, using the generation of electricity as an illustration. Underlying the whole discussion is the judgment that from the social point of view it is worthwhile producing output whenever it can be sold at a price covering its marginal cost of production. The question is really what is marginal cost and what principles should be followed in allocating overhead costs in conditions when plant may not always be used to capacity.

It is well known that the demand for electricity varies greatly; it is at its lowest in the summer and at its highest in conditions of intense cold in the winter. Such peak demands may last for only a short period even on a very cold day; there will almost certainly be considerable excess capacity available during the following night; and if adequate safety margins have been provided there may be little danger of the supply being interrupted at any time. The cost of the supply will vary however. It is the practice to use the newest and most efficient generators with the lowest running costs during the summer and gradually to bring others of higher running costs into use as the demand rises in the winter, perhaps to a sharp peak. Normally the last generating sets that are brought into use during the peak will have no more than scrap value; the cost of using them will be the cost of the fuel they use. Since they are less efficient than those sets in constant use the fuel they need per unit of electricity generated will cost more, but if the demand for electricity has been

---

[1] The appendix draws heavily on Ralph Turvey, *Optimal Pricing and Investment in Electricity Supply*, George Allen and Unwin, 1968.

expanding, so that even the most inefficient sets on standby are not grossly less efficient than the average, there may not be a very large difference in cost. Thus a price covering the marginal costs of generating electricity by the least efficient plants might not cover the total costs of generating a unit of electricity, after taking account of capital costs incurred in installing the equipment in the first place.

What ought an electricity undertaking to do in such circumstances? If it were to charge little more than the marginal cost of producing electricity, existing equipment would be more intensively used, the consumer would benefit and the undertaking would make a (perhaps small) marginal profit. But in total it might make a loss and while to some this has seemed permissible in the interests of producing more and obtaining a better use of resources in the economy, the various issues are not really so clear cut as has sometimes been supposed.

In the first place any loss would have to be financed in some way. Losses incurred by nationalised industries are often met out of general government revenues and if this were the case, consumers of electricity would be in the position of being subsidised by tax-payers in general. It is difficult to justify such a course. What is the case for the non-consumer of electricity subsidising the heavy consumer? Would not the effect of such a procedure be also to cheapen the cost of electricity (through the subsidy) in relation to that of coal and to encourage the use of electricity and the production of goods that required large amounts of electricity at the expense of other goods and services? Improvement in the allocation of the community's resources at one point might mean a consequent deterioration at some other point, which would be hard to justify and more serious than the initial distortion it was designed to correct. Moreover, it is not self evident that the consumer of electricity will gain very greatly from being able to purchase more electricity at lower prices except in so far as it affects his income. Some consumers whose demand for electricity is elastic may benefit greatly because cheaper electricity opens up possibilities previously denied to them; but there may be many other consumers whose demand for electricity is inelastic and who would not benefit greatly because lower prices encouraged them to consume, but more simply because lower prices saved them money. In other words the benefits to be gained from a reduction of price, as opposed to a consequential increase of income will depend on consumers' elasticities of demand.

The argument for marginal pricing as advanced so far also shows that marginal cost is not a clear cut concept. Differences between

marginal costs and average costs of production arise because capacity
is not exactly adjusted to demand. When there is excess capacity
marginal costs are less than average costs; but when capacity is
inadequate marginal costs may be much in excess of average costs.
The effects of marginal cost pricing on revenues depends on whether
capacity is adequate or so strained that marginal costs are high.

Changing capacity thus has an effect on marginal costs and it
may seem more reasonable to approach the pricing of electricity
from the point of view of the marginal cost of producing electricity
when capacity has to be adjusted to meet an increase in output.
In practice increasing generating capacity is a lumpy proceeding;
generating sets come in capacities of 500 megawatts or more and
they frequently have to be seen as part of a much larger installation.
Nevertheless, in principle the effects on marginal costs of investing
in generating capacity can be analysed as though they related to the
ability to produce an additional single unit of electricity throughout
the year.

Looked at in this way the marginal cost of producing electricity
in the long-run will be compounded of the cost of the equipment
needed plus the changes that the installation of the new equipment
makes in running costs when it is in operation. All this, of course,
has to be thought of as being in terms of the (marginal) cost of
producing an additional unit of capacity. The capital cost of adding
to equipment can be assumed to be known fairly easily, but the
changes in running costs resulting from installing the new equipment is not easy to arrive at. It cannot necessarily be assumed that
the new equipment will be run all the time; as it is likely to be
highly efficient it may be, apart from periods when it is due for
overhaul or if it breaks down; but some equipment is installed solely
to increase capacity at the peak. Whenever the equipment is in
operation it will reduce running costs below the level they would
otherwise reach, typically by reducing fuel costs. We have to think
of these savings in operational costs in relation to the whole of the
estimated life of the new equipment. Obviously this is not easy to
do but in principle estimates can be made. It will be necessary to
discount savings expected in future periods of time in such a way
as to estimate their present value. The method of doing this is
explained in Chapter VII. The marginal cost of providing for
an addition to peak demand for electricity can now be expressed
as

$$C-PW\ [(m-r)a]+PW\ [F]$$

remembering that all costs are in terms of cost per unit of electricity.
This expression may be explained as follows. C is the cost of pro-

viding the equipment; r is the costs that would have been incurred in generating electricity (over unit time) if the new equipment had not been available; m is the cost of operating the new equipment; $m-r$ is the saving in operating costs that results; and a is an indicator taking the value of 1 or 0 according to whether the equipment is in use or not for every unit of time of the equipment's life; F measures the cost per year of keeping the plant in being (maintaining and manning it). The symbol PW means simply the present worth of the time stream of savings; it indicates that all savings (whenever they arise) and all maintenance costs (whenever they will be incurred) have been reduced to their equivalent present value.

This is an extremely sophisticated concept of marginal cost requiring considerable calculation and estimation of future conditions to establish. But it is important in drawing attention to the need to meet all costs in the long run if investment decisions are to be soundly based, and in viewing marginal costs and their associated revenues from this point of view.

It still appears, however, to leave us with our previous difficulty. The new equipment will pay off if its marginal costs can be met and will presumably be ordered only if prices can be charged that will cover this. But at times generating capacity will be idle and the price to charge for electricity at such times remains to be decided. Can these points of view be reconciled? It appears that if the amount of equipment needed has been correctly anticipated this can be done by following two rules of pricing, a short run and a long run rule which are equivalent when capacity has been correctly determined.

The short run rule is: the price of electricity at each time, place and voltage is set equal to marginal running cost per kWh delivered or, if it be higher, at the level necessary to restrict demand to capacity. The long run rule is: an investment is undertaken if the present worth to consumers of the consequential changes in their supplies, less the present worth of the difference in total system costs with and without the investment, is positive.

The two rules boil down to the same thing when capacity is correctly adjusted to demand, for the following reasons. Consumers will pay more for units generated at the time of peak demand than marginal short-run costs of generation because their needs are urgent and because they are (in conditions of correct adjustment of capacity) prepared to pay the additional costs of having sufficient capacity to meet the peak demand they impose. In other words the cost of providing capacity to meet peak demands will fall on the consumer using electricity generated at peak periods. If such periods occur only for a few hours each year the element of capacity cost would be extremely heavy; but since we assume perfect adjustment of consumer's needs it must follow that they are willing to meet it. In fact the increase in cost will not be so onerous as might appear at first sight. The existing plant will have various degrees of efficiency in a realistic situation; the average direct cost of generation using the new plant will be less than marginal cost of using the old plant in most situations; thus the new highly efficient plant will be making a contribution to its capital cost through its comparative fuel saving (as is apparent from the formula) at most times. It is far from just a question of installing new plant to meet peak demands, if this were the case the capital costs falling on the peak period would be very great.

How nearly is it possible to fit electricity tariffs in practice to the kind of theoretical considerations outlined above? In the first place much more than generation costs are involved in fixing rates. The voltage at which supplies are to be delivered, the distance between consumers and other characteristics of their demand and distribution costs are all relevant. But too much complexity is to be avoided. Mr Turvey suggests that if marginal pricing is accepted as a principle the following factors might be taken into account :

(a) a connection charge for each new consumer equal to the capital cost wholly and exclusively incurred in connecting his premises to the system

(b) a rate per kW of contribution to peak at each voltage level of the distribution system, equal to the average annuitized cost per kW increment of capacity at that voltage level grossed up by the capacity margin[2]

(c) an annual charge equal to the marginal annual cost per consumer of consumer service, meter-reading, billing and account collecting

(d) a contribution to general overheads and to the annual cost of running, repairing and maintaining the system

(e) marginal running cost per kWh, grossed up to allow for incremental transmission and distribution losses, and varying from hour to hour as the total generating load changed

(f) incremental capacity costs per kW of contribution to peak generation calculated according to the concepts spelled out above.

In fact some simplification is inevitable. It is impracticable to relate consumers' price structure to peak demand at the time it emerges because it is scarcely predictable when it will occur, and

---

[2] These charges might vary with power factor or might be levied per KWh.

almost impossible to inform the general consumer in advance in order to give him time to adjust. Thus actual tariff structures are an approximation to the theoretical norm. When they include connection costs, some standing charge related to unavoidable system charges and the opportunity to take cheap supplies at off-peak periods, they may be sufficiently close to balance the needs for economic adjustments against administrative costs and complexities. Indeed, two part tariffs, as Mr Gabor has pointed out, can be devised to give substantially the same results for such purposes as a charge varying unit by unit with a consumer's use of electricity. They fulfil the dual purpose of securing an initial contribution to overheads and permitting users of large quantities of electricity to purchase subsequent supplies at little more than the marginal cost of providing the supply.[3]

[3] See 'A Note on Block Tariffs', *Review of Economic Studies XXIII*, 1955–56, pp. 32–41.

RESTRICTIVE PRACTICES AND MONOPOLY

THE interests of producers and consumers may often diverge. The consumer is interested in getting good value for money; but his choice in all these matters depends on what is offered by producers since he is seldom in a position to produce a variety of goods himself. Many producers set themselves the task of providing consumers with what they want and give good value for money; they concentrate time, attention and money on maintaining quality and improving their products. They may do this out of a sense of social duty or out of interest, or because if they fail to serve the consumer they will be unable to make adequate profits or to continue in business. To many people the welfare of the consumer seems most likely to be assured if the economy is run on competitive lines. Competition involves a mental image of a number of firms striving independently to provide the consumer with a better or cheaper product; those who succeed are able to expand their business and gain a greater share of the market, while those who fail to provide the same standard of performance are gradually driven out of production. Thus, not only does competition lead firms to strive to do better, but it automatically eliminates those who fail. There is a Darwinian process of selection with this system of the carrot and the stick.

The working of the economy does not always conform to this image. Sometimes there are a large number of firms all of which show little initiative in reducing costs, increasing sales, or introducing new products. Judging by the cotton industry, competition is as likely to produce morbidity as it is to promote vigorous life. In the jute industry, on the other hand, protection from foreign competition seems to have favoured economic progress and to have been conducive to considerable improvements in efficiency. Even if these paradoxical results seem to be contrary to the theory of competition it may be still true that the competitive process has the effect of transferring resources between industries, to the benefit of the community. But it would probably be as wrong to assume that in practice large numbers of firms are a guarantee of improvements in efficiency as to assume that monopolistic firms are necessarily the reverse.

In many industries small-scale production is economically

impossible. The generation of electricity requires a large-scale organization to link the various stations together and spread the load. The production of chemicals is generally cheapest on a large scale; an annual production of over 500,000 is desirable for motor cars; and so on. The creation of large companies has been inseparable from raising living standards over the past two centuries.

The larger companies are assuming a dominant position in their industries; there may be a mere handful of them and they may tend to act in concert. In the absence of competitive pressure on them to be efficient there is always the danger that they will be reluctant to extend themselves for the good of the consumer. If they choose to exert their monopoly power they have every opportunity to exploit the consumer. They may sit back and fail to promote research and development; they may be slow to take up new inventions or may even deliberately suppress those that threaten their livelihood; they may be tempted to exploit labour or, more likely these days, to provide the consumer with an inferior article at a price considerably above costs. History can show plenty of instances of monopolistic exploitation and many instances of monopolies functioning efficiently with the interest of the consumer at heart.

In economic literature considerable attention centres on an expected tendency for monopolists to restrict output in order to put up prices. It is not necessary to have a complete monopoly before it becomes worth while trying to keep prices on the high side. When there are a few producers of the same or closely similar products there may be another harmful effect, that of establishing production units that are below the optimum scale for the cheapest production.

Figure 6.1 illustrates these points. The marginal cost curve shows the cost of producing additional units of output in some undertaking operated on a small scale, say, a small printing establishment. It is assumed that the marginal cost of production at first falls as output increases, and then begins to rise after a period where it is fairly flat. The average cost of production is shown as being fairly high at first when the overheads of the plant have to be spread over a small number of units and then gradually falling as output expands, until a low point is reached; subsequently, it rises as marginal production costs increase because, say, increasing amounts of overtime have to be worked with the given size of plant. If there were a large number of active and knowledgeable producers there would be a tendency for costs to be forced down to their lowest point. If we include in costs an allowance for profit, output would be O_{PC} and this would be sold at a price P_{PC}.

If, however, there were only a few producers each with part of the market attached to him in some way, because, for example, some consumers imagine his product to be slightly superior to that of other firms, a different state of affairs would result. In these circumstances, each producer would find himself with a downward-sloping demand curve or average revenue curve such that if he reduced his price he would be able to sell more. We indicate such a demand curve on the diagram, along with a marginal revenue curve showing the additional revenue that a producer would get from selling an additional unit of output. Each producer following our pricing rule that marginal cost should equal marginal revenue would produce that output for which the marginal cost and marginal revenue curves intersect.

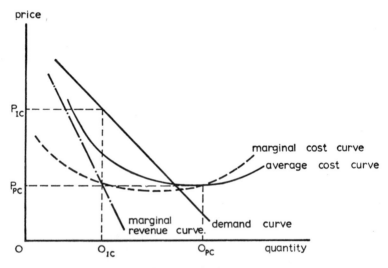

Fig. 6·1.   Price and Output under Monopolistic Conditions

This output is O_{IC} on the diagram and this would be sold at price P_{IC} which, of course, is higher than the competitive price P_{PC}. Thus, in conditions when there is only one or a handful of firms not competing vigorously, price will be higher, and output consequently lower, than it would be under perfect competition. In cases where there is a tendency for costs to fall with an increase in total output produced, substantial economies of scale might be lost.

Any natural tendencies to resist the rigours of competition are likely to be reinforced by collusion between producers, particularly to fix prices. In Chapter VI it was assumed that on the whole firms were free to decide what prices they would charge in the light of the objectives of their company. Few industrial countries nowadays are willing to allow firms complete freedom to fix prices, and legislation has been devised to make it more difficult for firms to operate restrictive agreements which act against the interests of others. The United States has a long record of legislation against monopoly, dating from the passing of the Sherman Act in 1890. This Act forbade all activities in restraint of trade except retail price maintenance practised by an individual producer or distributor. Exclusive dealing for the purpose of lessening competition and acquiring companies for the same purpose was also forbidden. The Act and subsequent Acts have meant that companies have often been restrained from amalgamation, and on occasion large companies have been broken up to promote competition and reduce their power. The threat of action under the anti-monopoly legislation has proved to be a means of curbing the power of large corporations, as happened when steel producers tried to increase prices contrary to Government policy in 1962.

Other countries have not been so anxious to attempt to curb monopolies by legislation as the United States. It was not until 1957 that an Act was passed in Germany against restraints on competition, the Cartel Ordinance of 1923 being designed only to prevent abuse. Under the 1957 Act certain restraints are permitted, for example arrangements to bolster a declining industry, to rationalize production processes and in the case of agreements concerned with export markets. In France legislation aimed at restrictive agreements, including Article 419 of the French Penal Code of 1810, which in effect condemned all agreements in restraint of trade,[1] had little effect until laws were passed after the Second World War prohibiting the fixing of minimum prices for goods and services (except for branded goods) and supervising the practices of cartels. It was not until 1958 that resale price maintenance was declared illegal. In other countries of the Common Market, Belgium, Holland and Italy, legislation against restrictive practices also seems to have been largely ineffective in influencing industrial behaviour. In Sweden, a non-common market country, anti-price law is also of post-war origin. A law passed in 1946 requiring the registration of restrictive agreements was strengthened in 1953 and supplemented in 1956. The general intention was to counteract restrictive business practices through publicity and negotiation.

The establishment of the Common Market led to a policy of unifying legislation against monopoly. Under the Treaty of Rome and subsequent Regulations such practices as fixing common prices,

[1] See G. C. Allen, *Monopoly and Restrictive Practices*, Allen and Unwin 1968.

market sharing and the imposition of restrictions on production and technical development were prohibited when these were likely to affect trade between member states.

Eventually, it is to be expected that some degree of unification of policies against restrictive practices will emerge in most European countries. At present, however, United Kingdom policy is being developed independently. Like other countries the United Kingdom was also late in the field of legislation against monopolies. In the inter-war years very little effort was made to control restrictive practices and in the 'thirties the climate was favourable to them rather than the reverse. In 1948 the Monopolies and Restrictive Practices Act was passed and the Monopolies and Restrictive Practices Commission was set up to investigate and report on matters referred to it by the Board of Trade. The Commission could be asked to investigate when over a third of the supply of a good in the United Kingdom market or a substantial part of it, was provided by one supplier or group of suppliers in such a way as to prevent or restrict competition. By 1956, when the functions of the Commission were altered, it had prepared a score of reports on such matters as the supply of electronic valves and cathode ray tubes, standard metal windows and doors, tea, linoleum and chemical fertilizers. The reports of the Commission did not always condemn the practices that they examined. The Report on the Supply of Insulated Electric Wires and Cables concluded that price competition would tend to lower standards, and that in view of the close technical collaboration between the manufacturers it was permissible for them to inform each other before changing their prices. Other practices that could not be condoned were the subject of negotiation between the industrialists concerned and the Board of Trade. It was the responsibility of the latter to negotiate changes of practice with those concerned or to decide if new legislation was required.

In practice very little impression was made on monopolistic practices by the Commission. It was left to another piece of legislation, The Restrictive Trade Practices Act, 1956, to put some teeth into the measures designed to promote competition. The Act provides for the registration of a wide number of restrictive agreements and all of these agreements have to come before the Restrictive Practices Court. *Prima facie* all restrictive agreements are considered to be against the public interest; if they are found to be so they automatically become void. If a restriction is not regarded as contrary to the public interest it must be proved that it confers certain advantages set out in the Act. These include conferring substantial benefits on purchasers, countering measures taken by other bodies to restrict competition, countering serious and adverse effects on the general level of unemployment in an area, and preventing a reduction in export earnings.

Very few agreements have been found to be in the public interest according to these criteria. Agreements to fix the price at which bolts and nuts could be sold were found to be in the public interest because they eliminated the need for users to go shopping to make sure that they were getting the lowest price (a strange decision!). In the cement case, the court found that the effect of the agreement was to keep prices below the levels that they would otherwise attain, because the greater certainty engendered by the agreement made it possible to attract capital on more favourable terms. In the Water-tube Boilers case it was found that an agreement which enabled a selected member to adjust the price it was proposed to quote for a contract to the lowest tender of members of the association was not contrary to the public interest : consultation in prices and market possibilities increased the chance of obtaining export orders. Other arguments that have been successful in the Court's hearings include advantages from standardization of products (glazed and floor tiles), reasonable prices being charged coupled with technical co-operation (permanent magnets), decline of outlets with consequent reduction of output (books), and the exercise of countervailing power (sulphuric acid). Study of the details of cases which have resulted in the upholding of agreements does not enable useful generalizations to be made about the principles involved. The record certainly shows that it is difficult to establish a case for agreements of a restrictive kind under the Act but over the whole period there does appear to have been some inconsistency in the decisions taken, and to the economic observer it might seem that certain restrictive practices that have been upheld should rather have been condemned.

More recently attention has centred less on the decision of the courts and more on whether the effect of the courts' decisions has been to prevent concerted action. It is not necessary to have agreements for common practices to be observed; it frequently happens that one manufacturer becomes regarded as a price leader and others in the industry follow the lead given with only small divergences. Such results may be achieved through information agreements whereby firms in the same industry circulate amongst themselves details of the prices they are charging. If this practice results in all firms charging virtually the same prices when a price fixing agreement has not been upheld by the court, it may be judged that price fixing is still taking place and legal action may be taken. This happened in the galvanized tank case when the parties concerned were brought before the court and fined for contempt in relation

o

to a previous agreement which had been rejected by the Court. Clearly, however, there are fine shadings in such agreements; price competition may be greatly tempered, although it may not be entirely eliminated, and in such circumstances it may be difficult to condemn the practices of the parties concerned.[2]

The 1956 Act made collective retail price maintenance illegal. This meant that manufacturers were forbidden to combine together to discriminate against retailers who did not observe resale prices. In some cases this meant the maintenance of common retail prices, but, more generally, agreements were designed to ensure that resale prices fixed by individual manufacturers were adhered to. Even after the passing of the Act it was still left open for manufacturers acting independently to insist on retail prices being maintained for their products. The Resale Prices Act of 1964 sought to reduce such price maintenance also. The Act was similar in broad outline to that of 1956, since it started from the presumption that it was necessary for those wishing to operate retail price maintenance to justify this course. Cases were heard, not product by product, but according to groups of products such as confectionery and domestic appliances. If retail price maintenance was not upheld by the Court its abolition applied to all producers of the products concerned. Agreements which had been upheld by the Court under the 1956 legislation were not again called into question, the Net Book Agreement being a case in point. It now seems clear that very little retail price maintenance will stand the tests imposed by the Court and be allowed to continue on the grounds laid down in the Act : that without price maintenance quality or variety of goods would be reduced, the number of shops reduced, the price of goods increased, health endangered or the provision of services in connection with the goods be reduced.

In some areas the virtual abolition of retail price maintenance is of considerable benefit to consumers both in the form of reduced prices and probably also in the long run by encouraging longer and cheaper production runs. But its effects should not be exaggerated; even before the passing of the Act many commodities were not subject to retail price maintenance. There are also observers like Andrews and Friday who saw advantages in resale price maintenance.[3] They argued that resale price maintenance protects the consumer against deterioration in the quality of products that is to be expected with intense competition; that price cuts on some

---

[2] See D. P. O'Brien and D. Swann, *Information Agreements, Competition and Efficiency*, Macmillan, 1968. The 1968 Act makes it possible to call up information agreements for registration.

[3] *Fair Trade* 1960, Institute of Economic Affairs.

articles are generally balanced by increases on others; that it reaches
the point of absurdity when two prices are printed on packets with
the old price crossed out and apparently replaced by a new and
lower price; and they quoted examples of price-cutting wars leaving
the public distrustful of products, to the point where a serious
decline in sales has resulted. They contended that the introduction
of resale price maintenance has sometimes resulted in a fall in prices
in practice, and its abolition in a rise. They added that abolition
would have the effect of concentrating more power into the hands
of large retailers who would tend to develop their own brands of
products made to their requirements by manufacturers, thus reducing competition between manufacturers. The net effect of changes
in the direction of larger scale distribution systems would be to
reduce consumers' choice and the service that he enjoys. Such conclusions may not be valid, but they are interesting as a defence
against the commonly held view that resale price maintenance is a
serious drag on progress.

The Restrictive Practices Court is not concerned with the operation of monopolies; this is still left to the Monopolies Commission.
The issues here are not restricted to the operation of existing
monopolies but also include the question of whether amalgamations
leading to the establishment of large units which might exercise
monopoly should be allowed. These issues were treated in the
Monopolies and Mergers Act passed in 1965. This gave the Board
of Trade power to prohibit proposed mergers and to dissolve existing monopolies on the recommendation of the Monopolies Commission, as well as to regulate prices and impose other restraints.
These powers are clearly not without effect; they enable mergers
involving the takeover of assets worth more than £5 million to be
investigated, as well as those likely to lead to monopolies. The
powers have been used, for example, to prevent a merger between
United Drapery Stores and Montague Burton, and to persuade the
Imperial Tobacco Company not to pursue a potential bid for
Smiths Crisps.

Under the original legislation against restrictive practices, the
provision of services was excluded. Powers were taken under the
Monopolies and Mergers Act 1965 to enable the Monopolies Commission, on a reference by the Board of Trade, to enquire into all
types of services where there appears to be a monopoly situation.

At the present time, the Restrictive Practices Court and the
Monopolies Commission are not the only bodies concerned with
price determination. The concern of the Restrictive Practices
Court and the Monopolies Commission with the determination
of prices has been supplemented by other legislative devices

from time to time. There have been a number of occasions in the postwar period when price and income policies have been applied. The Labour Government that was in power from 1964 to 1970 instituted the Prices and Incomes Board to exercise control in these spheres and it made recommendations that overlapped the working of the Restrictive Practices Court and the Monopolies Commission. Another innovation at this time was the Industrial Reorganisation Corporation set up in 1966 to facilitate mergers. It had wide powers to promote industrial efficiency and £150 million from the Treasury at its disposal for financing its operations. In 1967, for example, it made a £15 million loan to English Electric conditional on that company's taking over Elliott-Automation, and in 1968 it supported the G.E.C. take-over bid for A.E.I. It was also active in other fields.

Government intervention in industrial organisation has thus been many-stranded. At times contradictory policies of building up and breaking down industrial integration may seem to have been followed. Such actions are not necessarily inconsistent with pursuing a coherent policy. The form and size of organisation needed for industrial efficiency varies from industry to industry. There are no inviolable rules about how to secure workable competition.

CHAPTER VII

THE INVESTMENT DECISION

INVESTMENT decisions are among the most difficult in business. The value of capital employed in modern industry in 1954 may have been five times as big as annual expenditure on wages and salaries according to estimates by Professor Barna.[1] And since once money is sunk in buildings and plant there is little chance of recovering it for many years, investment decisions need to be taken with care.

In the simplest terms the investment decision is concerned with the question of whether adding to capital now will increase the profits that can be earned in the future by sufficient to justify the expense.

Firms invest to take advantage of apparently profitable opportunities which arise in various ways. Old plant may be wearing out and must be replaced if profits are to be maintained; new markets may be opening up if new products have been developed or new production methods discovered.

Investment decisions will not always present themselves in such simple terms. The need to replace old plant often gives an opportunity to change to something newer and better even if the old methods of production will still do. It is strange that at the one extreme firms virtually ignore such opportunities while at the other some firms with obsolescence in mind design their plant to have only a limited life. Age is not a virtue in capital equipment. Change is rapid, and piecemeal attempts to keep pace with it are often unsatisfactory, although complete modernization is only profitable in certain conditions.

So long as the prime (or variable) costs of operating existing plant are less than the total cost of operating new plant a change from one to the other is not worthwhile. Full account must also be taken of improvements in the product and other advantages that may result. But the possibilities of benefit should not

---

[1] See the *Journal of the Royal Statistical Society*, Series A, Part 1 (1957), Table 5, p. 24. Up to date figures of capital stock are given in National Income and Expenditure published each year by H.M.S.O.

be viewed too pessimistically. Progress depends on a willingness to do something new and perhaps to be a little over-optimistic about the outcome. There is room for both optimism and pessimism about the results of change because the outcome is seldom certain and often depends a great deal on the efforts and energies of those responsible for it.

The more investment is undertaken with the object of doing something new rather than continuing in the old pattern the more uncertain the results of it are likely to be. Even if it is known that the demand for a product will increase there is no guarantee that it will be worthwhile increasing production facilities to meet the expanding market. It is fairly certain that the demand for cars in the United Kingdom will rise as incomes rise and that the number of cars owned per head is so far below that of the United States that saturation is some time off. It might appear safe, therefore, to plan to increase productive capacity in the motor industry. But it does not follow that it is desirable for every firm in the industry to increase its capacity, or that the individual plans of car producers will be exactly co-ordinated so as to provide for the anticipated increase in car ownership and no more. The chances are that there will be over-provision, for the cost of producing cars falls as output increases and this will encourage firms to plan for a large increase in output in the hope of being able to increase their output at the expense of their rivals and thus sell more cheaply.

Excess capacity is sometimes a problem; in the 1930s for example, it appeared to be serious because these were years of depression and there was only a slow increase in output over the whole period. The solution really lay in increasing demand but it was scarcely surprising that many industrialists here and in other countries got together to try to rationalize production facilities and eliminate some excess capacity. Today the danger of excess capacity is less because the level of demand has been high. But it is not always avoided. The reduction of Government support to the aircraft industry when a decline in the air force was planned in the late 1950s left that industry with more capacity than it could hope to employ; producers of generating equipment undoubtedly found themselves with excess capacity when the output of the British economy, and with it the demand for electricity, failed to expand as foreseen in the economic plan drawn up in 1965. Excess capacity may result from the failure of firms to take account of the actions of their competitors and from the consequent overestimation of their own share of the market. In some cases the amount of investment may be quite severely limited by the capacity of the market to absorb output. In the United Kingdom two Corning 'ribbon' machines suffice for the production of all electric bulbs consumed.

The decision to establish a plant for the production of a new product involves different considerations from a decision merely to maintain capital equipment or to increase the output of some existing product. Major uncertainties exist about the qualities of the article that is to be produced and about the potential market for it, about the feasibility of the production processes that are proposed, and the intentions of competitors. Since much of the new investment carried out in the United Kingdom in post-war years has been in industries where there are considerable returns to scale and where oligopolistic competition is the rule, the intentions of competitors have been major considerations in the investment decision. This applies, for example to the production of tyres and synthetic fibres and in the refining of oil. If the product is slow to catch on or is threatened by a similar article, initial investment may turn out to be too large. If, on the other hand, the product is a success and the development of rival products is delayed, production facilities will be inadequate. This may still be true even when the market for the production can be viewed with confidence, as happened in the case of synthetic fibre production in I.C.I.

I.C.I. had the advantage in this field of close co-operation with du Pont which enabled them to obtain a licence for the production of nylon in 1939 and to join with Courtaulds in establishing British Nylon Spinners. On the strength of American experience the large-scale production of nylon seemed likely to be a profitable venture and it does not appear that any very close calculation of demand and cost conditions lay behind the decision to start production in this country. The potential market could clearly absorb the output contemplated and the scale of output was big enough to spread overheads. Production was first begun in a pilot plant in 1947 and the main plant started work in 1948. The original plant cost about

£6 million, but it was thought that an expansion of capacity sufficient to treble output would halve the capital cost per lb. of nylon. Before maximum output was attained, therefore, it was decided to carry out the investment necessary to increase output at Pontypool from 10 to 30 million lb.

Terylene was discovered by Whinfield & Dickinson and developed by I.C.I. who carried out experiments at considerable expense in time, money and ingenuity, to discover whether terylene was the most desirable fibre to produce on a commercial scale. After I.C.I. had secured a licence to produce terylene it took 3 years to get a pilot plant into production and by then a decision had been taken to set up a full-scale plant to produce 11 million lb of terylene per annum. At this stage £14 million had been committed to research and production but before the first plant was completed it was decided to set up another plant costing £18 million.[2] By 1960, however, production of synthetic fibres had greatly increased and there was temporary saturation of the market, giving rise to attempts to rationalize production, with I.C.I. bidding unsuccessfully for control of Courtaulds who are large producers of nylon. The check to expansion was short-lived and the prospect towards the end of the 1960s was for a great expansion in the consumption of natural fibres. This does not mean, however, that severe competition will not be experienced by synthetic fibre producers: profitability depends on the relationship between productive capacity and demand and when capital costs are a high proportion of total costs, price cutting to keep plants operating at a high level of capacity can be severe, unless major producers are restrained by a fear of provoking retaliatory action by unilateral price cuts.

Investment undertaken with the sole object of supplying export markets poses special problems in relation to demand. The development of countries where living standards are low is bound to disturb the structure of industry in other countries; many products currently supplied by industrial countries can be produced more cheaply where there is cheap labour, and the drive for national industrial development frequently disrupts markets for products even where cheap labour is no great

[2] See D. C. Hague, in *The Structure of British Industry*, ed. by Duncan Burn Cambridge University Press, 1958.

advantage. In order to keep their markets many companies have found it essential to establish branch factories in developing countries. Often such investment is encouraged by special tax remissions and assurances that in the event of nationalization full compensation will be paid. But the risks remain. Much overseas investment has resulted in loss; as a survey by Professor Reddaway has shown.[3] If on the other hand the decision is taken to export to overseas countries rather than establish production there, sales are at the mercy of import duties, import restrictions and competition from both within and without the country. In chemicals, for instance, such competition may accurately be described as cut-throat and prices fixed for many products may bear little relation to long-term production costs. Overheads are high in relation to prime costs and when several products are produced jointly the distribution of overhead costs in the prices charged for products may be largely arbitrary. Thus, to invest mainly in the hope of exporting a substantial proportion of output is to run the risk that profit margins will be extinguished by some competitor disposing of chemicals which to him are something between a by-product and a waste product.

There must be the prospect of high yields if businessmen are to invest in overseas markets. New money for investment in underdeveloped countries, with all the uncertainties involved including the major one of expropriation, may be available only if it is expected that the investment will give a return to the company of 20 per cent or more on capital, and companies wishing to invest in particularly risky undertakings in this category might have to offer investors a 20 per cent return on capital before they put up the money. Many plantation and mining shares have had to offer investors more than 20 per cent because of the risks involved, and this is without counting money put to reserves.

The choice of investment opportunities may be dictated by the existing interests and commitments of firms and individuals; firms look first for opportunities in their own industries and only then at opportunities in other industries in which their commercial interests or expertise are likely to give them some advantage. The profit records of industries vary greatly and

[3] *Effects of U.K. Direct Investment Overseas*, W. B. Reddaway et. al. C.U.P. 1968.

their current state of profitability is a factor encouraging or discouraging new investment in them.

The Economist regularly published figures of profits over a number of years and related them to the capital employed in various industries. One such measure takes gross profits, before tax, as a percentage of total net assets.[4] In 1952, the rate of return over the whole of industry was about 20 per cent, falling intermittently to about 12 to 15 per cent in the early 1960s and in subsequent years. The experience of individual industries and individual firms has been much more variable. The textile industry was very depressed in the inter-war period and while the return on money invested in it was quite high. at the end of the war it soon fell well below the return obtained in consumer trades; more recently the decline in profitability has been arrested with the organization and modernization of the industry so that it is now about average. The same cannot be said for the shipping industry for which the return on capital invested fell so catastrophically in 1959 to about 2 per cent, where it remained for some years. Shipbuilding also suffered a catastrophic decline in profitability; in 1965 and 1966 losses were recorded by many companies and it still remains to be seen whether effort to reorganize the industry will improve profitability. At the other extreme the return on shops and stores and catering and entertainment has been comparatively stable and higher than the average for all types of industry; in the former group returns of over 15 per cent on capital appear to have been normal. The return obtained from investing in property has been low. In some cases this may have been due to the effect of rent restrictions; for other types of property the explanation may be that investment in property is generally regarded as comparatively safe and investors are prepared to accept low yields. Part of the profit from such investment accrues in the form of capital gains and if these are taken into account the return would be much higher than profit figures indicate.

There is a fortuitous element in the profits recorded in any year, reflecting temporary market conditions, the effects of government policies, strikes and so on. The state of the economy vitally affects profitability but this has been less noticeable in

[4] Total assets *minus* current liabilities.

conditions of general prosperity than it was before the war. In general, we should expect firms in risky industries to continue only if they were able to obtain abnormally high profits, although it is possible that they might constantly underestimate the risks or overestimate the profits obtainable. Similarly we should expect firms engaged in industries where frequent innovation and changes of technique are a predominant feature to earn high profits, but reality frequently belies economic expectations. Probably the easiest way to secure high profits is by establishing a monopoly: the Monopolies Commission found, for example, that the British Oxygen Corporation made exceptionally high profits on capital employed by virtue of its monopoly position.

Table 7.1 shows the ratio of net income to net assets in quoted public companies in the United Kingdom for the four years 1964-1967. The figures have been prepared by the Board of Trade (not *The Economist*) and those for 1967 are provisional because not all company accounts were available for analysis.

A superficial interpretation of the various figures on profitability would suggest that investment in shops might be more profitable than investment in new ships or shipyards. Even if this is true as a generalization, individual companies will fare differently from the average and there may be opportunities to make substantial profits and obtain a satisfactory return on capital in industries which have shown an unprofitable record. The Norwegians do not seem to find the operation of shipping unprofitable and it may be suspected that if they were to take over British shipping companies profitability would be greatly improved. The record of the shipbuilding industry is a depressing one but this does not mean that investment must cease or that it will necessarily be unprofitable in the future. Those shipbuilders wishing to remain in the market for really large tankers have little alternative but to develop large building docks. The prospects for successful development along these lines were apparently favourable enough to persuade the Shipbuilding Industry Board to finance the construction of such a dock for Harland and Wolff. But in so doing they may have had regard to the social returns to be expected from keeping men at work in a shipyard as well as to the financial returns shown in the company's accounts on the money invested.

Present profitability is always an uncertain indicator of future prospects and determined and astute businessmen can make apparently unpromising ventures profitable on occasions.

TABLE 7.1

RATIO OF NET INCOME TO NET ASSETS IN QUOTED PUBLIC COMPANIES IN THE UNITED KINGDOM, 1964–67

	Net income as percentage of net assets			
Industry	1964	1965	1966	1967
Food	14.6	14.6	12.6	12.6
Drink	15.0	14.0	12.3	11.8
Tobacco	17.0	16.8	16.6	12.3
Chemicals & Allied industries	13.5	12.6	10.7	11.1
Metal manufacture	10.7	10.6	7.7	10.5
Non-electrical engineering	12.3	13.1	12.3	12.0
Electrical engineering and electrical goods	15.2	13.7	13.3	13.4
Shipbuilding & marine engineering	3.3	−4.3	0.8	5.8
Vehicles	16.1	15.3	12.0	8.9
Metal goods not elsewhere specified	17.9	16.4	14.8	14.8
Textiles	14.3	14.1	12.1	12.3
Leather, leather goods and fur	17.0	14.7	12.2	9.8
Clothing and footwear	15.2	13.0	10.9	12.4
Bricks, pottery, glass, cement	18.0	16.4	14.1	14.9
Timber, furniture, etc.	16.0	14.2	11.5	12.3
Paper, printing and publishing	14.0	13.4	11.8	10.8
Other manufacturing industries	15.3	13.5	12.2	12.4
Construction	21.6	18.4	14.6	16.6
Transport and communication (excluding shipping)	12.8	12.1	10.6	12.1
Wholesale distribution	15.5	14.8	13.2	12.4
Retail distribution	19.0	17.7	17.2	16.7
Miscellaneous services	15.9	13.7	13.7	13.6

Source: *Statistics on Incomes, Prices, Employment and Production*, No. 28, March 1969.

Note: Net income is gross trading income less depreciation
Net assets are total capital and reserves net of depreciation.

THE CALCULATION OF RETURNS AND COSTS

Once a potential area for investment has been identified it is necessary to assess its potential profitability.

It is now more than thirty years since Keynes set out in *The General Theory of Employment, Interest and Money*[5] the conditions under which a firm would maximize its profits from an investment project, but it is only recently that this method and variants of it have received recognition from the business community. At first sight this seems surprising but *'Thrusters*

[5] Macmillan, 1936.

and Sleepers[6] and the writings of Carter and Williams[7] indicate that many investment decisions are taken on an irrational basis. Reluctance to adopt Keynesian ideas may have been due to concern with other objectives than the maximization of profits, such as growth,[8] but the uncertain outcome of investment may have been more important in deterring businessmen from undertaking a thorough-going analysis on the convenient assumption that the element of chance outweighed the refinement of economic calculation. Investment decisions are particularly likely to suffer in this way because they have a long time horizon during which it appears that anything may happen to upset the most carefully laid plans; it is tempting to avoid the pains of analysis in such circumstances and to trust to luck, proceeding on the basis of hunch or follow-my-leader principles. It is better, however, to identify elements of certainty; to test them for sensitivity to alternative assumptions, and finally to decide whether to invest or not in the light of the analysis.

The necessity for some investments may be clear cut without any analysis—to meet a requirement of the Sanitary Authority for example—but in most cases there is some latitude. The investment decision in large companies often presents itself in the form of a choice between alternative projects which cannot all be accommodated within the funds available for investment, or which may not all meet the criteria of financial return laid down by the company.

The first step in choosing between alternative projects is to try to establish for all of them the costs and returns involved. Estimates may need to be prepared for a number of years, covering the full life of the investment. The preparation of such estimates is much more difficult than the application of investment criteria to the data.

We are concerned to estimate the cost of the investment itself, the running costs that will be attributable to it in each

[6] P.E.P. Study mentioned earlier.
[7] See for example, *Investment and Innovation*, Oxford University Press, 1958 and B. R. Williams & W. P. Scott, *Investment Proposals and Decisions*, Allen and Unwin, 1965.
[8] See W. Baumol in 'Measuring the Productivity of Capital,' an essay in *The Management of Corporate Capital*, edited by Ezra Solomon, p. 22, The Free Press of Glencoe, 1959.

year of its operation and the revenues that are expected. These will not all be easy to define. Some increase in overheads and in existing running costs may have to be taken into account as well as purchases of raw materials, wage payments, fuel costs etc. Depreciation of the capital equipment involved is not included as a cost in making these estimates because it is taken account of in the subsequent analysis in various ways. Against running costs it is necessary to set receipts; sometimes these will correspond to sales receipts, but in other cases the product will be processed further by the firm undertaking the investment and appropriate estimations of the value of the product will have to be made. When estimates of running costs and receipts have been prepared for each year net receipts may be calculated. They will not always be positive; restitution of land at the end of an opencast coal-mining operation will involve a net cost of considerable magnitude, and in other years losses may be made. The cost of the investment may often be established with greater assurance than the expected returns, but this is not always the case. With experienced surveyors the cost of constructing a building can often be estimated within a few per cent provided that specifications are adhered to and no unusual difficulties are encountered. Costs of machinery and its installation may also be estimated fairly closely from manufacturers' quotations. If, however, some radically new process is to be launched with no certainty that it will work full-scale without experiment and modification, ultimate costs may be far from certain. This is all the more likely in the case of countries at an early stage of development when the background information and experience for close estimation may be absent. It may well happen that the cost of a major project such as the construction of a dam will escalate to double the original figure between the time it was first given serious consideration and the time the final accounts are paid; the time taken for its construction may also be greatly underestimated and this affects costs and the viability of the investment itself. Sometimes costs are deliberately underestimated or little attention is given to circumstances that could arise to increase them greatly. Sometimes this may be part of the strategy of those committed to a new idea in order to get it accepted, as may happen from time to time in the case of industrial projects as well as defence projects put up to governments. It is a skilful administrator who can sense and establish that a project is radically under-estimated before it reaches the stage of acceptance in prin-ciple. If estimates are suspect it is not uncommon to appraise them in the light of the reliability of previous estimates from the same source, although this may fail either because the new project is different in kind or because by chance it deviates markedly from the general run of past experience. When a succession or group of projects can be regarded as a whole, as in the case of the adoption of a series of research projects by a company, it may be acceptable to concentrate on the average returns from the projects without attempting to appraise the probability of success or failure in relation to any one of them, thus looking to some kind of statistical averaging of estimat-ing errors. For this to happen there must be no general bias in the estimates prepared for the individual projects making up the series.

Most capital projects can be completed in a relatively short span of time; this makes it easier to estimate their cost. Running costs and earnings start only after the investment is completed and continue for many years. Since it is difficult to forecast for a long period operating results are correspondingly more in doubt; for example, the course of raw material prices or the price of the finished product and its market may develop differently from expectations.

It is possible to make too much of such uncertainties. Some of them may be reduced or eliminated by long term contracts; many investment decisions are concerned with improvement in existing methods of manufacture, or with the replacement of machinery used for the manufacture of some existing product where the element of uncertainty is less. In any case the results of the first few years of a plant's operations are more important than those of later years, when output may be running down or the prices of products may be falling to an unprofitable level; most systems of investment appraisal give less weight to the financial results in the more distant future.

Even so the element of uncertainty must be considered. Some analytical devices try to gauge the best and worst results that are likely to emerge on various assumptions and so try to narrow the area of doubt. The investment decision may then be considered in relation to the worst result that it is thought could materialize bearing in mind that this view may prove to be pessimistic.[9] In choosing between risky projects a maximin strategy may be followed, in which case projects with the risk of serious loss might be rejected even if there was the opportunity in favourable circumstances of large gains. Another approach might be to accept projects involving high risks only if the prospect of gain were substantially higher than average and it might be convenient to work out some convenient rule of thumb relating risks of increasing severity to gains of progressively increasing magnitude. Assessment of risks and the allowances to be made for them can often be made after analysing the potentiality of investment projects on the supposition that the costs and receipts estimated for them can be regarded as firm. If necessary, calculations can be made on the basis of alternative assumptions without attempting to incorporate all possible outcomes at every stage of the calculations. We proceed along these lines in the rest of the chapter, making no allowance for uncertain outcomes.

A number of techniques for appraising investment projects are in use, some of them representing convenient and first approximations to more refined analysis.

The most familiar of these in the *rate of return method,* which expresses the yearly net return from the investment as a percentage of the capital invested. The method may be convenient in relation to investment in financial assets but it is less easy to use in appraising the merits of investment projects. The reason is that earnings vary from year to year and must be averaged in some way; another is that provision must be made in the calculation for depreciation or writing down the value of the capital employed in order to arrive at a suitable average. In suitable cases the method will give approximately the same answer as yields calculated in a more sophisticated way; the analysis of the Victoria line discussed later in this chapter is a case in point. The method fails to take account of the time value of money.

Another approximate method of appraising investment pro-

---

[9] A good discussion of these matters appears in articles in the *Harvard Business Review* by John F. Magee, *Decision Trees for Decision Making* (July-August 1964) and *How to Use Decision Trees in Capital Investment* (September-October 1964.)

jects is to calculate the *payback period*. This simply consists of working out how many years will elapse before the cost of the investment is met out of the net expected receipts. The method is simple and widely used but it has serious analytical defects. It pays no attention to what happens after the payback period has been completed; it attaches no weight to the pattern of earnings within the payback period itself, and ignores the fact that an investment project with large earnings in the first few years and smaller earnings thereafter is to be preferred to one for which the reverse applies. Greater refinement of analysis is necessary if these defects are to be overcome.

The reasons for the continued use of the payback period as an investment criterion is that it may suffice to identify some obvious non-starters (or starters), to concentrate attention on the need to make money turn over quickly in times of financial stringency and to avoid long payback periods where risk of obsolescence is an important element. The method can be justified only on the grounds that in practice it does not give results radically different from those given by more refined methods with the added advantage of being easier to apply.[10] It also suffers from the defect that it may give insufficient attention to the change in the real value of money over time.

A possible practical compromise in such circumstances is to use the payback criterion (with all its defects) for small investment projects for which the responsibility of making decisions has been widely delegated, major investment decisions being decided by more refined criteria. One such method involves calculating what is known as the *internal rate of return* for the investment.[11]

The method is an attempt to take account of the present value of future sums of money. Money in the future is worth less to us than money in our pockets today, because between now and a future date it can earn interest. The opportunity cost of holding money is therefore the interest which could be earned in the period in which it is held. The process which takes account of this fact is known as discounting, which is most easily understood as the reverse of the process of accumu-

[10] For some indications of this see Myron J. Gordon, The Payoff Period and the Rate of Profit, in Ezra Solomon, op. cit.
[11] Keynes developed the concept under the title of the marginal efficiency of capital.

P

lating money at compound interest. If we have a sum of money A_0 and accumulate it for a year at a rate of interest r, where r is expressed as a proportion rather than a percentage (0.05 rather than 5 per cent for example), it will grow to $A_0 (1+r)$ at the end of the first year. We are assuming that interest is paid at the end of the year. If the principal plus accrued interest is left to accumulate for a further year, the total sum invested will increase to $A_0 (1+r) (1+r)$, and so on for as many years as we care to consider. We can express the sum that will be available at the end of any year in the form $A_0 (1+r)^n$ where n is the number of the year we are considering. The sum can be regarded as equivalent in present value to A_0, the sum we started with, because A_0 becomes $A_0 (1+r)^n$ after n years and it is in this sense that the two values are equivalent. Now suppose we think that at the end of year n we shall have a sum of money A_n and we want to find its present value. All that it is necessary to do is to divide this sum by $(1+r)^n$. We know that this will give us the right answer because in order to get the value of a present sum at the end of n years we would multiply by the same factor $(1+r)^n$. If we call the present value of the sum A_n (at the end of n years) A_0, we have :

$$A_0 = \frac{A_n}{(1+r)^n} \text{ or } A_0(1+r)^n = A_n$$

Thus whenever we have a future value we can establish a present value by using a rate of discount r.[12] What rate of discount r would equate the present value of the expected future net receipts from an investment with the present value of the investment outlay? This requires solution of an equation of the form given below in order to determine the internal rate of return. In effect this is a measure of the return expected from the investment; it can be compared with the interest that would have to be paid on money borrowed for the project, to give an indication of potential profitability, or used as one means of ranking projects according to profitability.

$$A_0 = \frac{A_1}{(1+r)} + \frac{A_2}{(1+r)^2} + \frac{A_3}{(1+r)^3} \text{ etc.}$$

[12] It is true that there is some degree of conventionality in equating future and present values in this way, for money invested at interest may or may not grow at an even rate. In business it seldom does.

In practice we shall not have an unlimited number of terms on the right hand side and this will make it easier to find a solution to the equation. One way of reaching an answer is to try some values for r, gradually getting nearer to the correct answer by a hit or miss procedure. There may be more than one value of r satisfying the equation as the following simple case illustrates. It assumes that the cost of the proposed investment is 1 and that this leads to a return of 7 at the end of the first year and a loss of 12 at the end of the second year. The internal rate of return is the value of r for which:

$$-1 + \frac{7}{(1+r)} - \frac{12}{(1+r)^2} = 0$$

In this case r can have two values, 3 or 2 corresponding to 300 and 200 per cent,[13] as may be easily verified by substituting the values 3 and 2 for r.[14] Even when only one value of r satisfies the equation circumstances can arise in which the rate is misleading.

One difficulty associated with the unmodified application of the method is that it relates only to internal conditions, thus failing to take into account the possibilities of borrowing money from banks or other sources of finance. It also assumes that all proceeds can be reinvested at the rate of return on the specific project. Projects ranked according to the internal rate of return may be ranked differently if borrowing is introduced as an element in the situation. Suppose, for example, that two investment opportunities Y and Z are contemplated, each involving an initial expenditure of 1; Y is expected to give a return of 0 at the end of the first year and 4 at the end of the second year while Z is expected to yield 2 and 1 in the first and second years respectively $(Y(-1, 0, 4), Z(-1, 2, 1))$. Using the internal rate of return criterion, Y yields 100 per cent and Z 141.4 per cent. Suppose, however, that the possibility of borrowing at 10 per cent is introduced into the problem. If Y is selected and 2 borrowed at the end of period one and repaid

---

[13] The examples are taken from Myles M. Dryden, Capital Budgeting: Treatment of Uncertainty and Investment Criteria, *Scottish Journal of Political Economy*, November, 1964, pp. 235–259.
[14] In practice it may be judged that the possibility of multiple solutions may not be very great.

at the end of period two with interest, the pattern of return becomes (−1, 2, 1.80). The return of 1.80 in the final year represents 4, the original return, less 2.20, the repayment of principle and interest to the lender. It now appears from inspection that Y is to be preferred to Z, for it gives the same yield in the first period and a higher yield in the second period.

An alternative criterion for the ranking of investment projects is the *net present value* criterion. It is similar to the internal rate of return criterion in so far as both methods reduce future to present values by a process of discounting; but it differs in the essential that the rate of interest used in the process of discounting is first determined. It might be determined either in relation to the cost of raising money or the alternative yields that could be obtained from lending the company's money to outsiders. Different projects are compared using the selected rate of interest. There is nothing to prevent the rate of interest being varied over the investment period if, for example, it is thought that interest rates will be higher or lower in the future than in the present, but such variation must apply to all projects. The interest rate selected for discounting purposes is the minimum rate of return acceptable either in terms of cost or opportunity. If the project provides a higher rate of return than this, the present value of the future stream of yields will exceed the capital expenditure needed; there will be a positive net present value. The rate of return may give a net present value of zero; in this case the acceptable rate of return coincides with the internal rate of return. Had a higher or lower rate of return been chosen the net present value would have assumed a negative or positive present value.

It will not always follow that the results given by the two criteria will indicate the same course of action. If the company is able to borrow money it will not be interested in the rate of return of a particular investment project so much as the net present value. Thus in choosing between two mutually exclusive projects the more expensive may offer the lower yield and the less expensive the higher yield. Provided that the lower yield is sufficiently greater than the cost of borrowing, the more expensive project may have a greater net present value, because in effect it may be possible to make greater profit in total by using a larger sum at a lower rate of return. This would not be the case if the company were unable to borrow and constrained to restrict its investment programme to the sum available; in this case the company would look for the greatest return that it could get from its own resources, and the internal rate of return would enable different projects to be ranked effectively, although difficulty would be experienced in comparing projects of different length of life and projects with different and incompatible capital requirements.

Too much should not be made of the differences between the internal rate of return criterion and the net present value criterion; in practice the differences are not likely to be a very significant item in the investment decision as a whole.

The process of comparing costs and receipts on the basis of present values may appear complicated and artificial, but all that it amounts to is deciding whether the net revenues attributable to the project will serve to repay the principal and accrued interest in the case of borrowed funds or to provide for depreciation and the required rate of return when internal finance is used.

This can be demonstrated fairly simply by taking as an example a project with a life of 3 years (it could be any number of years). The internal rate of return is determined from an equation of the following type:

$$A_0 = \frac{A_1}{(1+r)} + \frac{A_2}{(1+r)^2} + \frac{A_3}{(1+r)^3}$$

if all terms are multiplied by $(1+r)^3$ we have:

$$A_0(1+r)^3 = A_1(1+r)^2 + A_2(1+r) + A_3$$

In words, the sum expended on the investment accumulated at compound interest for three years at the internal rate of return is equal to the return at the end of the first year's operation, similarly accumulated at compound interest (but for only the two remaining years of the project), plus the return at the end of two years with interest accrued in the third year plus the final yield at the end of the project's life.

A critical factor in deciding whether to invest is the rate of return that is acceptable; this depends on the kind of investment that is being contemplated and on the body concerned.

Almost any rate of return reflects market pressures. It is scarcely practicable for a company to seek a return on an investment of 50 per cent if its competitors are going to be satisfied with 15 per cent; the rate of return sought by government is unlikely to be very different from the cost of borrowing money; similarly for industry the rate of return that is acceptable will be related to the cost of raising money from either banks, other financial institutions or shareholders.

From the point of view of the directors of a company investment seems worth while whenever there is a sufficient difference between the cost of raising money from investors and the expected return from the employment of additional amounts of capital in the business. The cost of raising money varies and depends on the purposes for which it is needed and on general economic conditions. In the post-war period it has been necessary to pay from 5 to 9 per cent for money to buy or build houses and the rate of interest that it has been necessary to offer on debenture issues has been of the same order of magnitude. The Government has generally been able to borrow more cheaply, but yields on some government stocks have exceeded 8 per cent for short periods. The range of yields on ordinary shares has been much wider. Investors have been willing to provide money for investment in some companies at a nominal yield of no more than 2 per cent. But they have done this in the hope that the profits of those companies would expand greatly and that future yields would be much higher in relation to the capital originally invested. For companies that offer no more than average growth possibilities in addition to providing a hedge against rising prices, but which are large, well known and well managed, yields have been rather higher. The yield on ordinary shares included in the Financial Times index has often been around 5 to 6 per cent, but in the autumn of 1968 after a remarkable rise in the prices of stocks and shares it was less than 4 per cent. These yields are, of course, dividend yields, expressing the value of the last dividend as a percentage of the market quotation for the share. Companies do not usually pay out the whole of their profits and the fact that part of the profits is put to reserve is an attraction to shareholders in addition to the dividends currently paid out, for they own the company and its accumulated profits. Investors, however, set more store on the amounts that are paid out,[15] and attach rather less importance to the sums put to reserve. Thus it is not unrealistic to picture a large company as being able to raise new money for its operations on the strength of an intention to pay a dividend giving the investor a yield of say 4 per cent in the conditions ruling in 1968.

The Economist's figures of the rate of return on capital show that for many industries the rate earned on existing capital, valued according to accounting conventions, was much greater than the dividend yields acceptable to investors. Thus we might be inclined to judge that in practice there is no close correspondence between the rate of return that can be earned in business and the rate at which investors would subscribe new capital.[16] It is not easy to be sure how great the difference is. The rate of return calculated on companies' assets may be misleading, because assets are revalued only periodically, and in inflationary conditions when costs rise continuously assets may be understated in terms of current prices; moreover the rate of return obtained by shareholders in the form of dividends may well be augmented substantially by an increase in the real assets of their companies, resulting from ploughing back undistributed profits, and an increase in their monetary value that may provide some hedge against inflation.

Another complication is that the rate of return on capital calculated from companies' profit and loss accounts and balance sheets is an average rate of return which may not correspond at all closely with the rate of return that can be obtained on new investment. It is this marginal rate of return that is relevant to the investment decision. There are theoretical reasons for supposing that it is likely as time goes on that the yield from investment would fall since it is reasonable to suppose that the most profitable investment opportunities are taken first, leaving less promising ones for later exploitation. But the real world does not reflect this expectation. Invention and innovation open up new production possibilities making large demands on investment resources, and it is not at all obvious how this will affect the demand for capital and the yield that can be expected

---

[15] See G. R. Fisher, 'Some Factors influencing Share Prices', *Economic Journal*, March 1961.

[16] From the point of view of welfare economics it may be noted that the return to investors is much reduced by taxation.

from new investment in an era when consumers' tastes and preferences are also changing. What is certain is that the opportunity for profitable investment shifts quite rapidly and that the apparent yield on capital assets varies from industry to industry and over time.

It is thus difficult to infer what rate of return should be sought by industrialists on the basis of past experience, and this is even more difficult to do when the question of the risks involved has to be considered in relation to yields.

Some general rules are clear : a company should not invest in its own affairs if it can obtain better results by investing somewhere else; it should invest when the expected yield, suitably discounted for risk, is greater than the cost of raising money for the purpose. It is not easy, however, to give a figure representing the application of these principles in any set of circumstances and quite impossible to do so for all sets of circumstances.

Basically the choice of an acceptable yield is for the company or individual concerned to make. A booklet prepared by the National Economic Development Council[17] draws attention to the need to consider the return on investment after tax. The reason for this is that the amount of tax paid does not depend on profits alone. The incidence of investment grants and initial allowances for depreciation increases the immediate return after tax on investments and this makes considerable difference to the outcome.

Table 7.2 draws on the NEDC booklet to give a practical illustration of how discounted cash flow calculations can be carried out and shows how they were related to the taxation imposed on companies at the time the booklet was written. Since then taxes have been changed and will no doubt continue to be modified in various ways. But the principles that are illustrated remain good.

Capital expenditure is taken at 1000. In the first year of operation an investment grant of 20 per cent of the initial cost is received under taxation and subsidy arrangements. Annual allowances for depreciation are also claimed in this year and they result in a saving in corporation tax on profits. If the company made no profits from its investment in the

[17] *Investment Appraisal,* H.M.S.O., 1967 edition.

TABLE 7.2

EXAMPLE OF A DCF COMPUTATION FOR AN INVESTMENT OF £1,000 IN NEW PLANT AND MACHINERY WHERE A 20 PER CENT INVESTMENT GRANT IS PAYABLE[1]

	A	B	C	D	E	F	G	H	I	J
Year	Capital expenditure	Investment grant	Gross profits before tax and depreciation	42½% corp tax on previous years' profits assuming no capital allowances C×42½%	Annual allowances granted against previous years' profits	Tax saved by allowances E×42½%	Corporation tax payable D−F	Company's cash flow after corp tax B+C−A−G	Discount factors for 7%	Discounted value of column H H×I
0	1000	200						−1000	1.000	−1000
1			165	71	160²	68	−68	434	.935	406
2			153	66	128	55	16	139	.873	121
3			144	61	102	43	23	121	.816	99
4			132	56	82	35	26	106	.763	81
5			121	51	66	28	28	93	.713	66
6			110	47	52	22	29	81	.666	54
7			99	42	42	18	29	70	.623	44
8			88	37	34	14	28	60	.582	35
9			77	33	27	11	26	51	.544	28
10			66	28	21	9	24	42	.508	21
11			55	23	17	7	21	34	.475	16
12			44	19	14	6	17	27	.444	12
13			33	14	11	5	14	19	.415	8
14			22	9	9	4	10	12	.388	5
15			11	5	7	3	6	5	.362	2
16					28	12	−7	7	.339	2
TOTAL	1000	200	1323	562	800	340	222	301		NPV = 0

Return 5.4% before taking investment grant and tax into consideration

7% after tax and grant

[1] The plant and machinery is for manufacturing not in a development area. It is assumed that the £200 investment grant is paid in the year following that in which the investment is made, i.e. year 1, and that in year 15 the capital has no scrap value. The rate of annual allowance is 20 per cent of the written-down value of the capital and the firm has profits against which it can be set immediately. Corporation tax is assumed to be at the rate of 42½ per cent in all years after a delay of about one year. (The delay between the accrual and payment of tax will vary from company to company depending in part on the date to which the annual accounts are made up.)

It is also assumed that gross taxable profits are equal to gross profits before depreciation.

² 20% of 800 (Investment grants are deducted from the original cost of investments in calculating annual allowances).

first year but had profits from other operations the tax saving would still be made. Column H shows the company's cash flow after paying corporation tax and the final column shows the present value of this after discounting by the appropriate factor for the year on a 7 per cent rate of return.

Present values of future sums can be easily calculated with the aid of tables of discount factors which are readily available. These cover a wide range of discount rates and greatly reduce the amount of arithmetic required in the analysis of investment decisions.

The figures have been so arranged that the discounted cash flow exactly equates the capital expenditure incurred. Thus at the rate of discount used the net present value is zero and is also equal to the internal rate of return. It is clear from the table how important the investment grant is in improving the rate of return. If no account were taken either of the investment grant or taxation the rate of return would be 5.4 per cent against 7 per cent after tax and grant; in effect, the investment grant and initial allowances reduce the capital the company needs to provide.

Variations in capital grants give government the opportunity to vary rates of return and to do this in a way that discriminates between areas. At the time the NEDC booklet was prepared the investment grant on new plant and machinery installed in development areas was 45 per cent and in Northern Ireland it was possible to get grants to cover 50 per cent of both plant and machinery and buildings. In a typical project this would have had the effect of raising the return on investment after corporation tax to about 10 per cent in a development district and to an even greater extent in Northern Ireland. The extent of this variation again illustrates the need to make calculations so that the correct policy decisions about the location of operations and investment can be taken. It is not just a question of re-doing calculations using the same earnings profile and making adjustments for differences in grants and other forms of assistance. Earnings themselves will depend on the location and may be affected by differences in transport costs, raw material costs, wage rates and on whether the region qualifies for the payment of the regional employment premium which is in effect a large subsidy on the employment of labour.

Table 7.2 illustrates the critical nature of the results of the first few years working. The earnings 'profile' is drawn realistically to suggest that the cash flow will be at its highest in the early years of the project and will gradually decline; the discount factor also by its nature increases progressively. Nearly 80 per cent of the total discounted value has accumulated by the end of the fifth year. The higher the rate of discount the more the profitability of the project depends on what happens in the first few years. Even if no decline in yearly earnings is assumed for a project lasting 25 years, 75 per cent of present value of the returns will accrue from the first 10 years of working if a rate of discount of 15 per cent is applied. Figure 7.1 shows the present value of £100 at future dates, illustrating how the discount factor operates. At a rate of discount of 15 per cent the declining importance of expected future yields is marked.

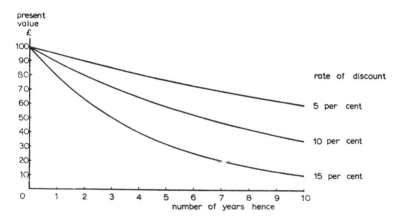

Fig. 7·1.   Present Value of £100 at Future Dates

The appropriate rate of discount may be much higher than 15 per cent. It is not uncommon in underdeveloped countries for industrial projects to yield 20 to 30 per cent. When this is the case the type of projects that qualify for acceptance in a development programme become severely limited. Projects which offer yields mainly in the long-term are unlikely to qualify unless the ultimate yields are very large. Emphasis will thus be placed on those projects which offer quick returns.

In some respects, risky investments may be regarded as being in the same category as investment decisions made when interest rates are high. The effect of high interest rates is markedly to discount the future; uncertainties about the outcome may be regarded as having the same effect as heavy discounting of future returns. This way of assessing risky projects is tantamount to saying that when a particular outcome is viewed with more than usual uncertainty it will be worth undertaking only if a successful outcome would produce a greater than usual yield.

The process of calculating discounted cash flows has a large number of applications and, suitably applied, is relevant to many types of industrial decisions. It can, for example, be used to resolve the question of whether to lease or buy some building or piece of capital equipment. Buying involves an immediate cash payment, leasing involves a succession of payments over the period for which the building or equipment will be used. It is again necessary to ascertain the terms on which money can be borrowed and to take into account tax allowances, capital grants etc.

Another example of the application of discounted cash flow techniques is in assessing the price to be paid for a firm. The basic approach is again to ascertain the value of future cash flows and to compare the discounted value of these with the purchase price contemplated. As A. J. Merret and Allen Sykes have pointed out[18] a number of circumstances peculiar to each contemplated purchase may have to be taken into account. Existing contracts with the firm's personnel may be relevant; if the firm to be purchased has made losses it may be possible for these to be offset against profits by the purchaser, so giving rise to tax savings; there may also be capital assets which can be realized because they will not be required by new owners who will put the firm's resources to different uses. Such factors need to be considered and evaluated; this is a question of establishing facts and establishing the range of possibilities that needs

[18] *The Finance and Analysis of Capital Projects*, Chapter 10, Longmans, 1963.

to be considered; once this is done however the discounted cash flow technique can be drawn on to appraise the advantage to the purchasing firm of the various courses of action open to it.

Another powerful use of discounted cash flow techniques lies in deciding how large a plant to build when demand is increasing. Large plants generally cost less to build per unit of capacity than small plants but if they are not operated to capacity for some time after they are completed, surplus capital is tied up in them. There is a point at which the increased costs of construction are balanced against the reduced unit cost of capacity inherent in the construction of larger plants. Too much excess capacity to begin with represents waste of capital; too little will mean that the possibilities of reducing capital costs per unit of output will not be fully exploited.

Professor Manne has shown how this kind of situation can be analysed in the case of an underdeveloped country.[19] He assumed that demand is increasing continuously at a constant arithmetic rate and that new plants are constructed at regular intervals. How long should these intervals be? A mathematical model can be used to give the answer.

Let D = annual increase in demand (tons/year) per year

x = time interval between construction of successive plants (years)

xD = plant size (tons/year)

$f(x$D$)$ = investment cost function for a single plant of size xD ($£$1)

r = annual discount rate, compounded continuously (per year)

e^{-rt} = present worth factor for costs incurred t years in the future

The function $f(x$D$)$ relates the cost of constructing a plant to the amount of output it can produce. Previously we have been assuming that interest is added at the end of any year; in this case interest is assumed to accrue continuously and the

[19] A. S. Manne, *Investments for Capacity Expansion*, Allen and Unwin, 1967.

corresponding discount factor is e^{-rt} corresponding to $(1+r)^{-n}$ in the previous analysis.[20]

It is assumed that every x years a plant will be built and that this process of expansion will continue indefinitely. Plants are assumed to last for ever, so no question of depreciation arises.

Now suppose a plant is constructed at some point of time which we can follow Professor Manne in calling a point of regeneration. The cost of construction is $f(xD)$. x years later a new plant will be needed because by that time the existing plant will be operating at full capacity. The present value of constructing this plant will be $e^{-rx} f(xD)$ (all plants are assumed to cost the same irrespective of the time at which they are constructed). x years later again another plant will be constructed with present value e^{-r2x} and this in turn will be followed with another plant with present value e^{-r3x} and so on infinitely.

Thus total discounted costs may be written:

$$C(x) = f(xD) + f(xD)e^{-rx} + f(xD)e^{-r2x} + f(xD)e^{-r3x} \ldots \text{etc.}$$

and this can be written

$$Cx = f(xD) + e^{-rx} \left\{ f(xD) + f(xD)e^{-rx} + f(xD)e^{-r2x} \ldots \text{etc.} \right\}$$

The expression in the curly brackets, which as before contains an infinite number of terms, may be seen to be $C(x)$ by looking at the previous line.

----

[20] The definition of e is the value that $(1+1/n)^n$ approaches as n tends to infinity. Consider a sum of money compounded at a rate of interest of r per cent per year paid n times per year (at a rate of r/n each time) as n becomes infinitely large. The capital plus accrued interest becomes $a(1+r/n)$ after the first payment of interest and $a(1+r/n)(1+r/n)$ after the second payment and so on. In any length of time x years, nx payments will be made so that at the end of x years the sum has become

$$y = a(1+\frac{r}{n})^{nx}.$$

$$= a(1+\frac{r}{n})^{\frac{n}{r}.rx}$$

$$= a\left\{ (1+\frac{1}{n/r})^{n/r} \right\}^{rx}$$

as n tends to infinity so does n/r, thus the expression in the curly brackets tends to e and the expression becomes $a.e^{rx}$. Thus y, the future value of a equals $a.e^{rx}$ and the present value a of the future sum y is given by

$$\frac{y}{e^{rx}} = y e^{-rx}.$$

Hence it follows that:

$$C(x) = f(xD) + e^{-rx}C(x), \text{ and } C(x) = \frac{f(xD)}{1 - e^{-rx}}$$

Now we can assume with some relation to actual cost functions in chemical industries that the cost function $f(xD)$ takes the form $k(xD)^a$ and this gives:

$$C(x) = \frac{k(xD)^a}{1 - e^{-rx}}$$

The problem now is to minimise this expression. Taking logarithms we have:

$$\log C(x) = \log k + a \log (xD) - \log (1 - e^{-rx})$$

Differentiating with respect to x gives:

$$\frac{d \log C(x)}{dx} = \frac{a}{x} - \frac{r}{e^{rx} - 1}$$

For minimum cost this expression equals 0.

If $a = 0.70$ and $r = 10$ per cent per year, $x = 6.75$ years.

If other values for r apply, the interval between the construction of plants will vary correspondingly. The higher r is, the shorter will be the intervals between the construction of plants; it costs more to have unused capacity and less of it can be justified in consequence. If a assumes a value of 1 there is nothing to be gained by constructing larger plants than those needed immediately; some simple rural industries might come in this category. Conversely if a is low the reduction in costs per unit of capacity in constructing large plants is very apparent and it will be worthwhile to construct plants at longer intervals even if this means that they have considerable excess capacity.

The principle of providing some excess capacity when demand is expected to increase can be justified in other cases than the production of chemicals. It applies to most 'lumpy' investments, to the building of motorways or to the provision of sewerage for a new and expanding town for example. Excess provision is often made in such cases as a safety margin and according to some customary rule of thumb; it probably does not cost very much more to put in the next larger size of sewer than one that would do; nevertheless it might be better to justify the decision by carrying out the appropriate discounted cash flow calculations.

Discounted cash flow techniques are not the final answer to all investment calculations. Linear programming is a powerful technique which may also be employed in appropriate circumstances, admitting the introduction of financial constraints into the calculation. For example an optimal solution may be sought, subject to the limitation of some desired level of liquidity throughout the planning period, and the requirement that the solution does not violate capacity limitations imposed by existing, associated plants. Receipts and outlays can still be discounted in reaching the solution. It may also be desirable to allow for leads and lags in payments and receipts and for feedback situations when the firm may wish, for example, to lend or borrow in order to maintain a required level of liquidity.

INVESTMENT IN THE PUBLIC SECTOR

Investment projects carried out by government or public bodies should be assessed in a similar way to those advocated for private business but the decision to invest should be governed by the costs and benefits that are expected to result to society. Thus the factors that must be considered are likely to have a wider range for the public than for the private sector of the economy and are to be regarded from a different point of view. First, many projects will be more politically orientated than those generally associated with private business and financial costs and benefits may be of less importance; second, many public investment decisions are likely to be less closely identifiable with the valuations of the market place; third, the State may be inclined to take a longer view than business. Many projects in the public sector may appear not to lend themselves to quantitative analysis. But even in apparently intractable cases, such as investment in education, numerical calculations can give some assessment of apparent yields, as has been shown for certain underdeveloped countries. The method followed is to try to relate the increased earning power of persons with certain educational attainments to the cost of providing the education needed. Calculations of this kind are imprecise but they may offer advantages over the arbitrary selection of administrative targets as a means to determine investment programmes, such as the attainment of universal literacy within a period of years, or the desirability of 25 per cent of the population having the advantages of advanced education. The wide ranging nature of public costs and benefits greatly complicates the investment decision. So far as the yields on investment are concerned the state is better placed to profit. The decision to invest in industry is made in relation to the returns anticipated by the firm, although other bodies will benefit in many cases. More capital is likely to improve workers' earnings; greater output at reduced cost will benefit consumers who can buy at lower prices and so on. Such additional returns do not accrue to the investing firm and probably in consequence it invests less than might be desirable on other grounds.

The state is better able to take the totality of benefits into account but will experience its own financial difficulties if it cannot increase its revenues as a result. However, it might be worthwhile for the state to invest at a loss or low cash return if it were satisfied that it was appropriate to finance the loss from general government revenues according to welfare or political considerations. Many of the benefits from government investment will not be easy to anticipate. The construction of a new transport route may have many repercussions beyond providing direct communications between places. It may be a factor in the establishment of industry as the Massachusetts Route No. 128 was in the Boston area of the United States; it will in many cases also be of benefit to those providing services such as the sale of petrol or the provision of catering. Nevertheless it is increasingly possible to identify some of the specific benefits to be obtained from public investment.

One such investigation, that of the cost-benefits to be secured from the Victoria line, has been described by Foster and Beesley.[21]

The construction of the Victoria line was authorized in August 1962, the first underground railway to be built in

[21] Estimating the social benefit of constructing an underground railway in London, C. D. Foster and M. E. Beesley, *Journal of the Royal Statistical Society*, Vol. 126, Part 1, 1963 p. 46. See also an article by the same authors, The Victoria Line: Social Benefit & Finances, *Journal of the Royal Statistical Society*, Vol. 128, part 1, 1965 and further discussion in vol. 129, part 2, 1966 of the same Journal.

Q

central London since before 1914. It was expected to take
5½ years to build and to cost some £56 million although
£8 million would have been incurred in any case in rebuilding
various stations along its route. The net cost can thus be put at
about £48 million. In calculating the benefits to be derived
from the line it was assumed as a first approximation that it
would have a length of life of 50 years. The tunnels and earth-
works may never need replacement, but there is always a
danger of obsolescence which makes it unwise to assume an
indefinite life. The precise assumptions about the span of operation do not, however, appear to alter the yields calculated for
the project very greatly.

Against the costs of construction must be set the benefits that
the line might confer.

It would have been wrong to have assumed that the benefit
derived from the line could be measured by receipts from travel-
lers, because fares are regulated by government and the transport tribunal in such a way that they bear little relation to
benefits. Another difficulty is that the whole structure of receipts
and costs in transport is distorted by the system of taxation of
motor vehicles. In addition non-users of the line were expected
to benefit from it because the diversion of traffic to it would
reduce congestion elsewhere.

Alternative methods of estimating benefits were used along
the following lines. The Victoria Line will save time for passengers; but what value should be placed on the time saved? Should
it be reckoned in terms of normal rates of pay or in terms of the
value which might be set on increased leisure? In the study it
was decided that journeys in working time should be valued at
7s. 3d. an hour and other journeys at 5s. It was also possible
to evaluate the increase in comfort and conveniences resulting
from the improved services in terms of time saved, on the
grounds that passengers could generally reach their destinations
in greater comfort if they travelled at some other time, either
before or after the rush hour for example. Estimates were
prepared of the value of time that would be saved by other
transport undertakings, because reduced congestion would
enable their vehicles to move faster, and so get through more
work in a given time besides saving petrol and tyres. The

calculation of savings resulting from these factors was complicated but sufficient data existed for it to be done.

As well as diverting traffic, the Victoria Line will have the effect of generating traffic because it is a new service offering additional and more comfortable facilities of travel. Time saving was again an important factor in estimating the benefits accruing to new users, on the ground that passengers had been deterred previously from making the journey because of the time it took. In addition, allowance was made for the fact that travel would be cheaper on the new line than on existing routes.

A further benefit was the saving in vehicle operating costs when traffic was diverted to the Victoria Line. This included, for example, savings in expenditure by private motorists when they travelled by train instead of car, and the reduction in costs following a reduction in public services which would no longer be needed.

The results of all these calculations are reproduced in Table 7.3 which shows the discounted value of benefits and costs using various rates of discount and arrives at estimates of the present value of net benefits. The social surplus rate of return expresses average net benefits over the whole period of operation and construction as a percentage of the capital invested. The figures shown are very close to the internal rate of return which was estimated to be 10.5 per cent.

Such rates of return are probably quite acceptable for investment in the public sector. Inevitably, however, with the method of calculating the benefits that had to be used, many of the benefits appear in the form of time saving and increased comfort and convenience; changes in the method of estimating these could affect the calculations quite considerably.

Another complication noted by Foster and Beesley in a re-appraisal of their estimations in 1965 was that a decision to raise fares in order to finance the line could greatly disturb the benefits accruing because it would have the effect of diverting traffic away from the rail system. This does not invalidate the form of the analysis but it shows the need to examine every aspect of the investment decision before deciding whether the benefits exceed the costs sufficiently to justify construction of the line.

TABLE 7.3

SOCIAL BENEFIT AND LOSS TABLE—VICTORIA LINE

| | Trend assumed | 5½ years' construction plus 50 years' operation | | | | | |
| | | Rate of interest 6 per cent | | Rate of interest 4 per cent | | Rate of interest 8 per cent | |
		Annual amount £m	P.D.V.† £m	Annual amount £m	P.D.V.† £m	Annual amount £m	P.D.V.† £m
(A) *Costs (other than interest charges)*							
Annual working expenses	0	1.413	16.16	1.448	25.07	1.391	11.14
Benefits							
(B) *Traffic diverted to V.L.*							
(1) Underground: Time Savings	0	.378	4.32				
Comfort and convenience	∅	.347	3.96				
(2) British Railways: Time savings	1½%C	.205	2.93				
(3) Buses: Time savings	0	.575	6.58				
(4) Motorists: Time savings	+	.153	3.25				
Saving in vehicle operating costs	+						
(5) Pedestrians: Time savings	++	.377	8.02				
	1½%C	.020	.28				
(B) Sub-total		2.055	29.34	2.055	45.30	2.055	20.35
(C) *Traffic not diverted to V.L.*							
(1) Underground: Cost savings	0	.150	1.72				
Comfort and convenience	∅	.457	5.22				
(3) Buses: Cost savings	0	.645	7.38				
(4) Road users: Time savings	0	1.883	21.54				
Savings in vehicle operating costs	0						
(C) Sub-total	0	.781	8.93				
		3.916	44.79	3.916	66.41	3.916	32.03

			.822	11.74	.822	18.65	.822	7.91
(D) Generated traffic								
Outer areas: Time savings	1½%C	.096		1.37				
Fare savings	1½%C	.063		.90				
Other benefits	1½%C	.375		5.36				
Central area: Time savings	1½%C	.056		.80				
Fare savings	1½%C	.029		.41				
Other benefits	1½%C	.203		2.90				
(D) Sub-total			.822	11.74	.822	18.65	.822	7.91
(E) *Terminal scrap value*				.29		.82		.10
(F) Total benefits (B+C+D+E)				86.16		131.18		60.39
(G) Net current benefit (F−A)				70.00		106.11		49.25
(H) Value of capital expenditure				38.81		41.14		36.68
(I) Net benefit (G−H)				31.19		64.97		12.57
(J) Social surplus rate of return §				11.3%		11.6%		10.9%

Notes: † P.D.V.s are present or year 1 values discounted at the relevant rate of interest set out in the column heading.
‡ The assumption is made that the trend will be 5 per cent for 15 years and 2 per cent thereafter.
§ Total benefits less costs other than interest charges (G) as a return on the capital invested (H), averaged over the whole period of operation and construction.
C compound
ø Assumed to fall to o at the end of 50 years of operation of V.L.

Chapter VIII

FINANCING

BROADLY, the firm has three main sources of funds: *internal funds,* or *self financing* derived mainly from the retention of past income in reserves, or through the sale of assets which the firm have acquired in the past; *long-term external funds,* in the form of loan and share capital; and *short- or medium-term external funds,* mainly in the form of bank credit, trade credit, hire purchase and similar shorter term obligations. The extent of the use of these sources in the United Kingdom is discussed in the Appendix to this chapter, pp. 257 ff.

There is a fourth aspect which is not a form of finance in the same way as the others, but is more strictly an allocation of available funds, or the improvement in the utilization and movement of funds within the firm. *Internal financial control or management* has the same aims as other financial decisions but the factors affecting it are different. The important point is that internal financial control, through the use of budgets, and attention to a number of appropriate financial ratios, enables the firm to augment and make better use of its internal resources.[1]

There is no such thing as an ideal way of financing a firm —the individual circumstances of each firm differ so much that each one has different requirements—but certain principles underly any financing decision.

There are four main considerations to be borne in mind:

1. The amount of money needed.
2. The time when it is needed.
3. The purposes for which the money is needed.
4. The form of finance to be used.

---

[1] Financial and operating ratios have two main uses. First is for comparison with other business briefly discussed in Chapter III; in this field, the service provided by Dun and Bradstreet and published in the journal *Business Ratios* gives information on key ratios for a wide range of industries and companies. Second is internal control, for which the ratios may provide useful guides to the utilization of resources.

There is a further consideration; whether it is profitable and worth while to undertake the expansion (or to start production at all). This question was considered in the discussion of the investment decision in the preceding chapter. Related to this, however, is yet another consideration: whether the proposed capital expenditure is to be used for the expansion of the business or in the maintenance of existing business (under which heading it is frequently convenient to consider not only replacement of assets but also such special requirements as safety and welfare).

Determination of the amount of money required is largely a matter of budgeting and forward planning. Overestimation of requirements is wasteful, since it involves the firm in payment of interest on funds which are not being put to any useful, profit-earning purpose; it is on the whole less serious than underestimation, which leads to the firm running short of funds before the project reaches a stage where it begins to pay its way. Not only does this lead to financial embarrassment *per se*, but it may also lead to greater difficulty in getting the extra funds which become necessary.

Timing is also largely a matter of budgeting: much capital equipment takes a long time to instal and reach the stage of profitable operation; it may also have a delivery date a long time ahead. At the extremes it takes several years to sink a coal mine, build a steelworks or a ship, or construct a power station or dam and even in less extreme cases the installation of much plant and equipment and the building of new workshops may take several months. Increases in working capital also need to be budgeted and provision made in good time, and possible seasonal variations in supplies and markets have to be taken into account.

The purpose for which the money is needed largely determines the form of finance which will be used. Long-term capital (internal or external) is almost always needed for the large-scale extension of productive capacity in the form of heavy plant, equipment and buildings. It is preferable, though not essential, that the capital for such purposes should be permanent, or, at the very least, not subject to withdrawal before the plant has started to pay for itself. The long term criterion of such finance is that the capital expenditure should pay for itself (or amortise itself) out of the profits earned from the plant.

Plant of a less durable nature—such as vehicles, contractors' plant, machine tools, etc., which can be written off over a period of 3 to 5 years—can be financed by medium-term funds; though it is possible and sometimes desirable to finance such equipment, along with durable plant, from long-term sources, and, in the case of a major investment decision, to bring all equipment into one long-term capital budget. Similarly, the financing of a very long contract—road building, factory building and so on—is often a good candidate for medium-term funds; the financing of the sale of capital goods (particularly in the export market) is also frequently undertaken from such funds.

Short-term funds are usually restricted to debt which is self-liquidating. Examples are the monthly payment of creditors, the financing of short-term contracts (up to 6 months), the financing of seasonal stock peaks, and the financing of production lags (of the seeds-to-harvest variety).

To some extent the form of finance used depends on the legal form of the firm. The unincorporated business initially has to rely for long-term capital on the contribution of the partners or the sole owner plus what it can borrow privately; later it may borrow from the bank, or it may acquire new capital *via* retained income, by bringing in new partners, or by a change to company status and the issue of shares; or it may at any time (if it can find lenders) raise funds by long-term borrowing on mortgage or by the issue of debentures. The private company can issue shares, but is restricted in the amount of capital it can raise in this way. The quoted public company can use the resources and contacts of the New Issue Market and can command access to much larger resources, both in total and proportionally, than its smaller brethren. Change from one legal form to another (e.g. from private to public company) may well be a way of raising funds by tapping new sources of finance, but before this is possible certain economic and legal conditions have to be fulfilled, and there are other implications, to which we return later.

Two further considerations have to be borne in mind: ownership and liquidity. Some forms of finance, of which ordinary share capital is the prime example, constitute a form of ownership, and raising funds in this way means that some ownership of the firm, and some degree of control, *via* voting rights, passes out of the hands of existing owners of the equity[2] of the firm. The degree to which this is acceptable to the firm depends on the existing structure of ownership and the attitude of the existing owners to any potential diminution of their power and control over the firm: one reason why many small firms are unable to expand is that their owners are loath to part with any share of the ownership—or, as they usually call it, their independence—and many of their potential lenders will not consider putting any money into the firm without receiving in return some degree of control. Other forms of finance, such as renting, hire purchase or any other form which requires payments at regular and specified intervals, whilst they do not raise the ownership problem, do represent obligations of the firm which may from time to time impair its liquidity, or its ability to settle its debts in cash or other acceptable forms of money at short notice: budgeting can avoid most of these problems.

PROFITS

Profit is the surplus of revenue from a trading operation left over after the expenses incurred in employing factors of production have been met.

The surplus is employed in the payments of dividends on equity capital (or risk capital), the payment of tax, and a transfer to reserves. Either in expectation or realization of high profits, 'top' management may get high salaries or bonuses in reward for its services; some of this the economist would regard as profit, the accountant would not, and most businessmen would wonder what all the fuss was about.

When it comes to the actual measurement of profit the economist and the accountant part company. Accountants adopt conventions in order to be able to do their work, economists disagree with the conventions because, they argue, they have little economic significance. Some of the disagreements relate to terminology and are not really very important, others to valuations and the treatment of items, which are more important.

Most of these differences can be highlighted by the use of

[2] Equity in this context means ownership and a right to a share in the earnings of the firm.

trading account and appropriation account (Table 8.1). This is an actual example, recast in such a way as to bring out the economic entities; in so doing it departs from accounting conventions.

TABLE 8.1

TRADING AND PROFIT AND LOSS ACCOUNT OF THE XYZ METAL MANUFACTURING COMPANY FOR THE YEAR ENDING JANUARY 12TH, 19....

			£
1.	OPENING STOCK		332
2.	PURCHASES less DISCOUNTS		3,206
	(Metal £2,234		
	Accessories £972)		
3.	CLOSING STOCK		597
4.	COST OF GOODS	(1 + 2 less 3)	2,941
5.	WAGES		31,549
6.	SALARIES		2,040
7.	OTHER COSTS		
	Advertising		233
	Fuel and power		1,996
	Rent and rates		1,636
	Repairs		106
	Carriage		839
	Packing		81
	Insurance		219
	Stationery		271
	Travel		48
	Cleaning		157
	Telephone, Postage		212
	Legal expenses		48
	Audit fee		63
	Interest		115
	Bad debts		2,136
	Sundry (car commission, etc.)		408
		Total other costs	8,568
8.	DEPRECIATION		1,769
		TOTAL COSTS	46,867
9.	NET SALES		53,637
10.	OPERATING PROFIT	(9–8)	6,770
11.	OTHER INCOME (Rent, interest, etc.)		515
12.	TOTAL RECEIPTS	(9 + 11)	54,152
13.	VALUE ADDED	(9 – 4)	50,696
14.	TOTAL PROFIT	(10 + 11)	7,285
	(INCOME FOR DISPOSAL)		
15.	DIRECTOR'S REMUNERATION		4,738
16.	TAX		1,194
17.	DIVIDENDS		863
18.	RETAINED PROFIT		490

The normal accounting definitions distinguish between gross and net profit. *Gross profit* is defined by accountants as the 'excess of sales (less returns) over the cost of goods sold directly attributable to putting the goods in a saleable condition. The cost of goods sold is the amount of the opening stock *plus* purchases (less returns) less the amount of the closing stock'.[3] *Net profit* is defined as 'the surplus remaining after charging against gross profit all the expenses, including depreciation, properly attributable to the normal activities of the particular business'.[4]

In contrast, economists usually consider gross profit to be much closer to the accountant's net profit; and net profit to be net of 'management salary', interest (both on borrowed money, and, implicitly on the company's reserves) and imputed rent on the buildings owned by the firm (if any).

Part of the difference is due to the desire of the economist to define his terms functionally in contrast with the accountant's desire to define them by enumeration. The accountant's gross profit comes somewhere between what the economist calls *net output* or *value added* and profit: it is the difference between sales and direct costs. In the example cited this is item 13 plus part of item 5. The *net profit* of the accountant is shown as item 10 (operating profit, or sales *less* costs): this is much nearer to what is generally thought of as profit.

To this is usually added the other income accruing to the firm in the form of rents, interest on securities held, etc., and the result can be called *total profit* (or income for disposal). From this sum certain allocations have to be made in the form of tax, transfers to reserves and dividends. Produced in this way the accounts show the composition of costs and sales, how the income resulting from the trading activities of the firm is distributed, and the pattern of costs is fairly clear.

But there are doubts about some of the items. This particular example was chosen because it illustrates one of the difficulties of profit measurement. The firm in question has less than 100 employees, and is controlled by three directors, one of whom is managing director. He receives one third of the *directors'*

---

[3] W. Pickles and G. W. Dunkerley, *Accounting* (2nd edn.) (Pitman, 1949).
[4] Ibid.

remuneration (item 7). The question is whether this directors' remuneration is profit (in the economist's sense) or whether it is all a sort of managerial wage. These three directors also own all of the shares of the company, and receive dividends of £863 (the reason why some of their reward is paid in the form of remuneration and some in the form of dividends is a function of tax law rather than logic: director's remuneration is earned income and taxed at earned income rates with appropriate allowances, a dividend is not).

Depending on how we classify these items, we get different measures of profit. If we include directors' remuneration as profit, the profit of the firm is £7,385, or roughly three times what it is if the item is excluded (£2,547).[5]

In many firms the managing director receives no salary but is rewarded entirely in the form of directors' remuneration: is this profit, or managerial wage? The accountant calls it all profit and indeed the Companies Act requires him to do so. Strictly, if we wish to assess profits accurately some allowance should be made for a managerial wage in these circumstances, the remainder being called profit.

In large firms, where most of the work of the entrepreneur is carried out by salaried managers, the difference made to the final profit figure by the method of calculation is proportionately much smaller since 'top' management salaries account for a much smaller proportion of total costs.

This particular question is, however, of little direct interest to the businessman, whose main concern is with the amount which he has available for distribution and retention, or more important still, what he will get in the future and what he must do in order to get it.

There are other points at issue which are of more practical significance. Most of these stem from a difference of viewpoint: the accountant is concerned with a factual historical record, the economist with the earning power of the business. An example of the sort of problem which may arise lies in the treat-

---

[5] For a further discussion of this point see James Bates and S. J. Henderson, The Determinants of Corporate Saving in the United Kingdom, *Journal of the Royal Statistical Society*, 1967, Series A, pp. 207–224, reprinted in P. E. Hart (ed.) *Studies in Profit, Business Saving and Investment in the United Kingdom, 1920–1962*, Vol. II. Allen and Unwin 1968. In this discussion, the salary or managerial wage, element in private companies in 1956 was estimated at £1,315 per annum.

ment of depreciation: in formal company accounts an asset is usually valued at its historical cost (i.e. what it cost to buy it), and written off over a period of years (a variety of methods is possible but they need not concern us here); the economist argues, however, that, in order to keep the value and earning power of an asset intact, it is often necessary to make further allowances. It is interesting that many firms find it necessary to revalue their assets in practice. An asset may depreciate in value through obsolescence, or through use, but if it is to be replaced in a time of rising prices further allowances may also be necessary to compensate for the increase in price of a replacement :[6] from all of these points of view it is more realistic to value assets at their replacement cost, and make the necessary adjustments to depreciation, than it is to use historical cost. The Inland Revenue authorities in Britain, in allowing depreciation (or 'wear and tear') as a cost do not permit firms to make any charge for obsolescence or rising prices. The firm wishing to maintain the earning value of its assets, however, has to make some such allowance, either annually or in the form of extra depreciation allowances; or, when it comes to replacing the asset, in the form of an extra large payment for a new asset. This extra amount must come from profit, on which the firm will have been taxed, but this is inescapable, and it means in effect that extra allowances have to be put to reserve to take account of the extra expenditure which will be needed.

Similar problems of valuation also apply to stocks which, strictly, should always be valued at replacement cost if the cost and profit figures of the firm are to have any real meaning. In times of rising prices, valuation of stocks at historical (or original) cost will mean that cost figures understate the true position, and profits are overstated; when prices fall the opposite occurs.

THE ALLOCATION AND FUNCTIONS OF PROFIT
After these adjustments have been made a surplus is available for distribution called TOTAL PROFIT, or INCOME FOR DISPOSAL

---

[6] There is a further complication: in a time of technological advance a machine will not usually be replaced by an identical machine but an improved model, frequently of higher price. Neither in theory nor in practice is it easy to sort out 'true' depreciation in a case like this.

in the specimen account; this is disposed of partly in the form of tax (which normally absorbs something over half the surplus), partly in the form of dividends and transfers to reserve. The two main functions of profits in the modern corporation are summed up in the last two appropriations. One function of profits is to provide a reward for the entrepreneur and the shareholder, partly in the form of dividends, partly as remunerations for directors. Dividends on ordinary shares, being non-contractual and residual, are more akin to profits than interest, and it is the ordinary shareholder who very largely undertakes the risk and uncertainty of business operations. Dividend on preference shares on the other hand is contractual and more akin to interest (from the point of view of the recipient) and a cost (from the point of view of the firm).[7]

The second main function is to provide for future expansion and to provide reserves for the expected and contingent future needs of the business. This is achieved by allocating the remainder of profit to reserves, either to some specially committed reserve (such as future taxation reserve) or to 'free reserves' —the actual allocation being largely a matter of book-keeping convenience. These reserves are rarely kept for long as a sum of money, but are continually used for the acquisition of assets (partly paper assets, such as securities, partly operating assets, needed for the actual running of the firm). The actual proportion of disposable income put to reserves depends on a variety of factors:[8] it is clearly influenced by the dividend decision in the first place, but considerations of prudence play a big part. The larger and less risky the company the more it is usually able to put to reserves, and it accordingly becomes even larger and less risky; but on the other hand many large and fairly speculative concerns tend to 'plough back' a high proportion of their profit in order to avoid having to go to the market for extra funds. In good years it is common to put by fairly large amounts to reserves, partly in order not to squander good

---

[7] Fixed-interest payments on long-term debt on the other hand are usually treated as a cost (and allowed as such by the Inland Revenue authorities) and not as an allocation of profit. Dividend on preference shares, although at fixed interest, is not allowed.

[8] See Bates and Henderson, op. cit.

fortune or the results of good management, partly in order to maintain dividend payments in times of adversity (some firms keep a 'Dividend Equalization Reserve Account' specially for the purpose) and in general to provide against possible bad times. In the years since the Second World War high company taxation has led to a substantial fall in the proportion of profits distributed.[9] Further, whilst the quoted public company sector as a whole has retained a slightly higher proportion of its income than before the war, large industrial companies have retained less. Small firms, which have proportionately smaller profits tend to retain a larger share in the firm, partly because they have to rely more on their own savings for expansion; the very biggest companies however plough back slightly more of their profit than do other public companies.

INTERNAL FUNDS

Internal funds consist of amounts retained from income in the past. The precise way in which profits are transferred to reserves is largely a matter of accounting convenience and convention, but there is a reasonably clear theoretical economic criterion of retained profit. Any amount of income transferred to reserves over and above what is required for the maintenance intact of the net worth of the firm (the assets of the firm, less the current liabilities; or alternatively, the equity or share in the firm of the shareholders or owners of the firm)[10] is retained profit. In practice, however, it is often difficult to determine this amount with any precision, and the determination of real net worth at any one time is frequently impossible. The answer may be in terms of earning capacity, or profitability of the assets of the firm, or of the replacement cost of the assets, but all of these are difficult to assess in practice; for example, the resale value of assets and earning power of assets both depend

[9] See S. J. Prais, 'Dividend Policy and Income Appropriation', in *Studies in Company Finance*, edited by Brian Tew and R. F. Henderson (National Institute of Economic and Social Research and C.U.P. 1959). Prais also shows (op. cit., p. 109) that in 1949 the one hundred largest companies earned over 25 per cent of total industrial profits, the remaining 2449 quoted companies earned 35 per cent, and private companies and unincorporated businesses earned 40 per cent.

[10] This is analogous to personal net worth (see Table 4.4), and it can be represented in balance sheet terms as the Total Issued Capital and Reserves of the Company (although in practice these only represent historical cost valuations plus any revaluations which may have been undertaken, and rarely represent real net worth).

on the fact that the firm is a going concern,[11] and are rarely related to the historical cost of the assets.

Part of the answer to these problems lies in the firm having a sensible attitude to and policy towards the valuation of assets, based probably on replacement prices, and making its accounting provisions for depreciation and replacement in accordance with such policy.

Strictly, therefore, depreciation provisions are not a source of funds, since they do not add to the net worth of the company; in a purely practical sense many firms treat such provisions as amounts of cash or resources becoming available in a certain period, and use them as a source of funds in the short run. In the long run this is not possible if assets are to be maintained intact.

The availability of internal funds depends on two things; past profits of the firm and its past policy with regard to the retention and distribution of profits. Policy in this respect may be complex: the firm cannot distribute all of its profits, even to keep shareholders happy with dividends, and indeed shareholders would themselves be unhappy to see nothing being put to reserve; but equally some dividend payments must be made and public companies in particular have to keep a healthy market in their shares if they are to use the capital market for raising new capital in the future. If too much is retained and used for the accumulation of liquid assets, mainly cash or marketable securities, the firm may lay itself open to the danger of take-over bids. The ability of small firms, whose directors own a majority of the shares, to pay out profits, up to a point, as directors' remuneration alters the form, but not the nature

[11] Contrary to what many accountants claim, this is a meaningful term. The valuation of a firm as a going concern is a measure of what the assets of the firm may be expected to earn in their present occupation; a historical cost valuation merely represents what the firm paid for the assets at the time of purchase. Historical cost valuations are economically meaningless: a firm's assets are either worth what they can earn or what they would fetch if sold. If the firm is sold as a going concern or if the assets are sold as working assets, they will fetch a sum calculated on a basis of what they could earn; if sold as scrap they would fetch another (much lower) sum. What the assets cost is irrelevant to either of these calculations. An experienced valuer should be able to put a 'going concern' value on the assets of a firm in the same way as he can assess the market value of a house or a motor car. From the book-keeping and auditing point of view historical cost valuations are perhaps reasonable, from the business point of view they are not. In any case, a reasonable compromise is a replacement cost valuation, which is not open to the objection that it is based on subjective elements.

of dividend policy. Taxation also plays a part, largely determining how much is left out of earnings for distribution: in the years following the Second World War, for example, high taxation led to a fall in the proportion of profits distributed as compared with the position before the war; but on the other hand, with the exception of the giant companies, who both distributed and saved less, public companies retained a higher proportion of their earnings than before the war.[12]

Internal funds are frequently the most important (sometimes indeed the only) source of long-term funds for small firms; and many of the industrial giants which we know today financed the early stages of their growth by this means, many of their owners going to what would nowadays seem extreme lengths in thrift and self denial in order to plough back profits for growth.[13]

Recent surveys[14] show that small firms tend to save more out of their profits than do large firms. They pay smaller dividends, less tax, and save more: private companies in 1954–56 saved 31.7 per cent of their trading profits, public companies saved 27.3 per cent; private companies saved 3.5 per cent of their net assets, but public companies saved 4.1 per cent. But more important, private companies relied on

[12] S. J. Prais, 'Dividend Policy and Income Appropriation', in *Studies in Company Finance*, edited by Brian Tew and R. F. Henderson (National Institute of Social and Economic Research and Cambridge University Press, 1959).

[13] The case of the Walker Brothers of Rotherham, iron founders, illustrates the importance of savings as a source of finance in the Industrial Revolution. They started business in 1741, both of the brothers working part time (Samuel teaching in a local school), in 1743 Aaron was employed full time, in 1754 Samuel gave up his school (the value of the concern was put at this time at £400); and from this time they allowed themselves 10s. per week each. Not until 1757, when the stock had reached £7,500 did they allow themselves a dividend—of £140, and throughout their lives dividends remained small. By 1774 their capital had reached £62,500; in 1812 the assets of Samuel Walker & Co. were estimated at nearly £300,000 (Samuel Walker had died in 1782, but his financial policies were continued by his heirs). See T. S. Ashton, *The Industrial Revolution. 1760–1830* (Oxford University Press, Home University Library, 1948), pp. 95–7. Ashton quotes many others who built up their firms in a similar way, including Wedgwood, Newton Chambers and others. He concludes: 'Industrial capital has been its own progenitor'.

[14] See J. S. Boswell, *I. C. F. C. Small Firm Survey* Industrial and Commercial Finance Corporation, 1968; Tew and Henderson op. cit., James Bates, 'The Finance of Small Business' *Bulletin of the Oxford University Institute of Statistics* (May 1958); James Bates 'The Finance of Small and Big Business', *Bankers' Magazine*, April 1961); and James Bates, *The Financing of Small Business*, Sweet and Maxwell 1964. These will be referred to in the remainder of this chapter as the National Institute Study (Tew and Henderson) and the 'Oxford Survey' (Bates).

R

retained profits to the extent of 44.7 per cent of total funds, public companies to the extent of 32.4 per cent; and within the private company group there was a tendency for small private companies to rely more on savings than their slightly bigger brothers.

This tendency for small firms to save more than big ones is partly due to the fact that they have to do so in order to grow at all (as will be seen later, they have particular difficulties in raising long-term capital). It is also partly due to the fact that they are less profitable than large firms, and simply in order to keep on relatively even terms they have to plough back a larger part of a relatively smaller sum. Even industrial giants, however, cannot rely entirely on external finance, even if they want to, and finance a large part of their expenditure internally. The large British oil companies for many years after the Second World War never went to the capital market for funds, but financed all of their growth from retained profits: this may have been partly due, as has been claimed, to the fact that their enterprises are rather speculative, and borrowing may have been expensive and difficult, but it also reflects the high profitability of such companies. The claim that the sums required were too large for the resources of the capital market is not substantiated.

It is sometimes argued that one of the major advantages of the use of internal funds is that they are free of borrowing cost, since the firm does not have to pay interest on its own money. The argument is illusory: the opportunity cost of initial funds is the alternative earnings from the money if it were put to other uses, such as purchase of securities or the buying of another firm. In some firms the rate of return on internally-financed assets is so low that the firm would have done better to purchase Stock Exchange securities or other paper assets. Failure to recognize this point may well result in bad investment decisions which do not reflect the true cost of capital.

LONG-TERM EXTERNAL CAPITAL

In this field the first distinction to be made is between Share and Loan Capital. Both involve the sale of some sort of security by the firm : share capital, as the name implies, is in the form of a share in the ownership or a prior right to a share of the profits of the firm; loan capital in the form of a prior right, both to interest and usually also over the assets of the firm, in the form of a mortgage or debenture. Share capital is never repayable save by permission of the High Court, though in quoted public companies it is marketable and is bought and sold on the Stock Exchange; long-term loan capital is repayable, the period varying from 10 to 50 years, and occasionally even longer; lenders cannot demand repayment before the 'term' of the loan, but are entitled to a fixed rate of interest, whether the firm is profitable or not; the security is usually marketable. If the firm defaults, loan creditors have the right to put it into liquidation in order to recover their principal and interest from the proceeds of the sale of its assets.

Share capital carries some share in the equity of the firm, and may be of two kinds. Ordinary share capital carries a vote proportionate to the number of shares held and receives a dividend in the form of part of the residual income of the firm after prior charges have been met. Preference shares rarely carry a vote, but have as compensation a prior right to dividend over the ordinary shares. There are several varieties of each of these types of share, but they need not concern us here; neither need the Stock Exchange implications of shareholding, but there are important policy considerations which affect the firm's attitude to, and distribution of, share capital.

First is the question of *gearing*. The gearing ratio (or leverage as it is known in the U.S.A.) of a firm may be defined as the ratio of the annual amount payable on prior charges, or fixed interest (on preference shares and long-term liabilities) to the annual income available for disposal; this acts as a limitation on the firm's freedom of choice in the raising of finance. The following calculation illustrates the point:

		1959	*1969*
A.	Fixed interest dividend payable	£25,000	£25,000
B.	Disposable Income	£50,000	£500,000
	Gearing (A/B × 100)	50%	5%

Clearly gearing matters less in good times (when a firm is making high profits, as in 1969 in the illustration) than in bad times (as in 1959 in the illustration), because fixed interest then represents a smaller burden on the firm. Since it is not always possible to predict profitability in advance, however, a reasonable guide to gearing may be obtained from the ratio of Preference Capital plus Long Term Liabilities to Ordinary Share Capital—where this is high, gearing is *potentially* high, and the owners and ordinary shareholders may be unhappy about the position—but in the last analysis it is the ratio of fixed interest to profit that matters. The gearing ratio in the National Institute study of quoted public companies in the years 1949–53 was 8.5 per cent; 60 per cent of companies had gearing ratios in the range 0 to 10 per cent; 18 per cent were in the range 11–20 per cent; 12 per cent were in the range 21–40 per cent; 6 per cent were over 40 per cent (and 4 per cent had negative income). Gearing was particularly high in the brewing industry. In the Oxford Survey half of the firms did not have any fixed interest commitments; 27.5 per cent had gearing ratios in the range 0.1–9.9 per cent, 7 per cent in the range 10–19.9 per cent, 4 per cent in the range 20–39 per cent, and 3 per cent were over 40 per cent.

From the ownership point of view most firms would prefer to issue preference shares, but they have to bear in mind that this would give them a high gearing ratio, which would commit an excessive proportion of their income each year, and would deter potential shareholders.

The possibility of obtaining fixed interest finance is also limited by the existing equity of the firm. Few outside investors would be willing to lend to a firm whose owners had what was thought to be an inadequate stake in the firm: this is particularly true in small firms with no long record of profitability; since many such firms are in particular need of funds and unable to contribute much in the way of self-financing, this may retard their expansion.

Ruling market conditions and the existing structure of interest rates in the country would influence the rate of preference interest which the potential preference share investor would want, and a time of high interest rates is rarely the best time from the point of view of the firm since, once committed to a rate of interest, this has to be paid regardless of the profitability of the firm or the economic climate and the later structure of interest rates. Tax considerations may also be important. In fact, the timing of any sort of issue is important and, since the raising of long-term external funds is in any case a fairly long drawn out procedure planned well in advance, the firm usually has a fair degree of latitude and within limits, can choose its time to suit market conditions. The raising of ordinary share capital is usually easier at times of good trade and high Stock Exchange share values, and it is in times like this that the issue of shares tends to be over-subscribed.

The New Issue Market in Britain is a fairly complex organization, consisting of a small group of issuing houses and merchant banks specializing in the issue of new share capital, whose prime function is to act as an intermediary between those who wish to issue share capital and those who are willing to invest in share capital. They will usually advise on the best form of capital, work out a financial plan, make sure that the complex Stock Exchange regulations are complied with, arrange any underwriting which may be necessary (under-writing is simply a guarantee by a financial institution to take up any part of an issue which is not bought), and—perhaps an important function as any—lend the weight of the house's name and reputation to an issue.

There are five main possibilities for the firm wishing to make a new issue of shares:[15] the offer for sale; the issue by prospectus; the placing; the Stock Exchange introduction; and the issue to shareholders. With an offer for sale, an issuing house buys the shares from the company and offers them to the public; with an issue by prospectus the issuing house undertakes to find subscriptions for the new issue of shares; both of these methods are expensive, and involve the issue of advertisements, and are rarely worth while for issues of less than £200,000 (the percentage of costs tends to be rather too high for smaller issues since there is a fairly high fixed-cost element). The private placing is a method by which an issuing house will sell shares through brokers or jobbers on the Stock Exchange, and thence to private investors (it is possible to do this without reference to an issuing house). This method is relatively cheap, and can be effected without a Stock Exchange quotation although, since the shares of unquoted companies

---

[15] The reader interested in a fuller discussion of these topics is recommended to read F. W. Paish, *Business Finance* (Pitman) and R. F. Henderson, The *New Issue Market* (Bowes & Bowes, 1951).

are not marketable, buyers are cautious of their issues, and the method is likely to succeed only if a firm's record and prospects are thought to be good. The Stock Exchange introduction is a method by which the issuing house makes application—on behalf of the shareholders—for the shares of the firm to be quoted on the Stock Exchange. The issue to shareholders (sometimes called a 'rights issue' if the company is public, since the existing shareholders have preferential treatment) is a relatively cheap method, since it does not involve a prospectus or advertisement; it is usually made in proportion to the existing holdings of shareholders. Whether or not this method is used depends partly on the size of the new issue and its relation to the size of the existing equity of the firm—if this is too large such an issue would be unlikely to succeed—and partly on the past record and prospects of the company. In general the main disadvantage of the issue to shareholders is that it taps existing sources of funds, and is therefore worth while only for relatively small issues, but for the small company it is frequently the only possibility in the field of long-term capital.

The small firm has particular difficulties in the field of long-term finance. Most small firms only require relatively small sums for expansion, and raising these may be too expensive for the normal processes: R. F. Henderson[16] estimated that the average cost of new issues in 1926, 1937 and 1945–47 ranging from £160,000 to £270,000 was between $7\frac{1}{2}$ and $15\frac{1}{2}$ per cent of the sums raised. Small firms are also handicapped by the increasing dependence of the capital markets on institutional investors, such as insurance companies, who prefer quoted and marketable securities, only want a limited number of equity shares, and do not in any case like small holdings of less than £10,000. The private company is further handicapped, as is the unincorporated business, by the fact that it cannot use the resources of the New Issue Market unless it becomes a public company; since its number of shareholders is legally limited to fifty, its field of influence is restricted and depends on the prosperity of shareholders (which to some extent depends on the prosperity of the firm).

Small firms rarely use the capital market at all; this is part of the explanation of their reliance on self-financing. Quoted

[16] Op. cit., p. 141.

public companies make much more use of this facility. In the Oxford Survey few private companies made any share issues at all, and these were usually small issues to shareholders; in public companies in the National Institute study, on the other hand, 32 per cent of firms made new issues between 1949 and 1953. Loan capital is subject to much the same considerations as share capital in this respect, and less than 1 per cent of private companies in the Oxford Survey made issues of long-term liabilities, compared with 10 per cent of public companies.

The problems of the small firm have been recognized for several years,[17] and the Macmillan Committee commented in 1931 : 'It has been represented to us that great difficulty is experienced by the smaller and medium-sized businesses in raising the capital which they may from time to time require even when the security is perfectly sound.'[18] Since then several institutions, of which the Industrial and Commercial Finance Corporation is the best known, have been established in an attempt to overcome the difficulties; they do valuable work but operate on a small scale and too selectively to do more than solve a part of the problem. The Radcliffe Report found it necessary to comment on the problem in 1959.[19]

There are two main sources of short- and medium-term finance for the firm: bank credit and trade credit.

British bankers have traditionally maintained that it is no part of their function to provide long-term funds for industry, and have concentrated in the past on the finance of relatively short-term needs of the seeds-to-harvest variety. In this they are sharply contrasted with German banks, which do have a large stake in German industry. Occasionally, however, within cautious limits, British banks are prepared to offer long-term finance.

The main disadvantage of the traditional bank overdraft is its relatively short duration : in practice banks usually review

---

[17] For a fuller discussion of these issues see James Bates, 'The Macmillan Gap— Thirty Years After', *The Banker* (July 1961); James Bates, 'The Macmillan Gap in Britain and Canada', *The Bankers' Magazine* (March 1962).
[18] *Report of the Committee on Finance and Industry* (June 1931) Cmd. 3897, para. 404.
[19] *Report of the Committee on the Working of the Monetary System* (August 1959), Cmnd. 827.

their overdrafts half-yearly, and once an overdraft has been granted it is not very common for it to be withdrawn, so that it is possible to use this form of finance for a longish period. But the bank usually wants to know what the money is wanted for, and bankers are not happy about lending for long-term projects. The fear of withdrawal of an overdraft, and its short-term nature in general make it a bad form of finance for anything requiring funds for longer than a year. Following a recommendation of the Radcliffe Committee the Midland Bank and its Scottish associate the Clydesdale and North of Scotland Bank introduced a scheme of term loans (loans of up to 7 years' duration, repayable in instalments); any spread of this type of finance is likely to be of help to the smaller firm, which often finds it difficult to raise finance for that sort of period. Unfortunately this particular facility was withdrawn at a time of credit restraint in 1961, and other banks have not introduced such measures.

In private companies in the Oxford Survey bank loans accounted for 6.5 per cent of total assets, compared with 2.8 per cent in public companies in the National Institute study.

Bank borrowing provides a convenient illustration of the need for realistic planning and control within the firm. It is always easier to borrow from banks if it is possible to indicate to the bank manager in advance that borrowing will be necessary. Good budgeting facilitates this, and shows the bank manager that the firm is not merely trying to borrow because it is in difficulties, but because of a planned and conscious intention to grow with adequate financial backing.

Table 8.2 shows the magnitude and direction of bank advances in the United Kingdom in November 1968.

Trade credit works in two directions: the firm gives credit to its customers, and this credit tends to vary directly with variations in turnover; it receives credit from suppliers, and this tends to vary with variations in stocks. In most firms debtors (accounts receivable) exceed creditors (accounts payable), partly because of the time lag between receipt of accounts and the payment of them, and partly because of the value added in production, which makes the price of finished goods higher than the stocks which go to their manufacture or processing. Both accounts receivable and payable tend to be higher in small

TABLE 8.2

ANALYSIS OF BANK ADVANCES TO MEMBERS OF THE UNITED
KINDGOM, NOVEMBER, 1968[1]

Industry	Advances (£million)[2]
Manufacturing	
Food drink and tobacco	289.6
Chemicals and allied industries	202.2
Metal manufacture	163.8
Electrical engineering	313.6
Other engineering and metal goods	538.9
Shipbuilding	110.4
Vehicles	222.2
Textiles, leather and clothing	239.1
Other manufactures	338.9
TOTAL MANUFACTURING	2418.9
Other Production	
Agriculture, forestry and fishing	533.4
Mining and quarrying	93.4
Construction	369.6
TOTAL OTHER PRODUCTION	996.4
Financial	
Hire purchase finance companies	128.9
Property companies	333.6
U.K banks	50.7
Other financial	430.4
TOTAL FINANCIAL	949.3
Services	
Transport and communication	171.3
Public utilities and national government	78.2
Local government services	60.9
Retail distribution	370.6
Other distribution	429.3
Professional, scientific and miscellaneous services.	560.7
TOTAL SERVICES	1671.0
Personal	
House purchase	373.8
Other personal	616.3
TOTAL PERSONAL	990.1
TOTAL U.K. RESIDENTS	7019.8

[1] Source: *Bank of England Quarterly Bulletin*, Vol. 9, No. 1. March 1969. Table 11.
[2] Excluding figures for Northern Ireland banks (£126.7 million in total).

firms than large: trade creditors form the major part of outside debt of firms in the Oxford Survey, accounting for 19 per
cent of total assets, compared with 14 per cent in companies in
the National Institute study, and 30 per cent in unincorporated

businesses; debtors account for 26 per cent of total assets in private companies and 19 per cent in public companies (and 30 per cent in unincorporated businesses).

To the extent that these two items balance each other, there is no net flow of funds within the firm, but one way of raising funds, in the short period at least (and it is a method that has dangers), is to take more money from creditors on loan than is lent back to debtors. Rapidly growing small firms tend to do this, pointing again to their special difficulties in raising funds. The biggest danger is that of overtrading, or expansion to the point that short-term commitments, notably in the form of wages and raw material accounts, exceed the liquid assets, or the ability to meet these payments. Budgeting can avoid these dangers.

Trade credit is a convenient and easy form of finance for stocks, and it has the additional virtue from the point of view of the entrepreneur that it is one of the less easily influenced sources of funds in times of credit restraint: one way in which some firms have avoided the effects of a credit squeeze has been by taking extra credit from suppliers, who, if the firm is doing well, are reluctant to apply excessive pressure. But since most trade credit is subject to a fairly substantial discount for prompt payment, this can be an expensive form of finance; it is also dangerous since it is always liable to dry up.

The use of trade credit as a source of funds demands sound financial control and a knowledge of the structure of the trade in which the firm is operating.

In the United States the importance of trade credit is more widely recognized than it is in Britain, and it is appreciated that the typical firm may well have large sums of money tied up in the form of accounts receivable (debtors).

Factoring has been slow to come to the United Kingdom, but in recent years it has developed rapidly and a number of specialized concerns are now operating in the field with some success. The principle is simple: the firm sells its trade debts to a factor; the factor then takes over the responsibility for the collection of the debt. The effect on the firm is an increase in cash resources, typically of the order of 15 per cent of annual turnover on a continuing basis. The main advantage to the firm is therefore that factoring liberates the cash tied up in debtors, with a resulting improvement in liquidity and a lessening in the need to raise extra funds from outside sources. The very small firm is not always in a position to make adequate use of factors, but many small and medium sized firms could take advantage of this relatively new and rapidly developing facility.

There have also been developments in recent years in the factoring of export credits, which are frequently long term and unreliable; one example is the Amstel Club, which is a series of reciprocal agreements between financial houses in Europe and the U.S.A. for the finance of exports and imports.

A new method of financing the sale of manufactured goods has also been developed in Britain: by this method, the manufacturer would not sell directly to the customer on credit terms but for cash to a specialized finance company, the finance company would then appoint the manufacturer as agent to sell the goods. This practice overcomes one disadvantage of ordinary factoring, which is that selling of debts in the ordinary way might suggest financial instability of the firm.

The Bill of Exchange is another way of financing trade credit: it is in essence a post-dated bill drawn by one trader on another. Although fairly common in the export trade and in some domestic trades where stock purchases are an important part of total costs, bills of exchange are rarely used by manufacturing firms.

It is possible to make other arrangements with creditors, who are usually the firm's suppliers, and debtors, who are its customers. Long term credit can sometimes be arranged with the supplier, particularly if the production cycle is fairly long. There is also a system in some industries, particularly engineering, where the customer with whom a contract is arranged provides the materials for fabrication without charge to the manufacturer, making provision for excess scrapping penalties. This system, known as the use of Free Issue Materials, is, however, restricted in its application. Similarly, large organizations sometimes finance their sub-contractors by making loans for the purchase of materials. Small contracting engineering firms can also come to arrangements for the finance of machine tools; sometimes the customer buys them and loans them, or charges the contractor at the completion of the contract; and there is a variety of possibilities.

Any of these formal arrangements is preferable to letting the bills run up in one direction or another and any arrangement which liberates cash tied up in trade credit is worth considering. The systematic control and financing of trade credit can make a substantial contribution to solving the financial difficulties of many concerns.

Hire purchase is another form of medium-term credit which may be used. Big companies rarely buy in this way, but hire purchase is frequently used by small firms[20] for relatively small purchases of machinery and motor vehicles. A quarter of the firms in the Oxford Survey used this method of finance: they were mainly small, rapidly growing concerns hungry for funds for their rapid development. It is an expensive source of funds, costing them 10 to 20 per cent per annum, but it is convenient and frequently easier to arrange than a bank loan, and many businessmen feel that the expense is amply compensated by the convenience and the fact that the earning capacity of the machinery is usually sufficient to meet the burden of repayment. Since the banks developed close links with hire purchase finance companies, bank managers are recommending their clients to finance part of their requirements by overdrafts and part by hire purchase.

Another possibility is that of leasing plant and equipment. For some years now a few large British firms have leased their cars, but it is only relatively recently that the idea has spread to equipment; the boot and shoe industry has long been accustomed to machinery leasing, complex office machinery has also often been leased, and bowling alley equipment is usually leased from the manufacturers, but there have been special reasons in all of these cases. Renting is similar to leasing save for the fact that leasing is usually for a specified period, whereas a rental agreement may be for any period which need not be specified in advance. The decision to lease, sometimes described as the lease-or-buy decision, which commits the firm to regular payments for a defined period, depends on an assessment of the advantages of capital economy weighed against the disadvantage of not owning the machinery and the possibilities of earning profit from the equipment. The total cost of rentals can be

[20] See James Bates 'Hire Purchase in Small Manufacturing Business' *The Bankers' Magazine* (September and October, 1957).

charged against tax; with leasing, however, since the leasing company owns the equipment, the lessee cannot charge wear-and-tear allowances. Leasing has other advantages; it avoids the problems of obsolescence of machinery to some degree, it requires no balance sheet entry (this is not important but it may well satisfy those who are more attached to the form of things than to their reality); it frees working capital and the bank overdraft for normal operating needs, and it makes budgeting easier. Like hire purchase, it also has the advantage that assets are earning their keep whilst the firm is paying for them.

Borrowing from individuals, such as directors or members of the family is not very common in large firms, but it is fairly frequent in smaller concerns and particularly in unincorporated businesses. About a quarter of firms in the Oxford Survey used directors' loans, but they accounted on average for only 1.3 per cent of total assets. Such borrowing may well help the firm out of a temporary difficult position, and it is a convenient way of borrowing from a director without giving him extra control in the company via the ownership of ordinary shares. But this last fact points to one of the difficulties: many directors will not do this sort of thing unless they get some such advantage, and it is not unknown for a lender to use his loan as a lever to get more equity, by threatening to withdraw the loan (or to enforce liquidation) unless some such offer is made. Bank managers, too, are rather suspicious of directors' loans on a balance sheet since they may well give a false impression of the liquidity of the firm, and managers are alive to the ruse of temporary borrowing of this sort in order to give a favourable impression.

A special form of finance, which does not fit readily into a classification by terms or period of borrowing, is the sale of assets. There are two main possibilities: the straight sale of an asset and the sale and leasing back of the asset. One form of sale of assets, the factoring of debts, has already been considered; it is also possible to sell real, operating assets such as plant, equipment, land, buildings, etc., and paper assets in the form of marketable securities. The general principle underlying such a straight sale is that the asset will be sold either if it is no longer needed, as in the case of a piece of equipment bought for a special purpose which the firm is not fulfilling any longer, or if it is not needed so urgently as the money. Sale of a security involves sacrifices of liquidity and of the interest receivable from the security, sale of an operating asset involves the loss of its earning capacity; both of these have to be weighed against the desirability of the finance and the prospective returns from the use of the money. As an alternative to borrowing this method has its advantages, but the scope is limited by the availability and value of such assets in the firm. Sale and leasing back is a form of external finance which has been popular in recent years, particularly in connection with take-over bids, the seller disposing of one asset in order to liberate the funds for the purchase of other assets. The method is largely restricted to buildings, and is particularly useful for firms whose buildings represent a substantial part of their assets, and hence of their illiquid capital. Since mortgages on industrial property are not common, such arrangements are frequently more practical than attempting to finance the continued ownership of the property.

Special problems are associated with the finance of innovations.[21] The Radcliffe Committee examined this problem and commented:

'There are certain special problems about the provision of finance for the commercial development by small businesses and private companies of new inventions and innovations of technique. One problem is that the amount of capital required to finance a development may be larger in relation to a small company's capital structure and apparent earnings prospects than the financial institutions would ordinary feel justified in putting up.'[22]

The problem of financing innovations is essentially one of reconciling the risks with the long period of development and the attendant wait for rewards; the rewards may never accrue, or, when they do, may not accrue to the person responsible for the innovation. The risks are in development, the rewards are in marketing; the major risk is that the innovation may not be a commercial propostion.[23] Larger firms can usually take care

[21] See James Bates, 'The Finance of Innovations', *The Bankers' Magazine* (July 1962).
[22] Cmnd. 827, para. 948.
[23] The experience of the National Research Development Corporation in Britain and similar organizations overseas suggests that 5 to 10 per cent of suggestions put to them succeed in this sense.

of the risks of innovation; they have specialized research facilities, the cost of which is justified by the scale of operation, and the finance of innovations is part of the process of growth of larger firms. Small firms can rarely do any of these things. A survey in the U.S.A.[24] showed the advantages of larger firms: only 8 per cent of manufacturing companies with less than 100 employees had research programmes, compared with 94 per cent of companies with over 5,000 employees.

Technical Development Capital Ltd. was formed in London in 1962 to cater for some of these problems; one of the functions of the National Research Development Corporation is also to assist inventors, and one of its successes has been the hovercraft (which unfortunately did not yield very much for its inventor). It is still doubtful whether what has come to be known as the 'Radcliffe Gap' has disappeared.

There are still other financial possibilities which need not be considered in detail. The Exports Credit Guarantees Department, a British Government institution, helps the exporter by insuring his export credits; this is an extremely valuable function in some of the more unreliable export markets. There are also some special factoring concerns specially concerned with exports, and in general the finance of exports has attracted a great deal of sympathetic attention in recent years.

The Government is also prepared to offer help to firms in development districts (areas suffering from or threatened with large-scale unemployment) by means of grants, loans, tax-concessions such as the Regional Employment Premium refund, provision of premises at low rents, provision of houses and grants for key workers, preferences in the award of contracts put up for tender, and, in Northern Ireland in particular, capital grants.

But these schemes in the development areas and the field of exports, are for particular problems: where they are applicable they are useful, but such schemes only exist because of the particular problems involved, and these problems in themselves may constitute sufficient disadvantages for the firm not to consider operating under conditions where they might be eligible for such assistance.

[24] National Science Foundation *Science and Engineering in American Industry* (U.S. Government Printing Office, 1956).

Many firms dislike the use of additional external finance, whether long term or short term, and some even go to the point of restricting expansion to the availability of cash from retained earnings, even though this may mean ignoring profitable earnings. This reflects a desire for independence, not only of outside ownership, but of any form of control; even bank loans sometimes carry restrictions on the use of funds, and many other lenders insist on a seat on the board. It is also sometimes argued that there is another factor which owes its existence to the Managerial Revolution and the consequent divorce of ownership and control. The rewards of professional management usually consist of a salary plus some share of profits (which may be small in relation to the salary) and promotion. These rewards are not always closely geared to the profits of the firm, and since managers frequently regard their security both from dismissal and from the bankruptcy of the firm as fundamental, they are disinclined to take extra risks (such as change of ownership) involving the use of external finance. The importance of this motive is questionable.

The decision about the financing of the firm depends first on the expected profits or gains from the expenditure balanced against what may be termed loosely the costs of borrowing. In terms of theoretical economics, the entrepreneur balances the marginal efficiency of capital against the marginal costs of borrowing. These costs include not only interest and repayment obligations but also considerations of the use to which the money is to be put, the actual amount required, the timing, and the form of finance to be raised; these in turn raise questions of ownership, control, convenience, liquidity, capital structure, field of influence and to some extent, personality.

APPENDIX TO CHAPTER VIII

TABLE 8.3 shows the frequency of use of various sources of funds in the United Kingdom in the early 1950s. The tables are now out-of-date, but they contain the only comparable figures currently available; regularly published data on private companies is not available. A more up-to-date comparison of a restricted group of private companies (financed by ICFC) and quoted public companies is shown in Table 8.6. This provides additional evidence which does not conflict with that from the other tables; ICFC firms showed a higher level of stocks and work-in-progress, a more important role for trade credit, heavier reliance on bank borrowing, a higher proportion of post-tax profits retained in the business, lower liquidity and a similar use of long-term fixed-interest capital.

There are also differences between non-quoted public companies and quoted public companies.[1] Non-quoted companies rely more heavily on current borrowing, make infrequent use of long-term external capital and depend heavily on retained profits. They are also lower-geared and less liquid than quoted companies. Part of the difference in the structure of current debt is explained by the fact that much of their trade credit and borrowing is either from parent companies or others in the group to which they belong; some of this may fairly realistically be regarded as essentially long-term in nature.

[1] See James Bates, *Company Finance in the United Kingdom, Bankers' Magazine* May 1965, and *The Accounts of non-quoted companies, Economic Trends*, February 1965.

TABLE 8.3

SOURCES OF FUNDS OF SMALL FIRMS, 1950–56

Source	Number of firms using source
A. *Retained Profits*	
No retained profits	29
Profits ploughed back in:	
1—3 years	39
4—6 years	253
Not ascertained	14
TOTAL	335
B. *Overdraft*	
No overdraft	162
Overdraft in:	
1—3 years	49
4—6 years	121
Not ascertained	3
TOTAL	335
Average duration of overdraft:	
Up to 6 months	143
6 to 12 months	27
C. *Other sources of funds*	
New shares issued to shareholders	35
New shares issued outside firm	16
Debentures, etc., issued	10
Loan from parent company	15
Directors' loans	76
Other sources:	
Institutions	37
Other	9
Hire purchase of plant and equipment	108
Total other sources	306
No other sources used in period	193
TOTAL*	499

Source: James Bates, 'The Finance of Small Business' *Bulletin of the Oxford University Institute of Statistics* (May 1958).

Notes: This table includes unincorporated businesses.

*Since more than one source may be used at once (i.e. sources in group C are not mutually exclusive) total sources exceed total firms.

TABLE 8.4

BALANCE SHEET AND SOURCES AND USES OF FUNDS OF PUBLIC
AND PRIVATE COMPANIES, MARCH 31ST, 1956

| | Percentage of total assets | |
	Public	Private
Capital and liabilities		
Issued capital	28.9	26.4
Reserves	37.0	38.8
Long-term debt	10.0	2.2
Bank loans	2.8	6.5
Director's loans	Nil	1.3
Trade creditors	14.4	18.9
Other	7.0	5.9
TOTAL	100.0	100.0
Assets		
Fixed assets	39.3	32.2
Stocks	30.2	32.1
Trade debtors	19.0	25.8
Liquid assets	11.5	9.9
TOTAL	100.0	100.0
Average amount	£4,855,000	£97,546

| | Percentage of total sources/uses | |
	Public	Private
Sources of funds		
Issued capital	16.9	33.4*
Bank loans	0.4	−3.9
Directors' loans	Nil.	1.6
Creditors	12.0	−16.6
Other accruals	3.0	1.0
Retained profit	32.4	44.7
Depreciation	24.8	34.3
Further tax reserves	3.2	−9.5
Other	7.3	15.0
TOTAL	100.0	100.0
Uses of funds		
Fixed assets	54.5	71.8
Stocks	16.3	−25.6
Trade debtors	16.2	37.0
Other capital payments	6.1	0.2
Liquid assets	6.9	16.6
TOTAL	100.0	100.0
Average amount	£466,300	£5,546

Source: Data from Small Business Survey of Oxford University Institute of
Statistics, Tew and Henderson, *op. cit.*, and *Economic Trends* (February 1957).

*This total is inflated by large issues by three companies.

TABLE 8.5

THE SAVINGS OF PUBLIC AND PRIVATE COMPANIES, 1954–56

Profit and Loss Account (annual average)

	Percentage of total profit	
	Public	*Private*
Trading profit	117.9	110.1
less Depreciation	21.4	24.5
plus Other income	3.5	14.4
TOTAL PROFIT	100.0	100.0
Tax on current income	53.8	49.8
Dividends (net)	18.9	18.5
RETAINED PROFIT	27.3	31.7
(N.B. Director's remuneration	2.0	40.0)
Annual total profit	£536,800	£7,823

	Average annual profit as percentage of net assets	
Trading profit	17.2	13.1
Total profit	14.5	11.9

Source: As Table 8.4

TABLE 8.6

FINANCIAL STRUCTURE—U.K. QUOTED
COMPANIES AND 300 I.C.F.C. FIRMS, 1964

A. Balance Sheets	Quoted	I.C.F.C.
Tangible fixed assets	57.7	55.4
Goodwill, etc.	3.7	0.9
Trade investments	4.8	3.4
Total current assets	71.4	101.0
Stocks and Work-in-progress	34.0	50.2
Debtors	29.0	45.2
Cash	5.3	2.8
Investments	3.1	1.8
Other current Assets	—	1.0
Total current Liabilities	37.6	60.7
Creditors	23.1	33.7
Other current Liabilities	7.3	8.8
Bank Loans and Overdrafts	7.2	18.2
Net current assets	33.8	40.3
Total net assets	100.0	100.0

Representing:		
Long-term loans	13.1	14.5
Minority interests	3.0	0.6
Future tax reserves	4.4	5.9
Preference shares	5.9	8.4
Ordinary shares	33.6	26.0
Capital and revenue reserves	40.0	44.6

B. Appropriation of income		
Total income (after all expenses including director's remuneration)	100.0	100.0
Depreciation	24.0	21.2
Interest	3.8	6.4
Net profit before tax	72.2	72.4
	100.0	100.0
Taxation	48.2	43.5
Net profit after tax	51.8	56.5
	100.0	100.0
Distributions	50.0	27.0
Profit retained	50.0	73.0

Notes:
1. It will be seen that for purposes of this comparison bank borrowing has been treated in the same way as that generally used in quoted company accounts and elsewhere: as a current liability.

2. Source for quoted companies, 'Income and Finance of quoted companies', 1964, Annual Abstract of Statistics. The above comparisons involve certain approximations and are intended to reveal only the broad magnitudes. Thus 'long-term loans' for the I.C.F.C. firms include loans from Directors, and H.P. and Mortgages. 'Interest' for the quoted companies is only on long-term liabilities—since in the Annual Abstract interest on bank borrowing is not included —whereas for the I.C.F.C. firms this is included. The ratio of distributions and retentions for the I.C.F.C. firms represents an estimate.

3. Source: J. S. Boswell, I.C.F.C. Small Firm Survey, Industrial and Commercial Finance Corporation, 1968.

Chapter IX

PLANNING, FORECASTING AND CONTROL

KNOWLEDGE, THE FIRST REQUIREMENT FOR EFFECTIVE CONTROL

THE first requirement for effective control is knowledge; the second is the means to use this knowledge for the formulation of policy; the third is the means to ensure that what is intended materializes.

TABLE 9.1

A COMPANY BALANCE SHEET

Liabilities	£000 Year I	Year II	Assets	£000 Year I	Year II
Share capital	210	210	Fixed assets	416	655
Revenue reserves	392	431	Current assets:		
Future taxation	92	83	Stock on hand	152	175
Current liabilities	148	257	Debtors and payments		
			in advance	122	149
			Deposit on leasehold		
			property	23	—
			Government securities	29	—
			Cash	100	2
	842	981		842	981

One conventional way of providing financial information about a company is to draw up a balance sheet which sets out the assets and liabilities of the company and shows, when compared with similar statements prepared for earlier dates, how the company's position has been changing.

Table 9.1 shows a condensed balance sheet. Liabilities of the company are shown on the left-hand side of the statement and assets on the right-hand side. The liabilities of the company are shown under four main heads; liability for the share capital of the owners of the business; liability for the reserves that have been accumulated over the life of the company (for on dissolution these belong to the shareholders); provision for future taxation (a liability to the Board of Inland Revenue); and current liabilities, to creditors, bankers, shareholders and for taxation payments. On the credit side are placed first property and plant, after allowing for depreciation; and second current assets consisting mainly of the stock of raw materials, semi-processed and finished goods owned by the company; cash (largely in the form of bank balances); and the debts owed to the company by its debtors, which are claims to the receipt of cash in the future.

For the sake of comparison, figures are shown for two financial years. Some substantial changes are noticeable between the two dates. On the side of liabilitities there has been an increase in revenue reserves (which have to be accounted for to shareholders) and to this extent the shareholders' stake in the company has been increased; there is a considerable increase in the amounts owing to creditors. The increase of liabilities has been matched by an increase in the property owned by the company, partly offset by a fall in holdings of Government securities and a marked reduction in the amount of cash available. The picture given is one of expansion of the firm's activities, imposing some strain on liquid resources and tying up shareholders' reserves in the business. In fact, at the end of Year II the company was holding no reserves of cash and would have been dependent on bank finance to maintain its liquid position.

The change in the balance sheet reflects the results of the previous year's working as well as changes resulting from expenditure on capital account. The profit and loss account is shown in Table 9.2. Profits have fallen from the previous year, and there was some fall in taxation. After paying dividends, a substantial sum remained for transfer to reserve and this helped to finance the investment that was made.

The shareholder might examine the accounts of a company in order to see if it was profitable, if it appeared to be adding to its assets in a desired way and if it were in a position to continue to do so in the future. He might well feel satisfied with the progress that his company was making; without more information he would only rarely be in any position to suggest changes in policy, much less to put them into effect. It does

TABLE 9.2

PROFIT AND LOSS ACCOUNT

	£000	
	Year I	*Year II*
Trading profit	294	279
Deductions for directors' fees, depreciation and bank interest	41	57
Profit before taxation	253	222
Deduction for taxation	119	113
Deduction for dividends	70	70
Transferred to reserve	64	39

sometimes happen, however, that balance sheets and profit and loss accounts throw up facts that are apparent to shareholders and apparently ignored by company boards. Shareholders in Courtaulds might well have inquired from their board why at the end of March 1962 net current assets had reached some £44½ million, and whether it would not have been wiser to have used some of these resources in the extension of their manufacturing activities in earlier years. In a wider setting, information along the lines given in company reports and covering a number of years might enable shareholders to review their company's operations to greater purpose; economists are used to drawing conclusions and suggesting policies from historical series of figures, and investment analysts sometimes use the same techniques. But very little can be said about the operations of a company on the basis of the limited information contained in a single set of accounts, and for the most part shareholders and would-be shareholders should be chary of drawing conclusions from them. The following comment by the *Daily Telegraph* (August 18th 1961) on the report of a Select Committee on the gas industry illustrates the point. Consider how much additional information would be needed before the conclusions could be accepted without question. 'In particular the report convicts it of the besetting sin of all nationalized industries—that of failing to return enough profits to maintain and develop its capital equipment. Nationalized gas started with a capital of £187 million, and has raised £424 million from outside sources.

It has increased its borrowed capital by over 120 per cent but the amount of gas sold has increased by only 6 per cent.' Such a sweeping conclusion cannot be reached on the basis of the four figures adduced in its support. What happened to profits? Was it possible to justify the expenditure on the grounds that costs were reduced? What was the state of the gas industry before nationalization? Presumably this comment rested on wider appreciation of the operation of the gas industry than was possible in a brief leader. Shareholders would often be misled if they attempted to control their companies on the basis of such limited information, and more complete and illuminating company reports are often needed to keep shareholders informed about their company's position. But it is also true that many of them would pay little attention to more informative reports; the bulk of private shareholders are more likely to guide their appreciation of a company's progress and potentialities by reading the chairman's speech or digesting financial commentaries than by detailed statistical studies. The latter they may well leave to those who operate the companies they own.

THE FLOW OF INFORMATION IN A FIRM

The directors of companies are in a vastly different position from the shareholders. They are able to devote themselves much more exclusively to the affairs of their company and they command the means to secure the knowledge, both internal and external, which is necessary for company control. Information about matters external to the company is required for setting the wider objectives of the firm; to help in suggesting profitable lines of production; to enable an appreciation to be made of the prospects of getting labour; to allow the firm to anticipate changes in the Government's economic policy; and so on.

Information about the internal working of the firm must be sufficient for:

1. Objectives to be set for the firm, bearing in mind, of course, that external factors must also be considered.
2. A plan to be prepared for attaining the objectives.
3. Management to be able to verify whether objectives are

being attained and to see what deviations have occurred from the plan.

4. Management to be able to establish the causes for deviations and either remedy them or adjust the plan to changing circumstances.

Much of the information needed for these purposes is financial. The performance of a firm is measured in terms of profits or, if expansion is the main aim of the firm, in terms of additions to the value of assets. By the criterion we are using, firms are successful if they earn profits and increase the value of their assets.

PLANNING

Planning may be directed to near or distant horizons of time. Long range planning is concerned with the general direction of a firm's development; it is strategic in nature, designed to identify objectives and examine in broad terms how they may be achieved. One of the functions is to open managers' minds to future opportunities and dangers that might otherwise go unperceived or be only dimly comprehended.

Long range plans may be expressed in financial terms such as planned turnover, profits and investment, but they are concerned much more with the type of products and markets that the firm intends to exploit and with the effect of technological innovation on production methods and the creation of new wants. Such plans seek to show how the firm can adapt itself to new situations and opportunities, how existing resources whether of plant, management or business connections can best be used, and how weakness and insufficiencies can be overcome.

Exercises of this kind have relevance for short term planning. They indicate what steps must be taken even in the short term to prepare the way for long term developments and, sometimes just as important, may reveal that short term plans may prejudice the ultimate objectives of the company.

In a small company planning can be carried on without any great apparatus. In the one-man business there is no great need to commit much information to paper. But for the larger business a formal plan is indispensable. Sir Alec Cairncross has described how programmes (or plans) serve several distinct functions: they register and communicate decisions and allow decisions to be delegated; they serve the purpose of clarifying and forcing decisions and provide a measure of success.[1]

A fully developed plan of business operations has thus considerable administrative advantages. The various departments can regard budgetary plans (discussed later in this chapter) as a basis for their operations. The rate and amount of purchases is written into the plan; the production scheduled gives an indication of the number of men that will be required during the period for which the plan has been drawn up; and financial requirements can be mapped out. This will not eliminate the need to co-ordinate activities, but it will facilitate it by ensuring that conflicting requirements are reconciled within the context of the plan. The plan is also an important means of administration since it sets limits to the expenditure of departments or individuals. An increase in expenditure over the levels laid down in the plan requires authorization, and in consequence is brought to notice earlier than would otherwise occur.

The administrative uses of plans must not be allowed to obscure the importance of a plan as a formulation of policy. A good plan is an essay in imagination as well as an administrative instrument, for it concerns itself with what the business can become as well as with what it is, and it incorporates arrangements for development as well as for continuation. Those who belittle planning often do so because they think too much in terms of continuation of the present and too little in terms of the need to shape events as well as to accept them.

The starting point to the formulation of a plan may be a consideration of what modifications need to be made to some previous plan, or it may be an intention to improve on previous performance. Sometimes the starting point will represent a radical departure from what has gone before, for example the desire to expand on a grand scale, or an opportunity to move into some new branch of industry. In many cases one aspect of the operation of a business will appear to be dominant, for example, the need to expand sales or make the best use of productive equipment. But whatever the starting point may be, all aspects of a business operation must be seen as a

[1] *Scottish Journal of Political Economy* (June 1961) p. 88.

whole; production, sales and stocks must be consistent with each other; costs, returns and profits must be related and so on.

FORECASTING

Any form of planning involves some view of the future. It may be an optimistic view, a pessimistic view, one based on hunch, or a simple assumption that the future will be rather like the past. Sometimes the precise view taken is not critical; if it proves to be wrong plans can be easily and speedily adjusted. But on other occasions, when resources have to be irrevocably committed to some purpose, accurate forecasting may make a great deal of difference to the fortunes of a company or the economy of a country. The price of natural fibres can vary by 10, 20 or even 50 per cent in the space of a year; the same is true of certain other materials, such as silver, lead and rubber; and of foodstuffs such as butter and tea. A view that the market will rise or fall is in effect a forecast even though the extent of the rise or fall anticipated may never be precisely formulated.

Some of the most important forecasts in business are connected with sales. Most production is carried out in advance of sale; to produce too much is expensive, to have too little on hand may be to miss substantial profits if demand proves to be unexpectedly high. The demand for some products varies markedly; economic crises cause the Government to cut back on demand and this falls heavily on certain types of goods; hire purchase sales fluctuate with some regularity; the demand for oil increases from year to year but by varying amounts. Uncertainty about the course of demand vitally affects investment decisions. An unexpected turn of events can make past decisions appear wrong in retrospect. The ships that were laid up in 1959 as soon as they were completed would not have been built by their owners if it had been realized that too many ships would be seeking cargoes in that year.

Mistakes of this kind are costly (however justifiable the original decisions may have been) and it is worth seeing whether techniques can be developed to give greater accuracy of prediction. Reluctance to undertake this kind of analysis often stems from the belief that economic events are unpredictable. Some are: political actions of governments do not lend themselves to easy prediction; the closure of the Suez Canal for the second time in 1967 could scarcely have been predicted; and political observers differ so greatly in their views about the date that Britain will be accepted into the Common Market as to suggest that this economic event is also unpredictable. Many natural events with economic consequences fall into the same category. The weather that reduced the yield of jute grown in Pakistan in 1960 could not have been forecast with the knowledge and techniques then available, but the reaction of jute growers to the high prices that resulted in that year might have been predictable and the same is true within limits of many other economic events.

Forecasting is concerned with the future, but we have information only about the past and present. The future is uncertain; how far it is capable of prediction depends on the extent to which it is related to the past and whether the relationships between past and future events can be discovered. In the natural sciences the future does appear to be deducible from the past for many relationships; we may feel confident that the sun will rise tomorrow and that the proportions of oxygen and hydrogen contained in water will remain the same. So far we have not been disappointed in these beliefs. But many of the relationships established for the natural sciences are approximate: they are useful generalizations that may have to be modified as time goes on and as our understanding of the true relationship grows; economic relationships established at one time and having all the appearance of an acceptable approximation may cease to be so as the nature of the economy alters or as knowledge about it becomes more complete.

The view that economic events can be forecast depends on the reasonable assumption that economic events have some continuity. If there were no relation between the past and the future there would be no basis for forecasts and we could only guess at what would happen. This is thought by some observers to be true of stock exchange forecasts, for example.

The purpose of forecasting techniques is to exploit the relationships that are thought to exist between past and future. Although forecasts are sometimes made as though the value of the variable to be forecast will, or will not, attain a particular value, complete accuracy is not to be expected. A point fore-

cast should be taken to convey the notion that the future value
of the variable is uncertain, but that of all the different values
that could have been chosen one appears to be more likely
than the rest. A forecaster might be rather surprised if, in the
event, his point forecast proved to be dead on. But equally
he would be surprised, or at least disappointed, if the value
materializing proved to be remote from the forecast figure.
Ideally, a forecast would take the form of giving a picture
of all the values that might be assumed by the variable to be
forecast with an estimate of the likelihood that they would be
attained. This type of information might be summarized by
saying that the most likely value for the variable would be v
and that it would be unlikely to deviate from this value by
more than a certain amount. The accuracy of forecasts could
be improved in this sense if an alternative value of the variable
could be shown to be more likely; if it could be shown that the
possible range of values was smaller than supposed; or if it
could be said that the variable would lie within given limits
with a greater degree of certainty.

It is sometimes said in business that it is no good trying to
forecast because forecasts are almost always bound to be wrong.
There may be some truth in this observation if the accuracy of
a forecast is thought to depend on its coinciding exactly with
what transpires. But this is not what a forecast is intended to
do. One forecast is to be regarded as more accurate than
another if it reduces the margin of uncertainty about future
events, and the test of whether forecasts are to be preferred
to guesses is whether on the average they lie nearer the truth.
In business, the criterion to be used in judging a forecast
is whether it enables better decisions to be taken. In the evaluation of the usefulness of forecasts account must be taken both
of the consequences of the forecast being successful, that is of
the forecast event falling within some critical range, and of the
possibility that the forecast will fall outside. A number of
good forecasts may not be enough to compensate for some
disastrous deviation from the expected value.

Pursuing this general line of reasoning, the decision of a
business to spend money on forecasting should be based on the
following considerations. If the use of forecasting techniques
increases the accuracy of assumptions made about the future

for planning purposes, and improves the quality of managerial decisions in consequence, forecasting may be worth while. But it will be so only if the increase in profits that results from improved foresight exceeds the cost of making the forecasts. If the forecasts result in no better profits than would have been realized without them there is no point in forecasting, just as there may be no point in planning if policy changes are costless. If profits can be increased by greater accuracy in forecasting, it will be worth while increasing expenditure on the preparation of forecasts up to the point that the additional cost just offsets the increase in returns that results. Some forecasting techniques are relatively costless but, if accuracy involves nation-wide surveys, costs can mount rapidly.

METHODS OF FORECASTING

The methods of forecasting used will depend very much on the objective. Some things are appropriate for a business to forecast, others are not. All businesses are affected by the rate of growth of the economy, but few businesses in this country have the resources to devote to estimations of this kind. In most cases it may be best to rely on forecasts made by bodies specializing in this field, such as the National Institute of Economic and Social Research, or to take guidance from forecasts done by other research teams with the specialist knowledge required.

The first step in forecasting the growth of output in the economy is to attempt to understand the inter-relation between major sectors of the economy. What, for example, determines the level of consumption? In the model used for forecasting in the Dutch economy, consumption is decided according to the amount spent by wage-earning and entrepreneurial families and it is assumed that each of them spends different proportions of their incomes remaining after taxation. The proportions spent broadly reflect past experience. Similarly prices are supposed to depend on wage rates, the price of imported goods and tax rates. The relationship between the various types of price index and the variables explaining them are again constructed from past experience, modified if necessary to take account of any changes that can be foreseen in these variables in the period for which the forecasts are made. In all, the 1955 system for the Dutch economy consisted of twenty-seven equations, twelve of which were definitions, and these equations acted like a working model of the economy.[2] It was possible to tell from them what might happen if, for example, wage rates rose, production increased, or a number of changes took place simultaneously. Prediction proceeds by feeding into this system a number of plausible guesses or assumptions, about certain variables, for example, wages rates, stock changes, and import prices and the consequences of these changes for the development of the economy can then be estimated in detail. Models for the U.K. the U.S.A. and other countries are constructed on similar principles. They are all examples of the use of multiple regression techniques in forecasting.

Models of economies are complicated devices but the principles underlying their design are fairly readily understood and represent a sophisticated application of a basic scientific approach, that of stating a theory and testing it for applicability and validity. Since theories are no more than useful approximations and simplified summaries of relationships, we must not hope for perfection. One of the tests of theories applied to forecasting is whether they work in a useful way.

An essential ingredient of any forecast is the establishment of a relationship between the variable to be forecast and the passage of time. Such relationships should be grounded on experience of the working of the economy to which they apply. If such a relationship has been established for the variable in which we are interested we have our prediction, but the issues are not always so simple. It may be necessary to relate the variable in which we are interested to some other variable for which we have a prediction and so to forecast at one remove.

How this can be done may be illustrated from the discussion of the determinants of demand in Chapter IV. These included the price of the commodity in question, the price of other commodities and income as well as other factors. The relationships varied from commodity to commodity. For foodstuffs, elasticities of demand were rather low; for cars, price elasticity of

[2] See H. Thiel, *Economic Forecasts and Policy*, (North Holland Publishing Company) p. 52.

demand is low but income elasticity of demand quite high.[3]

In forecasting we might be justified in reaching the conclusion on the basis of past experience that the demand for food was not likely to change very much in total and that the demand for cars would depend on changes in incomes which would have to be separately forecast. In these instances simple relationships may suffice, because only a limited number of variables contribute to the forecast; when a wider range of variables is involved, as in forecasting income, it may be possible to use a forecast prepared by some other agency. Income is a major economic variable in a whole complex of variables which are mutually determining, as in the model of the Dutch economy.

Official forecasts simplify the task of the business forecaster; even without such forecasts it is sometimes possible to form a view based on leading series of economic statistics. It should not be assumed, however, that leading series will always maintain their validity for prediction.

Post-war stock exchange indices, for example, appear to have lost their validity and other indicators have had to be developed for forecasting purposes. Direct inquiry from a representative sample of businessmen is now carried out in a number of countries. In this country the Confederation of British Industries asks businessmen what changes they anticipate in business conditions and whether, for example, they anticipate increasing the level of their investment in some future period or whether it will fall or remain unchanged.

The search for leading series is of general application. A rise in import prices in the United Kingdom does not affect retail prices immediately but will do so after a lapse of perhaps 3 months. A decision to construct a new dam will give rise to orders for new generating equipment at some later date; a fall in new orders for ships will affect steelmakers only when existing orders have been completed. An increase in the rate of

---

[3] See 'Demand for Cars in Great Britain', C. St. J. O'Herlihy, *App. Stats.*, *Journal of the Royal Statistical Society*, Series C. Vol. XLV, Nos. 2 & 3. 1965, p. 183. Similar studies for the U.S.A. have suggested an income elasticity of demand for new cars of 2.5, much the same as the figure of 2 found by O'Herlihy for Britain; but price elasticity appeared to be higher, 1½ against 1/3. (See G. Maxcy and Aubrey Silberston, *The Motor Industry*, George Allen & Unwin, 1959). O'Herlihy's relationships were long term ones. The short run changes (that is in the current year) were thought to be three times bigger.

T

utilization of plant and capacity is likely to give rise to orders for some new plant; a rise in the population will affect the demand for houses, and so on. Relationships of this kind, though they may be obvious, are valuable. They are likely to play an important role in business forecasting.

There is a relationship between the area of land planted for jute in one year and the relative prices of jute and rice in the previous year. Research carried out by the Food and Agriculture Organization of the United Nations shows that an increase in rice prices or a fall in jute prices will tend to reduce the acreage put down to jute in the following year. A high price for rice will make farmers increase the output of it, either on the supposition that high prices will continue to rule in the following year, or because the high price is a sign of hunger and it is not intended to run the risk of starvation the following year in the hope of maintaining previous proceeds from the cash crop. A relatively low jute price will reduce the value of the cash crop and suggest a change to the production of apparently more worthwhile crops. A 1 per cent increase in the price of jute relative to that of rice increases the acreage put down to jute by about half per cent. Thus the supply of jute is in some measure determined a year ahead of its harvesting.

The relationship for jute does not hold exactly from year to year. For a more complete explanation additional variables have to be introduced. Perhaps some measure of the opportunity to prepare land for sowing, having regard to the incidence of floods and rainfall, or the addition of other price series to that for jute might improve the 'explanation'.

Generally greater confidence is felt in a forecast that depends on some understandable relationship. It is reasonable to proceed on the assumption that the jute acreage is related to prices in the way that has been indicated. Forecasting the jute acreage by the above method would not, however, necessarily be ruled out even if no easily understandable explanation of the relationship could be advanced. If observation suggests that two series are related in some way it is perfectly possible to use the one as an explanation of the other. But considerable doubts might well be felt about the reliability of such forecasts if the variables involved could not be connected with any kind of economic model. The relationship might be a chance one,

holding over a limited period of time but without real underlying validity.

There may be some justification for comparatively simple
forecasting procedures. The demand for some article may
be forecast on the assumption that it will increase in the future
at much the same rate as it has done in the past, and a more
complicated forecast may be built up out of a number of such
simple assumptions relating to separate items in a composite
whole. Such relationships sometimes seem to rest on insufficient
foundations but they may be more reliable than alternatives
that would otherwise be used. One company found, for example, that they were more reliable indicators of sales than the
expectations of their salesmen.

Another example of the future course of a series of figures
being related to values assumed at some earlier date arises in
the case of the replacement demand for certain types of capital
goods. Thus, if machines have a life of x years and n of them
were installed x years ago, n will now be due for replacement.
Relationships of this type are generally of a much more variable
form than that postulated above. The life of capital equipment is not predetermined; the decision to replace some existing machines depends on a number of uncertain events,
such as the cost of repairs as the equipment becomes older, the
extent to which replacement may be advanced or retarded,
obsolescence and the state of the market for the products being
made by the machines. Nevertheless economists have related
orders for new ships to the need to replace those approaching
certain age limits, and this is also a factor in the demand for
aircraft.

Similar types of relationships may exist for hire purchase
expenditure. Mr. J. R. Cuthbertson has suggested that individuals tend to sustain a certain level of hire purchase payments so that the completion of a series of payments on one
article tends to be followed by the conclusion of another hire-
purchase agreement.[4] If such a relationship held, it might be
possible to expect a resurgence of demand for durable consump-

[4] 'Hire Purchase Controls and Fluctuations in the Car Market', *Economica*
(May 1961) p. 125. See also: A. Silbertston, 'Hire Purchase Controls and the
Demand for Cars', *Economic Journal*, (March 1963).

tion goods in the future from looking at the anticipated maturities of existing contracts.

Observed relationships are not always so simple as this. For many years economic forecasts of saturation of the demand for durable consumer goods have proved to be wrong because young consumers in the middle and upper income brackets were willing to enlarge their instalment debt for the sake of upgrading their possessions.[5]

It is sometimes useful to relate demand to the existing stock of the commodity in question or to the concept of saturation of the market. New purchases of cars depend in some measure on second-hand prices, which in turn are related to the number of cars existing and to their condition. O'Herlihy used an extremely sophisticated model to predict registrations to 1966. His forecast is shown in Figure 9.1. The estimated line represents the values for registrations given by the equation explaining purchases between 1948 and 1961. The explanatory variables were income, price, supply, time trend, and hire purchase regulations. Various assumptions were made about the values that these variables would assume in the years 1962 to 1966 and demand was predicted by inserting these values into the equations developed from the data of earlier years. The actual registrations are plotted on Figure 9.1.

In the United States it appeared that a 1 per cent increase in the level of disposable income increased expenditure on new cars by 2.5 per cent; and a 1 per cent increase in the ratio of the prices of new cars to the index of consumer prices was associated with an average decrease of $1\frac{1}{2}$ per cent in new car sales.[6]

A motor car agent might do well to consider how the main factors affecting the demand for cars would be likely to move before ordering cars for a new season and in planning expansions to capacity of sales premises or repair shops.

Saturation of demand is important in those cases when demand can be regarded as being met progressively. If one refrigerator per household is regarded as normal, saturation

[5] See George Katona, 'Changes in Consumer Expectations and Their Origin', *The Quality and Economic Significance of Anticipations Data*, p. 81, National Bureau of Economic Research, 1960.

[6] See G. Maxey & Aubrey Silbertson, *The Motor Industry* George Allen & Unwin, 1959.

will be reached when all householders have a refrigerator. The percentage of families owning various appliances increases rapidly at first then more slowly, with obvious implications for sale prospects.[7]

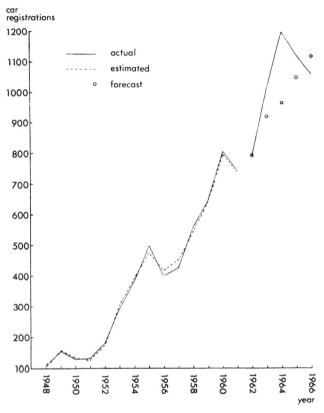

Fig. 9·1.   Forecasts of Registration of Cars in Great Britain.

Source: 'Demand for Cars in Gt. Britain'. C. St. J. O'Herlihy, Applied Statistics. 1965.

In *Planning Production, Iventories and Work Force,* Holt, Modigliani, Muth and Simon describe how they set about forecasting sales of paint 1 month ahead. They found that

---

[7] See Lohnas H. Knapp, Forecasting Appliances, p. 376 in *How Business Economists Forecast* Prentice Hall 1966. The original source was *Electrical Merchandising Week.*

sales in the first half of a calendar year could be accurately forecast from sales from the second half of the preceding year. Sales for the full year could be forecast from the real gross private domestic investment component of the gross national product. Monthly forecasts could be obtained by applying seasonal adjustments to the half-yearly data, which effectively allowed for the variation of the sales pattern from month to month. The key to the success of the method devised was the use of the series for gross private domestic investment.

Asking salesmen and businessmen what they think is likely to happen is one way of getting a lead on the future. But special techniques are needed to get the best results and care must be taken to avoid getting biased responses. Salesmen may be naturally chary of giving their opinion about the market and if asked about the prospect for sales they may be inclined to underestimate possibilities so that their actual performance will stand up well against the apparent difficulty of the task that they were asked to undertake. On the other hand many salesmen are extroverts and optimists and this might lead them to exaggerate sales prospects. In appraising the views of businessmen, allowance must be made for the fact that opinions are catching and that it is safer to ask a businessman what he intends to do than what he thinks will happen. The views of businessmen may be determined in some considerable measure by what has been said in official quarters, in financial circles or on television.

Expectations, however, are clearly an important element in forecasting. Research done by Miss Eva Mueller appears to suggest that consumer attitudes to the purchase of consumer goods may be a very good indication of future purchases. But it is desirable not to look too far ahead; expectations are often short run. A number of techniques are available for assessing consumer attitudes. It is possible, for example, to get some indication of buying intentions of consumers by asking them about their financial expectations in the coming year, their views of the long-term outlook, and so on. Another approach is to ask consumers what they intend to buy and this technique was used in the 'Quarterly Survey of Consumer Buying Intentions', published in the *Federal Reserve Bulletin,* as an indication of the prospects for consumer sales in the United States

during the next half-year. Some of the work in this field prom-
ises well, but it is necessary to assess the reliability of new forecasting techniques before great weight is put upon them, and
this is what research workers are trying to do. Consumer attitudes may be better than buying intentions as an indicator
of actual expenditure.[8]

It should not be assumed that the most complicated forecasting model is necessarily the best. At first sight complicated
relationships between a large number of variables might appear
to hold out the greatest chance of success, and it may be possible
to establish such relationships more easily in the future with
the development of new statistical series and the use of
computers. But there are good reasons for believing that forecasts will be better if they are reasonably simple. All economic
series are subject to unobservable and indeterminate error.
These errors accumulate when a large number of statistical
series are combined in calculation, they also interact and multiply. Apparent connections between variables may be derived
from errors incorporated in the data used and may not have
any real economic significance. Another difficulty is that the
more variables are used to 'explain' some series, the easier does
it become to fabricate an explanation in statistical terms, even
though that explanation may not really represent the causal
factor at work.

A relationship between variables may not be comprehen-
sible in intuitive terms but it may still be acceptable if it with-
stands statistical testing. A predictive system may be good simply
because it works. Exponentially weighed averages may not explain relationships, but they are useful for forecasting in some
circumstances.

The logic underlying exponential smoothing techniques is
that future values of some variable are related to past values,
with the more recent observations exercising greater influence
than those taken earlier. The value forecast for some variable,
such as sales, is based on an average of previous values, weighted
in an exponential manner and adjusted in other ways. If
previous values of sales are $S_t, S_{t-1} S_{t-2}$ where t is the present

[8] See Eva Mueller, 'Ten years of Consumer Attitude Surveys; their Forecasting
Record', *Journal of the American Statistical Society*, Vol. 58, 1963, p. 905.

time and $t-1$, $t-2$, etc. are earlier periods, an exponentially weighted average is calculated according to the formula:

$$A = aS_t + a^2S_{t-1} + a^3S_{t-2}$$

The value a is selected so that the sum of the geometric progression $a + a^2 + a^3$ . . . etc. is equal to 1. a itself, of course, is less than 1 and the weight given to earlier observations thus diminishes progressively in constant proportion, with remote observations contributing very little to the average. The 'best' value for a can be determined from past observation in such a way as to minimise the difference between the actual observations recorded over some period and the values given by the exponentially weighted moving average system. This process is simpler than might seem because once some average is accepted as an approximation to the first exponentially weighted average of a system, subsequent moving averages incorporating more recent observations are easily calculated. In fact the new average say F^n is derived from the old average F_{n-1}, and the new observations S_a according to the formula $F_n = F_{n-1} + (1-a)$ $(S_n - F_{n-1})$

In words, the new average equals the old average plus $(1-a)$ times the difference between the new value (of sales) and the old average. This follows from the form of the geometric progressions[9]. If necessary the best value for a can be determined by a process of trial and error.

When a has been determined, forecasting may consist of no more than taking the value of the latest exponentially calculated mean as the expected value for subsequent periods. While such procedures may work and have the advantage of smoothing and perhaps averaging out chance variations in the data for recent months, they suffer from the defect that they make inadequate allowance in the averages themselves, as well as in the forecasts, for any trend that may be present. If an upward

---

[9] $F_n = aS_n + a^2S_{n-1} + a^3S_{n-2} + a^4S_{n-3}$ . . . etc. The sum of the weights $a + a^2 + a^3$ . . . etc. (a geometric progression) comes to $a/1-a$. This can be made equal to 1 by the expedient of dividing each of the weights a, a^2, a^3 etc. by $a/1-a$ which is equivalent to writing the expression as

$$
\begin{aligned}
F_n &= (1-a)\,(S_n + aS_{n-1} + a^2S_{n-2} + a^3S_{n-3} \ldots \text{etc.})\\
F_{n-1} &= (1-a)\,(\quad\;\; S_{n-1} + a\;S_{n-2} + a^2S_{n-3} \ldots \text{etc.})\\
F_n &= aF_{n-1} + (1-a)S_n\\
&= F_{n-1} - F_{n-1} + aF_{n-1} + (1-a)S_n\\
&= F_{n-1} - F_{n-1}(1-a) + (1-a)S_n\\
&= F_{n-1} + (1-a)(S_n - F_{n-1})
\end{aligned}
$$

trend is present the moving average will always be less than the most recent value recorded while it will be greater for a declining trend. Thus the base from which the forecasts are made really represents the situation at some earlier time and moving averages may thus require adjustment when a trend is present if they are to serve as forecasts. Moreover, if a trend is present it will be incorrect to give the same forecast for any future month as for the present value of the average since with an increasing trend future values will grow.

This can be corrected by superimposing an estimate of the trend on the moving average. Such a trend can be calculated in a number of ways; one way is simply to compare the average of two periods separated by a reasonable length of time. When such a trend has been calculated it may be added to the moving averages calculated for forecasting purposes with various degrees of refinement. Naturally forecasts for more distant periods will be more affected by the trend than those for shorter periods ahead.

The test of the usefulness and validity of using exponenential moving averages as a forecasting tool is, as always, whether experience shows that the forecasts are better than those obtained by other methods and whether the benefit from using them outweighs the costs involved in their preparation and use. The method is usable only for short term forecasts for which it may be operationally successful even though the underlying model is neither fully explained or understood.

A variety of other methods of forecasting are available. Those discussed in this chapter are only illustrative.

Since the susceptibility of forecasts to error is often advanced against attempts to chart the future, it may be useful to examine how it is that forecasts go wrong. Errors can arise for fundamental reasons inherent in the methods of forecasting in use. Many forecasts start off with the assumption that some variable can be expressed as a linear relationship of some other variables: that sales, for example, will vary proportionally with income or that sales will be equal to some fraction of income plus a constant. In the first place this relationship will be established from past data. Even if the relationship postulated is a true one in the sense that it correctly represents economic relationships, it does not follow that it will emerge from a consideration of data relating to past periods. These data are subject to error and the relationship calculated from them is almost certain to be only a rough approximation to the true relation. Secondly, irrespective of the quality of data, it is unlikely that the form of the relationship postulated between sales and income is the true one. Thus, in addition to saying that sales are equal to some proportion of income, plus a constant, we have to make allowance for the fact that the relationship with which we are working is inexact in some measure, and insert a term representing error in the equations. Thirdly some variables that are liable to affect the relationships between sales and income may lie outside our system of prediction (exogenous variables). Changes in hire purchase regulations may fall into this category, for while it may sometimes be possible to anticipate changes in Government regulations it is seldom possible to predict the exact form that they will take.

Another possible source of error may be described as economic. Errors of this kind may arise partly out of inadequate formulation of the relationships between the variable in which we are interested and other variables. In an effort to do something an inappropriate relationship may be selected. In earlier explanations of the trade cycle it was suggested that cycles were closely correlated with the activity of sunspots. There were reasons for thinking that there might be some connection between the two, but in fact the connection is of slight importance. Forecasts of economic activity related to sunspot activity would obviously be doomed to failure if the relationship postulated in the first place was incorrect. Another class of economic errors arises in what is measured or what it is possible to measure. Income as measured may not be the variable that we would like to consider in forecasting sales, but the nearest we can get to a variable that would give an exact relationship. In some instances we may be forced to leave out of consideration certain variables that we would like to take into account if they were available. In addition to considering income we might like to consider buying intentions expressed by consumers, but these may be impossible to compile.

Statistical errors also require consideration. Estimating procedures used to establish the connection between two variables may be based on the assumption that the errors in variables are independent of the values that the variables assume. If, in fact, the errors are larger for larger incomes than for smaller ones, appropriate methods of estimation will have to be used. Many statistical techniques assume that the observed values of variables are independent, i.e. that the choice of one does not affect the other; if this is not the case, serious errors may result. Errors in statistical data have already been touched upon; they may be caused by clerical mistakes, by a failure of those compiling data to interpret their instructions correctly, or even in some instances by a disregard for what is required.

It is frequently necessary to collect data by sampling. This can introduce its own quota of errors. The sample may not be well drawn and may be unrepresentative of what is being measured. The sample may become unrepresentative if some of those asked to fill in the questionnaire do not respond. There is generally some systematic reason for non-response; so that non-respondents often prove to have different characteristics from those who complete the questionnaire. A second request for the completion of a questionnaire may sometimes improve the response rates of those who failed to return the questionnaire on the first appeal. It is possible that those who respond eventually will be more representative of those who fail to make any response than those who replied in the first place, and this may enable a more representative sample to be compiled. If, however, no means can be found of getting any response from those who are reluctant to answer the questionnaire, the sample is bound to remain unrepresentative.

Even if the sample has been correctly drawn and response to it is complete, the characteristics of the sample may not be the same as the characteristics of the population from which the sample was drawn. To question twenty housewives about whether they would buy a product will not necessarily give the same proportion of would-be buyers as would emerge if 200 housewives were questioned, or all housewives in the country. It might be that all the twenty housewives first questioned were potential buyers, even though if all housewives had been consulted it would have emerged that only half of them were ready to buy. It would be most unlikely that a sample of 200 housewives would be misleading in the same degree. Up to a point the larger the size of sample the more representative it is likely to be. Errors due to unrepresentative samples can be estimated by statistical methods within certain limits.

It might be inferred that accuracy of estimates based on samples can always be improved by enlarging the size of the sample. Formally, this is true; but in practice other considerations have to be taken into account. A small sample can be taken with great care, perhaps by a team specially selected and trained for the purpose. For larger samples, it may not be possible to maintain the same care and attention to detail so that errors of observation are increased at the same time as sampling errors are being reduced. The net effect of increasing the coverage of the sample may be to reduce its accuracy, and more money may have been spent in an effort to improve the sample only to have the opposite result in practice. Thus, when only limited resources are available, it may pay to concentrate on taking a good sample rather than to attempt to spread inquiries too widely.

ACCURACY IN PRACTICE

In the face of such a formidable array of sources of error it might seem impossible to make forecasts of any value. Before considering what constitutes a valuable forecast for various purposes it may be useful briefly to see what accuracy has been attained by some economic forecasts in the post-war period.

The National Institute of Economic and Social Research examines the economic situation at intervals in its *Economic Review* which is a very useful source of information about the economy; every year it presents a full-length review of the economic situation. In one of the reviews an appraisal was made of the accuracy of some previous forecasts: Table 9.3 summarizes a number of comparisons of what actually transpired with the forecasts of the Institute.

The forecasts were made for less than a year ahead for both the January and May forecasts; yet both the forecasts show substantial differences from what actually transpired. Other forecasters fared no better and a forecast based on a mathematical model developed at Oxford, similar to that described earlier for the Dutch economy, was no improvement.

TABLE 9.3

CHANGES IN DEMAND, FORECAST AND ACTUAL

1959 Fourth Quarter to 1960 Fourth Quarter.

	Per cent change over 1959 Change forecast in		Fourth quarter Actual change
	January	May	
Consumers' expenditure	+3½	+3½	+1½
Of which durables	+9	+6	−2½
Public authorities' current spending	+4	+3½	+6
Gross fixed investment	+8	+7	+6½
Export of goods and services	+6½	+5	—
Total demand excluding investment in stocks	+4½	+4	+2½
Total final demand	+4	+3½	+3
Less imports of goods and services	+7	+7	+8
Less factor cost adjustment	+6	+6	+6
Gross domestic product (from expenditure)*	+3½	+3	+1½
Gross domestic product (from output)*			+2½
Industrial production	+6 or 7	+6	+2½

Source: *National Institute Economic Review* (May 1961)

*The difference is due to statistical discrepancies in the method used.

The May 1968 Review compared forecasts of components of the gross national product prepared by the Institute with ones prepared by the Treasury (see Table 9.4). The latter were published on March 12th, 1968, and must have been compiled somewhat earlier than those of the Institute. In fact the Institute's forecasts must have been made in the light of fairly firm information about what had transpired in the first few months of the year, and so were more in the nature of estimates than forecasts. This explains to some extent why the forecasts for the first half of the year were close to what was subsequently recorded. The two sets of forecasts differed appeciably for the second half of 1968. In part this reflects the differing dates at which the forecasts were prepared, but the state of the economy was changing rapidly and it is less easy to forecast in these circumstances than in more stable conditions.

It is evident from the comparison of forecasts with actual results that there were considerable divergences as well as agreement in some instances. Consumer expenditure was greatly underestimated; in fact consumers indulged in a spending spree in the second half of 1968, prompted by fears of continuing increases in prices and fed out of higher incomes. Underestimation of imports was offset, so far as the balance of payments was concerned, by underestimation of exports. There are instances of the actual figures recorded falling well outside the range of both sets of forecasts.

These illustrations indicate that forecasting cannot be expected to be too accurate using present methods. There is an acknowledged need to improve forecasting techniques. Nevertheless, even present techniques may give much better results than pure guesses.

Some measure of success appears to have been achieved by the Dutch forecasters using their economic model. Dr. Theil has shown that the percentage change of various economic indicators forecast for the Dutch economy averaged about 0.7 of the percentage changes actually recorded.[10] The corresponding figure for forecasts made for Scandinavian countries was generally somewhat smaller, typically about 0.5. There was, however, in all cases a considerable variation in the accuracy of individual forecasts. Nevertheless, the forecasts were invariably better than the results that would have been attained if it had been assumed that the changes of the previous year would exactly repeat themselves.

The tendency to underestimate the amount of change taking place is a common feature of forecasts. The recognition of this tendency does not mean, however, that this error can be corrected by the simple expedient of increasing all forecasts in some proportion. While this would improve the average performance it would make some forecasts worse and it might destroy the basis on which the forecasts were constructed in the first place.

In assessing forecasting performance it is necessary to distinguish between future projections that are in the nature of targets and forecasts that are expected to be realized. In the post-war period the United Kingdom Government was much more concerned with the preparation of targets than of forecasts and there was an element of wishful thinking in the projections made. It is scarcely surprising that there were often appreciable differences between what was predicted and what transpired.

Forecasts concerned with capital goods are particularly likely

[10] H. Theil, op. cit., Chapter 3.

to be in error. One reason is that many capital goods take a long time to make and most are extremely durable. Forecasts are likely to be of decreasing accuracy the longer the period they cover, and those concerned with the profitability of capital goods must cover some considerable span of time. The durability of capital goods also makes forecasting difficult, because the replacement demand for capital goods may be rather small and a moderate increase in the demand for products requiring particular types of capital goods may represent quite a large proportion of normal output.

TABLE 9.4

COMPARISON OF FORECAST OF COMPONENTS OF THE GROSS NATIONAL PRODUCT WITH ACTUAL FIGURES

(the second half of 1967 = 100)

	1968 first half	1968 second half
Consumers' expenditure		
NIESR	100.9	98.2
Treasury	99.6	98.1
Actual	100.9	101.1
Public Authorities *Current Spending*		
NIESR	101.4	102.6
Treasury	101.7	103.0
Actual	101.4	100.7
Exports		
NIESR	113.4	116.3
Treasury	112.8	113.1
Actual	113 5	119.0
Gross Fixed Investment		
NIESR	101·6	105·8
Treasury	102.7	105.7
Actual	101.9	103.0
Imports		
NIESR	107.7	105.9
Treasury	102.3	100.6
Actual	106.3	108.0
Gross Domestic Product		
NIESR	102.0	103.5
Treasury	102.0	103.6
Actual	101.6	104.2

Estimates of the state of the market for ships, prepared early in 1959, indicated a strong possibility that almost as much as 15 million gross tons of shipping might be laid up in 1961. In the event, laid up tonnage amounted to less than 3 million tons, partly because of much greater increase in world trade than had been expected and partly because of enhanced rates of scrapping.[11] The estimates might have been improved if they had paid greater attention to the rate of increase in world trade that was likely in the short term and less to the customary life of ships.

Forecasts of energy requirements in Western Europe over two decades again illustrate the difficulty of making accurate forecasts over long periods. An expert committee examining Western Europe's requirements in the mid-1950s for imported fuels in 1975, increased its estimates by over 25 per cent within 2 years.

The very factor that caused the revision of the committee's estimates of oil requirements—a readiness to allow cheaper sources of energy from overseas to compete with domestic fuel resources—was instrumental in increasing world trade in oil more rapidly than had been assumed. Government decisions to allow greater oil imports were an exogenous factor that could not easily be taken account of in the predictions.

Both the forecasts of energy requirements and the state of the market for ships rested in the last resort on assumed rates of increase in national income, which are not easy to forecast. Difficulties in forecasting national income over an extended period of time—in the case of the oil estimates, 20 years—would have been quite sufficient to disturb both forecasts substantially with the passage of time.

If shorter forecasts are all that is needed, there is a greater chance of achieving an acceptable standard of accuracy. The estimates of paint sales prepared by Holt *et al.* showed an average forecast error for the first half of the year of less than 2 per cent and in the second half of the year of less than 4 per cent. The average for the year as a whole was less than 3 per cent with a maximum of 6 per cent. This suggests that there is a good opportunity for developing useful short-term forecasts of the demand for certain types of consumer durables. In some cases the best estimates might result from combining

[11] See J. R. Parkinson, 'The Demand for Ships', *Scottish Journal of Political Economy* (June 1959).

statistical estimates of the above kind with the results of attitude surveys.

Few business decisions have consequences only for the present. Many are concerned largely with the future and involve the formation of some view about the course of events. It is seldom possible to take a decision about the future that will be optimal in all circumstances, and decisions involve commitments that cannot be modified or avoided without cost. There are thus good reasons for taking forecasting seriously and for being ready to go to considerable trouble and expense to make sure that the best methods are being used. It does not follow that the best methods are always the most sophisticated. If experience shows that the forecasts of someone knowledgeable in business are as good as, or better than, those produced by specialists using advanced techniques, the former are to be preferred. But it is as well to establish such superiority before deciding against the use of alternative methods; and it might be worth while exploring whether the experience of those in the trade could be drawn upon to improve forecasts. It may be, of course, that improvement is not possible or that superior methods of forecasting would cost more than they were worth.

The value of forecasting has become more apparent with the spread of organized planning and, as the more progressive business firms have demonstrated the usefulness of forecasts, competitive pressures have stimulated the others to follow suit.[12] The fact is that many business decisions depend on what view is taken of the future, and forecasts of sales, for example, may virtually regulate a factory's operations.

In using forecasts it is important to recognize their limitations; no forecast is exactly right except by chance. Thus business plans must take into account the uncertainty that is attached to a forecast and provide for a degree of flexibility in operation that will take account of a range of outcomes. It may be cheaper to provide for this flexibility than to improve the accuracy with which forecasts can be made.

The accuracy of forecasts depends on the length of period for which the forecasts are required. Short-term forecasts stand

[12] See Charles C. Holt, 'Forecasting Requirements from the Business Standpoint', *The Quality and Economy Significance of Anticipations Data* (National Bureau of Economic Research).

u

a better chance of being right than ones for very long periods. There is some tendency for forecasts that have been constructed for a medium period ahead to be valid for a shorter period, say for the next quarter of the year rather than for the quarter after that.

It is desirable to consider what forecasting horizon should be adopted. It is seldom necessary to forecast the whole life-span of an operation. If it is planned to build a dam, it may appear natural to consider the whole life of the dam in estimating its profitability, but this is not really necessary. The results of operating the dam must be increasingly heavily discounted the more we attempt to peer into the future. Unless the rate of interest is low it is the first 20 years of the dam's operation that really count; and if the rate of interest is low the decision to build the dam is likely to be taken on other than purely economic considerations. When the installation of plant and machinery is at stake there will be no point in preparing forecasts beyond the life of the assets. And, in practice, the relevant period to consider is probably far shorter than this, both because it is necessary to discount the more distant future rather heavily, and because the reliability of the forecasts will almost certainly decrease as they are extended into time.

Long-term forecasts must look to the establishment of trends; short-term forecasts, on the other hand, may be concerned largely with deviations from trends. This does not prevent some long-term forecasts from being greatly influenced by the conditions ruling at the time they are made. Very often there is a strong subjective streak in forecasting and a tendency to picture the future as being related to the immediate present rather than to a sequence of years. Errors of this kind might be reduced if greater reliance were placed on relationships established mathematically and less on adjustments involving personal judgment. But it is to these elements of personal judgment and to knowing when to reject or modify a mathematical model that the Dutch planners attribute some of the success of their methods.

There is room for much improvement in forecasting techniques. But prediction can be carried out in a number of business situations with sufficient accuracy to make a sizeable contribution to profits by improving the quality of business decisions. The uncertainties that remain are reasons for attempting to improve forecasting techniques rather than for complaining that they do not always give the right results.

CONTROL

Various analytical tools are available to managers for determining company objectives and for ensuring that they are attained.

As we have seen, knowledge is the first requirement of control and this involves the collection and use of information relating to happenings outside the firm as well as the use of data relating to its own operations. Reliable statistical data are essential.

It is common experience that flexibility is needed in the preparation of statistical data. Data that is adequate for one purpose may not be suited to another; figures that have proved to be perfectly adequate in the past need to be developed and analysed in greater detail as events change or the emphasis of the company alters. This suggests that the aim should be to collect data in a form that permits of variety in analysis if this can be done with economy. In the case of sales, the company may want to know the value of everything it has sold in a given period, or in divisions of that period; it may want to know how the total of sales was distributed between products, salesmen or districts; it may require totals grouping products according to certain main characteristics, say, according to whether they were affected by a change in hire purchase regulations or by the weather. It is a great advantage if a variety of analyses can be made available with a minimum of effort even if many of them are required only occasionally. There is a need, however, to strike a balance between extreme flexibility and keeping statistical operations within bounds. Some managers prefer to collect the minimum of routine information and rely on *ad hoc* compilation of data for specific purposes. Fortunately, the mechanization of statistical work and the use of electronic computers is tipping the balance in the direction of being able to provide copious statistical information in useable form with the minimum of delay. But although it is desirable to make provision for a variety of statistical analyses, particularly in order to have sufficient information for the formulation of policy, the actual amount of detailed information considered by individuals will depend on their functions. A foreman

U*

will need detailed information about the operations for which he is responsible, but the production manager will be most concerned with the totals relating to his department. Attention to ten or a score series of key aggregative figures is likely to be all that is needed to keep the managing director in touch with what is happening in the business, and will give him warning of points that require attention and suggest additional information that is needed to follow up indications of deviations from anticipations. If the statements he receives are well chosen and prepared, he will often be able to assimilate the figures while removing his coat in the morning.

It is not possible to prescribe in detail the figures that are necessary to run individual businesses. Information on sales and orders, on purchases, production, manpower, costs, stocks, credit and capital expenditure will be required in concerns of any size. Much more information may also be needed since requirements differ very greatly in detail. The guiding consideration is that the data must be as adequate as is economical for the determination of policy, for the preparation of a plan of operations, and for the supervision of the execution of the plan once it has been prepared. The latter requirement means both that the data provided and the plan itself must be related to the administrative divisions of the company; otherwise it will be difficult to integrate the company's operations with the plan of operation prepared for it.

Finally the more speedily data can be compiled the more use it is likely to be. Data relating to periods long since past serves neither as a warning, a means to put things right nor as a starting point for future planning. Information needs to be presented at sufficiently frequent intervals for changes in the circumstances affecting the company to be discernible with little delay. It also follows that information which gives a more up-to-date view of a company's operations is to be preferred to a series that is up-to-date and speedily available but refers to events taking place some time ago; thus figures of sales are generally of more value than figures of receipts, which reflect sales in some previous period.

The results of a company's activities are recorded at yearly or shorter intervals in the form of profit and loss accounts and balance sheets, discussed earlier in this chapter.

Such statements are non-operational; they record the results of past operations and as such are an account of stewardship. They yield information about the future of the company only so far as it is reasonable to suppose that the immediate future will resemble the immediate past or so far as they might serve to throw up obstacles to development or opportunities for expansion.

If financial statements are to serve as a useful instrument of planning and control they must be drawn up for some future period in order to show the results that it is intended to achieve.

A plan for a company's operations requires integrated information about many aspects of its operation.

Integration can best take the form of a series of interlocking budgetary accounts. These provide a means of formulating a plan and serve as instruments of execution and verification. The future operations of the business will be portrayed in a series of financial accounts for the next operating period or periods.[13] For the whole of the company's operations these will show the total expected expenditure and forecasts of the value of sales and profit. In a large company the budget will have to be spelt out in considerable detail. Each major department will have its own budget, which will lay down what is expected from it in operating results during the budgetary period. The budget for the sales department will specify the value of sales required and underlying this figure will be estimates of the quantities of various products that can be sold and the prices that will be realized. Expenditure by the sales department will also be budgeted, the figure allowed depending on the number of salesmen to be employed, the average salary and commission earned and selling expenses. The authorized expenditure will be judged adequate for the task in hand and the sales department will be expected to adhere to its budget. For the production department output will take the place of sales, and expenditure will be based on the supposition that production programmes are adhered to. Table 9.5 shows the expenditure budgeted for a production department during the current year and shows how expenditure and the budget compared after 9 months of the year had been completed.

The costs of the Production Department were roughly in

[13] See, for example, Harold C. Edey, *Business Budgets and Accounts*, Hutchinson.

TABLE 9.5

MANAGEMENT ACCOUNTING STATEMENT

Production Department costs for 9 months to August 31st

	Year to date				Total budget				Per cent of total budget used(1)			
	Basic labour cost	Overtime cost	Expense cost	Total	Basic labour cost	Overtime cost	Expense cost	Total	Basic labour cost	Overtime cost	Expense cost	Total
	£	£	£	£	£	£	£	£				
Production administration	8,325	225	296	8,846	12,444	400	400	13,244	66.9	56.3	74.0	66.8
Manufacturing departments	114,313	45,303	17,254	206,870	203,853	42,500	29,000	275,353	70.8	106.6	59.5	75.1
Assembly departments	50,359	13,284	2,605	66,248	67,395	13,100	10,000	90,495	74.7	101.4	26.1	73.2
Plant engineering	26,058	9,140	30,496	65,694	36,185	9,300	31,000	76,485	72.0	98.3	96.4	85.9
Production control	79,183	18,868	2,882	100,873	112,721	18,800	5,000	136,521	70.2	100.0	57.6	73.9
TOTAL PRODUCTION COST	308,238	86,760	53,533	448,531	432,598	84,100	75,400	592,098	71.3	103.2	71.0	74.9

(1) To be compared with the completion of 75 per cent of the budget year.

line with the budget after the elapse of three-quarters of the budgetary year but overtime costs were somewhat in excess of what had been planned. This deviation would certainly call for explanation. Was it due to difficulties in recruiting, excess rates of overtime pay, failure to keep production on target without excessive overtime, or slowness in installing new machinery? What effect on ultimate costs and profit might the deviation be expected to have? And what remedial measures, if any, should be proposed? Management by exception, as it is known, consists of finding out the reasons for deviations from intention and taking action on them. Not every departure from plan is necessarily bad. In the illustration, more intensive working of existing machinery through working additional overtime might have had the effect of reducing costs rather than increasing them as might be assumed at first sight.

In order to establish the causes of the deviations additional information would have to be sought. Some of this might be contained in supplementary budgets on which the accounting statement was based. The rate of pay for overtime working, for example, would almost certainly have had to be specified in preparing the budget, as would the number of operatives it was intended to employ. The causes of the deviations may be known to those responsible for operations without the need for detailed scrutiny of budgetary figures. There might have been a problem of recruitment throughout the year that made overtime working unavoidable and efforts to remedy this might have had little success. But whatever the cause, the departure from the accepted norm calls for inquiry and consideration of accepted views.

By no means all control is exercised through budgetary statements and in some senses the budget is the end-product of control. Many critical operations will almost certainly be controlled without immediate reference to the budget. It is often simpler to control output in terms of the number of units produced than in terms of the financial contribution that is being made to the affairs of the company, and comparison of the output produced with the target rate of production laid down may be all that is needed to keep operations according to plan. If a high rate of operation is the key to success, which is likely to be true if there is a rapidly expanding market for some product, control may centre on output statistics. Sometimes performances may be so critical that hourly reports of the number of units produced may be required; it is not that the loss of an hour's production would be irreparable so much as that even momentary relaxation of efforts to increase output can destroy the accelerating tempo of working up to a high target.

This is a relatively simple control statement. Departmental budgets are often prepared in considerable detail and rest on a number of assumptions about the distribution of work, wage rates, scrap percentages and so on. The departmental budget itself may be broken down further into sub-departments and foremen may also be required to work within a budget. In a large company there may be a large number of such budgets covering every aspect of the company's operations.[14]

They should also cover such matters as the investment programme for the company. Investment cannot be planned on a hand-to-mouth basis and it is necessary to estimate what money can reasonably be expected to be available for this purpose for a mumber of years ahead and to specify the sources of the funds that are likely to be available. A cash budget is no less essential to make sure that the company will not be impeded in its operations by an avoidable shortage of cash, and that it makes proper provision for overdraft facilities as a precaution against financial stringency; indeed, the fact that budgets have been prepared to cover all the operations of the company, and particularly its financial requirements, may be of considerable help when seeking an overdraft from a bank because it is possible to show that the company's requirements have been carefully worked out.

Budgetary planning is less formidable than might appear; plans seldom grow out of nothing and must generally bear some relation to what has gone before; as a properly conducted planning exercise they will incorporate the view of those who are expected to carry out the plan as well as those who have responsibility for the formulation of policy. Departments will be asked for estimates of their proposed future expenditure in

---

[14] Those interested in the details of budgets are referred to *An Introduction to Budgetary Control, Standing Costing, Material Control and Production Control*, The Institute of Cost and Works Accountants.

relation to certain broadly determined objectives; after verification and sifting these will be incorporated in the draft budget. If these methods are followed, it is possible for the plan to be fully accepted by those who have to carry it out, thus avoiding the lack of co-operation which could completely nullify budgetary planning.

As all the individual departmental budgets are drafted a picture for the operations of the business as a whole will emerge. This picture will be compared with what the directors of the company would like to see. There may be harmony between the views of the directors and the results expected by departments, but there may also be divergences of view and objectives. The directors will wish to achieve certain results. They may want to secure some minimum rate of profit on the capital employed in the business, based on past experience of what is possible or on what can be earned in other activities; they may wish to aim at some target increase in sales, to cut costs or to provide funds for the development of new products or additional investment.

The directors of the company are always likely to press in their planning for a little more than what seems to be obviously feasible; they may aim at a slightly higher profit than they expect to get, or try to raise sales or production as close to full capacity working as seems reasonably possible. Partly in self-defence, those who have the task of carrying out the directors' intentions are likely to press for less rather than more, and some compromise may have to be reached. In the event the directors may be pleasantly surprised or disappointed; the future seldom turns out completely as expected but a good plan will be sufficiently flexible to take account of most eventualities and may provide for a variety of outcomes.

Flexible budgeting is designed to be responsive to changes in activity that are due to outside and uncontrollable influences. It would be absurd for a production manager to refuse to produce more than was provided for in his budget if capacity and markets were available for additional production and enhanced profit. Such an eventuality can be covered in budgetary planning either by developing a number of plans for different levels of output or by making it explicit in the first place that departures from the budgets laid down are permissible within certain limits. In the latter case fulfilment of the budgetary requirements will depend on adhering to recognized standards of productivity, and on costs varying with fluctuations of output in a reasonable way. Thus, adherence to a budget becomes more a matter of comforming to certain norms than of achieving certain expenditure figures and particular totals. The use of standard costs in budgetary control is one aspect of the establishment of recognized but not unchanging norms. If major departures from plan are made the whole of the company's operations will need reconsideration if they are not to become unco-ordinated.

The essence of budgetary control as a check on operations is to compare what has been achieved with what was intended. Routine checks are needed to verify whether the company's operations are going according to plan or whether there have been significant deviations. Some deviations are to be expected; sales may not materialize; new capacity may be late in coming into operation; raw material costs may rise or fall. If deviations from plan are due to factors outside the control of the company there is nothing for it but to accept the fact that the plan is unlikely to be fulfilled and to modify it accordingly; but if the deviations are due to factors within the control of the company, remedial action is possible and, if the plan was well conceived in the first place, desirable.

The use of budgetary control and planning is by no means universal in British industry. The P.E.P. inquiry[15] showed that out of forty-seven comparatively large firms only thirty operated budgetary control and for a number of these it was a recent innovation. Surveys carried out in Northern Ireland and the Republic of Ireland, where firms tend to be comparatively small, have shown that the use of budgetary control is even less widely spread.

Control is rigorously practised in the cigarette industry and the application of budgetary control to the operations of Carreras in Northern Ireland provides an example. Two basic views about the functions of management underlie the importance of budgetary planning; the first is that management by delegation does not mean management by abrogation and there is thus a strong compulsion to shape the affairs of the firm; the

[15] *Attitudes in British Industry.*

second is that a major objective is to attain a specified return on capital. Another reason for the emphasis on control is that after the imposition of duty, tobacco is a costly raw material, which must be conserved and used effectively.

As a first step in determining policy and exercising control, a plan is prepared for a five year period. Within the context of the five year plan two other plans are prepared, one covering three years and the other one year only. The time span covered by the plans is bound up with the time needed to see major changes completed: five years may be necessary to branch out into some allied form of manufacturing, three years necessary to develop a new machine and a one-year plan essential in relation to the purchase of tobacco and for more immediate operations.

Any set of forecasts prepared initially may prove to offer an unacceptable rate of return as judged by comparison with the rates of return being earned currently by other companies or in other industries. If so, it is necessary to see what can be done to change the plan and the concepts behind it in such a way as to improve returns. This may involve examining other ways of using the company's resources than in cigarette manufacturing, for the view is held that the company is not committed to its existing interests and is free to diversify its activities.

No plan is accepted until it has been fully examined in all its details so that there is every assurance that when it is finally put into action it will be possible to implement it. This means that the plan is realistic, but it does not avoid the need for action to restore the situation or the need for re-thinking from time to time in the light of changing circumstances. If this has to be done it is carried out comprehensively in order to avoid the short-term decision which is not consistent with long-term objectives.

The Board of Directors of the company includes a high proportion of full time executives. They tend to be fully conversant with the operations of the company and the way in which the planning operation has been carried out. They are thus unlikely to find it necessary to examine a plan in detail provided that it appears to meet their objectives; they can concentrate their attention on major issues.

The plans themselves are expressed in budgetary accounts,

but behind these lie all the physical plans for production related to forecasts of the movement of demand and the growth of the company's activities. The capital budget is a vital part of the whole operation; technical change in cigarette-making, particularly the development of new high speed machines, continues to reduce costs and to justify expenditure on re-equipment.

So far as the productive processes themselves are concerned budgetary control finds its expression in frequent checks on machine performances, including the automatic monitoring of quality standards.

INDEX

301